CHRISTMAS SPIRITS AT HONEYWELL HOUSE

GHOSTS OF ROWAN VALE BOOK 3

SHARON BOOTH

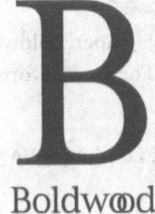

Boldwood

First published in Great Britain in 2025 by Boldwood Books Ltd.

Copyright © Sharon Booth, 2025

Cover Design by Rachel Lawston

Cover Images: Rachel Lawston

The moral right of Sharon Booth to be identified as the author of this work has been asserted in accordance with the Copyright, Designs and Patents Act 1988.

All rights reserved. No part of this book may be reproduced in any form or by any electronic or mechanical means, including information storage and retrieval systems, without written permission from the author, except for the use of brief quotations in a book review. This book is a work of fiction and, except in the case of historical fact, any resemblance to actual persons, living or dead, is purely coincidental.

Every effort has been made to obtain the necessary permissions with reference to copyright material, both illustrative and quoted. We apologise for any omissions in this respect and will be pleased to make the appropriate acknowledgements in any future edition.

A CIP catalogue record for this book is available from the British Library.

Paperback ISBN 978-1-83656-768-4

Large Print ISBN 978-1-83656-767-7

Hardback ISBN 978-1-83656-766-0

Trade Paperback ISBN 978-1-80635-300-2

Ebook ISBN 978-1-83656-769-1

Kindle ISBN 978-1-83656-770-7

Audio CD ISBN 978-1-83656-761-5

MP3 CD ISBN 978-1-83656-762-2

Digital audio download ISBN 978-1-83656-765-3

This book is printed on certified sustainable paper. Boldwood Books is dedicated to putting sustainability at the heart of our business. For more information please visit https://www.boldwoodbooks.com/about-us/sustainability/

Boldwood Books Ltd, 23 Bowerdean Street, London, SW6 3TN

www.boldwoodbooks.com

*True love is like ghosts, which everyone talks about and few have seen ~
Francois de La Rochefoucauld*

1

Despite the clamour of voices doing their very best to distract me, I somehow managed to pull up safely in the school car park without pranging anyone else's car. Miracle.

'I need a pack of Christmas cards.'

'Mum, can I have burgers for tea?'

'I've got loads of mates and they're already sending out Christmas cards. I've got three in my bag from yesterday. They'll think I'm tight if I don't send them one!'

'And beans. Not peas. Yuck! I hate peas.'

'Don't get soppy ones though. Or cutesy ones. Or religious ones.'

'And chips! I want chips! Crinkly ones, please.'

Bloody hell! I took a deep breath, steadied myself, then turned to face the kids in the back seat.

'It's only just December, Declan. You don't need Christmas cards yet.'

'But Mum—'

'And we're having stew for tea, Freddie. It's your dad's favourite and I've already promised him.'

'But *I* want burgers,' Freddie wailed.

'Should have got in quicker then,' I said heartlessly, steeling myself against the pleading look in his big, blue eyes. 'Sorry. Right, get your bags or you'll be late.'

'What's new?' Declan grumbled, opening the car door. Nine years old, he was already at that awkward age. Actually, he'd been at that awkward age since he was nine *months* old. God help me when he hit his teens.

I scrambled out of the car and waited for Freddie, who was taking his time collecting his school bag from the floor.

'What have I got for lunch?' he demanded fiercely, as he clambered out of the car. Evidently, it would be a while before he forgave me for the stew.

'Your favourite,' I assured him.

He narrowed his eyes suspiciously. 'Peanut butter?'

'Yes,' I said firmly, mentally crossing my fingers. 'Peanut butter.'

'My favourite's cheese spread,' he said accusingly.

'It's peanut butter *and* cheese spread,' I said.

'Together?' He gave me an astonished look, then shrugged. 'Okay.'

Bloody kids! I wondered what he'd say when he opened his packed lunch to discover ham sandwiches. Oops.

I bundled the boys towards the school building, although Declan quickly broke away from us and hurried over to where some of his classmates were making their way inside, laughing and joking with each other. He certainly didn't want to be seen with his mother.

Six-year-old Freddie, thankfully, was still at the age when I didn't embarrass him. Give it time.

After removing his coat and hanging it on the peg in the cloakroom, I steered him into his classroom. I mumbled a hello to the teacher, Mrs Crawford, who was faffing about at her desk, and the teaching assistant, Miss Lemming, who was hovering by the door. She looked cheerful and greeted us warmly. Mrs Crawford, on the other hand, looked as if she was utterly exhausted, and barely managed a smile.

I knew how she felt. I'd have happily crawled back into bed the moment I got home, if only I could.

'Not long to go,' Miss Lemming whispered to me.

She said it like it was a good thing. The end of term wasn't something I was looking forward to, Christmas or no Christmas. It was the *start* of term I lived for. Although even then, life was one big hassle, what with getting the two youngest boys to school in Kingsford Wold, and making sure my eldest, Ashton, was ready in time to catch the school bus to the academy at Chipping Royston.

I kissed Freddie on the cheek and gently turned him towards his seat at a table that was already occupied by several children. They'd possibly overdosed on sugary cereal that morning, given the way they were bouncing up and down on their chairs and shrieking at each other.

'Mum, did you pack me some crisps?' Freddie demanded suddenly. Honestly, the boy was obsessed with food.

I gave Miss Lemming a nervous look, aware of the school policy on junk food.

'Now, Freddie, you know we don't eat crisps,' I said, praying he'd go along with my outrageous lie. 'I've packed you some raisins. You like raisins.'

Miss Lemming gave me an approving smile. Mrs Crawford, who was taking books out of her briefcase, slid me a knowing gaze but said nothing. She was a mother, too. Solidarity.

'Right, I've got to dash,' I said hastily, just in case Freddie decided to ask if I'd packed him one of the KitKats out of the fridge. 'Loads to do at home. Be a good boy and I'll see you later.'

Luckily, he'd spotted Sophie, who was his current *bestest friend*, and barely acknowledged me as he ran towards her, leaving me to smile awkwardly at the two women before I turned and fairly galloped out of the classroom, making my escape before one of them thought of something that would delay me further.

Freedom!

Well, I thought, heading towards my car, keys jangling in my hand, not really. I wasn't joking when I said I had loads to do at home. The house looked like a municipal tip right now, and Toby would need walking. I had a stack of washing to do, too.

I shivered and pulled my coat tighter. I hadn't zipped it up because I wouldn't have been able to breathe properly if I had. Whenever I sat down, it rode up to my waist. I needed to go on a diet, I thought ruefully. I'd really let things slip all round. Just another thing to add to my never-ending to-do list.

* * *

I knew the house was a mess, but looking round at the kitchen, my heart sank. It was worse than I'd remembered, and that was saying something.

Toby, our big, beautiful Bernese mountain dog, came ambling over to me, sniffing at my pockets hopefully.

'No treats today,' I said, feeling a twinge of shame as I realised he'd come to expect that I'd arrive home from school with my pockets bulging with tasty snacks. Well, the shops in Kingsford Wold were way too tempting. There was a fudge shop right near the school gates, for goodness' sake! And there was a pasty shop just across the road, and nine times out of ten I hadn't had time to eat breakfast before I dropped the kids off, and the smell of hot food drifting from the open door of Auntie Pat's Pasties was just too much to resist.

Except, today I had. Having made one more attempt to zip my coat up before getting in the car, and failing dismally, even I'd had to accept that it was time to cut down on treats.

I patted Toby on the head and sighed. 'You look as miserable about it as I feel,' I told him. 'Right, where shall we start?'

Dishwasher, I decided. Honestly, I couldn't even complain that I had to wash the dishes by hand, because I had a machine to do it for me, but even the thought of loading it made me feel exhausted. With enormous effort, I opened the door, only to discover yesterday evening's dirty plates and cups still in there. I'd forgotten to switch the dishwasher on.

'I think,' I told Toby, 'that before I do anything else, I need a strong cup of tea and something to eat. After all, I haven't had breakfast. You should never start work on an empty stomach.'

Although, as I switched on the kettle, I thought gloomily that the last thing my stomach looked was empty. It was all my own fault. I'd discovered the joys of jogging bottoms and leggings, with all the freedom and comfort elasticated waists brought. There was no going back after that.

Unfortunately, that meant I hadn't noticed how rapidly the weight was creeping on.

'Clara Milsom, fashion icon. Ha!' I muttered, smothering newly popped granary toast with butter and strawberry jam. 'It's all the fault of my hormones. Bloody perimenopause.'

Toby was positively drooling, which should have been enough to put me off eating, but I was too hungry to care.

'You've had your breakfast,' I reminded him. They'd *all* had their breakfast. Jack had devoured poached eggs on toast before leaving the house at five-thirty for work. The two youngest boys had descended on the kitchen an hour after he left, and between them had practically emptied a box of cornflakes and the fruit bowl. I'd been too busy mopping up spills, pouring cereal, making drinks, doing last-minute ironing, and trying to drag Ashton out of his pit to eat anything myself.

I carried my plate of toast and jam and a mug of hot tea into the living room. There was dog hair all over the carpet. Again. I noticed a layer of dust on top of the fireplace and along the bookshelves. Those windows really needed cleaning too.

I flopped onto the sofa and, balancing my plate on my knee, I reached for the remote. Just half an hour watching something inane on the television while I had my breakfast. Then I'd start work properly.

By the time Jack got home, the kids would be back from school, the stew would be simmering on the hob, the house would be spotless, and the windows would gleam. I might even pop to the shop on my way to collect the two youngest boys and buy a pack of Christmas cards to please Declan.

I just needed this half an hour. That's all.

2
AGNES

'You know, I've never really understood the need for an advent calendar,' Agnes said, 'but I've come to accept that this is now a tradition, as are so many strange and improbable things. But this—' she waved a hand dismissively at the one that hung on the kitchen wall in Harling Hall, 'I completely fail to see the point of. There isn't even a pretty scene behind the door.'

'Chocolate, Mrs Wyndham,' Imogen told her patiently. 'Chocolate's the point!'

'A chocolate advent calendar.' Agnes shook her head. 'I've never heard anything so ridiculous.'

'All the shops are full of them,' Imogen's mother, Callie, explained. 'It's harder to find an advent calendar that *doesn't* have chocolate in it these days.'

Agnes sighed. 'Disgraceful.'

'Didn't you have an advent calendar when you were a kid?' Imogen asked.

Agnes snorted with laughter as the eleven-year-old girl gazed at her with eyes full of curiosity. These youngsters knew nothing about history, clearly.

Back in the early nineteenth century, when Agnes had been alive, there had been no such thing as advent calendars. She understood they were a German invention, but though poor King George and the Prince Regent were, after all, of German blood, such things were unheard of – certainly in Agnes's circle. She pondered that so many things associated with Christmas in England these days had originated in Germany. She doubted Imogen had any idea.

Dear Florence was just as ignorant of the facts, even though Agnes had tried her best to teach her. Maybe, now that she was having lessons with Walter Tasker, her daughter might finally start to learn something. Walter might be a pompous ass, but as he had once taught William Shakespeare himself, no less, Agnes had to concede he was probably worthy of Florence.

'There were no advent calendars in my day,' she told Imogen. 'Indeed, I don't remember seeing one in this house until Sir Edward was a little boy, and it looked nothing like this one. And after that...' She thought for a moment. 'No, no I believe they vanished again. Probably something to do with the wars and the shortage of cardboard. Now, let me see. Did Lawrie have one when he was a child? No, I really don't believe he did. I think, perhaps, William was the first to have what you'd consider an advent calendar in this style, although there was certainly no chocolate in it.'

'Is William Brodie's dad?' Imogen checked.

Agnes nodded. 'He is indeed. Ah, it's been a long time since I saw him, or his dear wife, Katya. Brodie must miss him dreadfully. It's a shame he never visits, though I suppose it's a Herculean task, travelling from Australia.'

'Not that difficult,' Callie told her. 'He could get a flight here any time, but he's so busy. And we can hardly complain, since we're too busy to go over there.'

Agnes gasped. 'I should think not indeed! Why would you want to travel to Australia, of all places?' She shuddered at the thought of being perched in the belly of an aeroplane for all those hours. So vulnerable. How could they possibly stay up in the air all that time? 'Although,' she conceded, 'it is a shame that so many miles separate Brodie from his parents. And, of course, you've never met them, and you really should, since you and Brodie are courting.'

'Courting!' Immi – as she insisted on being called, to Agnes's disapproval – wrinkled her nose, her hazel eyes bright with laughter.

Agnes frowned. 'Have I said something amusing?'

'It's that word,' Callie explained, giving Immi a reproving look. 'It's a bit old-fashioned. No one says courting any more.'

'Then, what *do* they say?' Really, Agnes couldn't believe how many things had changed. She'd always prided herself on keeping up with modern developments, but sometimes the ways in which things altered bewildered her.

Callie shrugged. 'I don't know really. I suppose you'd say, Brodie and I are going out.'

'Going out? Going out where?'

Immi giggled. 'Just going out. Or dating.'

'Dreadful term.' Agnes sniffed. 'Courting is a much more elegant and suitable phrase. You are, after all, in a period of courtship which will, one assumes, lead to marriage.'

Callie visibly gulped. 'Steady on, Agnes. We're a long way from that.'

'I don't see why,' Agnes said. 'After all, it must be on your minds. I'm quite sure it's on Brodie's. He is not one for trifling with a woman's affections. Why else would he woo you?'

She reared up indignantly as Immi collapsed in a fit of giggles.

'Now what have I said?'

'"Woo"!' Immi managed, clutching her sides in mirth. 'What the heck does "woo" mean?'

'Good gracious,' Agnes said huffily. 'Am I here simply to be an object of your ridicule, young lady?'

'Immi, don't be rude,' Callie said sternly.

'But – but *woo*?' Immi wiped her eyes. 'Isn't woo the noise a ghost makes?' She flapped her hands in some dreadful attempt to impersonate a ghost, and made a spooky noise, which, it had to be admitted, did rather sound like a distorted 'woo'.

'Immi!' Callie said, shocked.

'Well, really!' Agnes shook her head. 'I can't believe you're mocking me. What have I done to deserve it, may I ask? That was in extremely poor taste, Imogen.'

Immi's laughter died. 'Sorry, Mrs Wyndham. I wasn't mocking you, honestly. I really didn't mean it.'

As Callie and Immi gazed sorrowfully at her, a spark of mischief ignited within Agnes. She threw up her arms in an imitation of Immi's earlier actions and uttered a bone-chilling cry of, 'Woo!' making them both jump and leap back, alarm on their faces.

'Agnes!' Callie burst out laughing. 'I never knew you had it in you.'

'Not such a fuddy-duddy after all,' Agnes said, nodding her head vehemently.

'Well, well, what's all the jollity?'

They all turned to see Aubrey striding into the kitchen, looking the very picture of a Victorian gentleman, with his dark, grey-streaked hair, almost white at the temples, and an impressive beard, moustache and sideburns.

Dressed in a black frock coat and grey trousers, with a stiffly starched white collar and a wide, blue necktie tied in a loopy bow, he was the epitome of elegance, unlike poor Agnes who, in a white cotton nightdress, woollen stockings, a flannel bed jacket, and a white linen nightcap, was doomed to spend eternity looking as if she'd just got out of bed.

'Agnes just played a joke on us,' Immi said, her eyes still wide with shock at such an unexpected event.

'Did she indeed?'

As Agnes looked sheepishly at Aubrey, she noticed the twinkle in his eyes, and yet again imagined that her long redundant heart fluttered wildly. After all these years, he still had that effect on her. Had there ever been a more handsome man than Aubrey Wyndham?

'She did *this*.' Immi demonstrated Agnes's actions, which caused Aubrey to laugh heartily.

Agnes peered up at him, feeling almost shy at his obvious approval.

'That doesn't surprise me in the least,' Aubrey told Immi and Callie, while never taking his eyes off Agnes. 'She has the most delightful sense of humour, haven't you, my dear?'

Agnes dimly registered Immi's incredulous gasp of, 'She *does*?' but she was too busy basking in Aubrey's loving gaze to care.

Callie cleared her throat.

'We, er, were just discussing advent calendars,' she said. 'Agnes tells us there wasn't really one in this house until Brodie's dad was a child.'

With seeming reluctance, Aubrey turned to face Callie, and Agnes pulled herself together, tugging at her bed jacket and adjusting her nightcap, as if it had somehow slipped.

'I don't think there was, no,' Aubrey considered. 'I remember young Brodie always had a chocolate advent calendar. Ah, much like this one here,' he added, peering at the one on the wall. '"An assortment of chocolates, toffees and chocolate Santa figures",' he read. 'Sounds marvellous. Vegetarian and fair trade, too. Splendid.'

'Do you know what fair trade is, Mr Wyndham?' asked Immi.

'Of course he does!' Agnes said indignantly. 'Mr Wyndham is an extremely well-educated man. I do wish,' she added wistfully, 'that we could give one of those to Florence. It's hard enough at any time of year, but I feel it at Christmas most of all. Not being able to give her gifts. Not being able to feed her all manner of delicious treats. Oh, she would have loved plum pudding, I'm sure.'

'Plum pudding.' Aubrey gave a longing sigh. 'And roast goose...'

'It must be awful,' Immi said sadly. 'It doesn't seem fair that we get to do all those nice things at Christmas, and you can't.'

'Well,' Agnes said thoughtfully, 'we still have each other. Our little family. And home.'

'Exactly, my dear,' Aubrey said. 'What more do we need? And you must remember, Immi, that Agnes and I have had our turn at living. We've enjoyed many Christmases. We've sung carols, eaten the delicious food, and given and received gifts. Now it's your turn.'

Agnes said nothing, but her eyes misted with tears that could never fall. She remembered Aubrey's last Christmas before he died. He hadn't been able to see her, of course, and had no idea that she'd been with him that day. She knew what it had been like for him. She would hardly have called it a merry Christmas.

As usual, whenever she remembered those days, she was filled with rage at the injustice of it all. Even so, she did her best to subdue her feelings. She had never let on to Aubrey what she had witnessed, though she supposed he must have realised. He was a man, after all, and had his pride. She cared far too much about him to take that from him, unlike certain others who seemed to have derived great pleasure from trying.

'I've never had plum pudding or roast goose,' Immi admitted. 'What *is* plum pudding anyway, Mum?'

Callie shrugged. 'I've never had it either. I couldn't tell you.'

Agnes tutted at their ignorance. 'It's the most delicious, steamed pudding, rich with dried fruit. And are you seriously admitting that you've never had roast goose? You must try it! You should order a goose for Christmas this year.'

'I don't really fancy it,' Callie confessed. 'I've heard it's a bit fatty. I like my turkey. Christmas just wouldn't be Christmas without a turkey.'

'I remember having roast beef as well as goose,' Aubrey said dreamily.

'We had venison,' Agnes remembered. 'Roast goose, roast beef, and venison. And wassail!'

'Mulled wine.'

'Mince pies.'

'What's wassail?' asked Immi.

Aubrey and Agnes blinked and pulled themselves together.

'Wassail,' explained Agnes, 'was a sort of spiced cider. Delicious.'

'You had a lot of exotic things to eat and drink for Christmas,' Immi observed.

'But you must remember,' Agnes told her, 'that our celebrations didn't start on the first of December – unlike yours.' She nodded at the advent calendar. 'The festivities in my day began on Christmas Eve and ended on Twelfth Night, though of course we always marked Advent. These days you begin the celebrations far too early. It spoils the whole thing.'

'Quite,' Aubrey agreed. 'Too long a build-up.'

'Those advent calendars were in the shops straight after Halloween,' Callie told them.

Aubrey shook his head sadly. 'Not everything has changed for the better, if you ask me.'

'It'll be Easter eggs in the shops by January,' Immi said cheerfully.

'Anyway,' Callie said hastily, no doubt noticing the horror in Agnes's eyes, 'it may seem like Christmas has started too early in this house, but bear in mind we've got a whole village to get ready. The market huts are arriving at the weekend, and we're going to start transforming Rowan Vale into a winter wonderland.'

There was to be a Christmas market for a whole fortnight in the run-up to the big day, and the last weekend before Christmas was going to be Dickensian themed, with everyone dressing up in costumes.

'I'm so excited,' Immi said, clapping her hands. 'Me and Florrie are going to watch them putting the huts up. You're going to love it, Mr Wyndham, what with there being a Victorian weekend. You *will* come, won't you? Florrie really wants you to.'

Agnes swallowed as Aubrey's gaze fell on her. Her hands flew to the ribbons on her bed jacket, which she fiddled with as she always did when she was nervous.

Aubrey stifled a sigh and said, 'We'll see, Immi. We'll see.'

He looked so sad that it broke Agnes's heart. She might not wish to hurt his pride, but she knew she was hurting him in other ways and hated herself for it.

But what can I do? I have no choice. He mustn't go into the village!

She was a coward, and she knew it, and her cowardice was keeping him a prisoner at Harling Hall. Well, she would do her very best to give her beloved

Aubrey the best Christmas she possibly could, to make up for the pain she was causing him.

It's only because I love him. So much.

She couldn't be without him. If she didn't keep him close, she might lose him forever. She simply couldn't take that risk.

3

Saturday morning was one of those bright December days, where the sky's blue, but the air's so cold it almost strips the skin from your bones. I was pretty sure my nose was glowing like Rudolph's as Jack and I headed into the paddock and began to inspect the model village.

It was something we did periodically, making sure that everything was okay, and taking note of anything that needed repairing or repainting.

The model village was an exact replica of the Harling Estate as it had been in the 1930s, when Jack's great-grandfather had started building it. A trained craftsman, he'd drafted in some of his colleagues to help, and together they'd created an amazing feature that, somewhat inconveniently, covered the entire paddock behind our house.

Recently, the new owner of the estate, Callie, and her boyfriend, Brodie – who was the grandson of the previous owner, Sir Lawrence, or Lawrie as he preferred to be called – had decided that the model village would be a great asset to the village and had suggested that we open it up to the public.

I'd thought that was a great idea. With Freddie now at school, it meant I had some time to myself at last, and I was keen to get back into the world of work. I had to admit, my confidence was low, having been fortunate enough to stop working when I'd had my first baby twelve years ago. I'd been a stay-at-home mum ever since, which was what Jack and I had both wanted, but now it was time to go back to work I was a bag of nerves at the thought.

Running our own attraction, right here in the village, meant I wouldn't have to go for interviews, or try to find a job that I could work around the kids' school hours. I'd be my own boss. It seemed like a win-win situation to me.

Jack still wasn't so sure. He was worried about the lack of privacy, for one thing. The paddock backed onto our garden, which was quite small. The kids would be in full view of the tourists, he pointed out. Any visitors wandering through the model village would be able to watch them playing in the garden. He was far from happy about that and took the opportunity to remind me of the fact as we did our inspection.

Naturally, I felt the same, but I thought a six-foot fence would solve that problem.

'And block our view across the fields beyond,' Jack said grumpily.

'Only from downstairs.'

'And there's still the issue of visitors having to traipse through our outbuildings and garden to get to the paddock in the first place.'

That was true. Honeywell House had been constructed very oddly – from the outside, at least. Situated down quiet Honeywell Lane, you entered the property through a five-barred gate, finding yourself in a courtyard, edged on three sides by buildings. To the left was Honeywell House. Straight ahead and to the right was an L-shaped block of outbuildings.

We could access the garden from our kitchen door, but everyone else had to go through the outbuildings to get to it. That made it nice and secure for us, but it was far from ideal for paying visitors.

'Thing is,' Jack said, 'we're going to have to make a path at the side of our garden that people can follow to the paddock. And that means fencing down that side, too. It's going to take another chunk of the garden, and we can't really afford to lose any. It's small enough as it is with three boys and a dog the size of a grizzly bear.'

'He's not *that* big,' I said, glancing round and seeing Toby watching us forlornly from the garden. Well, actually, he *was* pretty hefty. 'It's just a matter of getting used to it, that's all. And it's not like we live in a city and there's nowhere for the boys to run around and let off steam, is it? There's the playground just up the road, and they can walk for miles round here.'

'But it's not ideal, though, is it, love?' Jack frowned as he picked up a model of what was supposed to be the ghost of Isaac Grace, the former landlord of

The Quicken Tree Inn in the village. 'Hello, he's looking a bit worse for wear. I'll have to give him a coat of paint.' He dropped Isaac into a bag and gave a heavy sigh. 'I'm not trying to pour cold water on the idea, honest I'm not, but I do think we need to give this more thought.'

'But it's all arranged!' I protested. 'We said yes to Callie and Brodie ages ago. Think about it. I can finally go back to work! And you'll be able to quit your job and work with me. We'll be a proper team. Self-employed, too. Imagine being our own bosses, Jack! It's the dream, isn't it?'

'It's a lot of hard work and insecurity, if you ask me,' Jack said. He'd never been the most adventurous of men, it had to be said, but I'd honestly thought I'd managed to talk him round. 'What if it doesn't attract as many paying visitors as Brodie forecast? And what about in the winter, when the tourists stay away because of the bad weather? What if we get a bad summer? What if—'

'What if, what if, what if,' I said sulkily. 'We can't live our lives worrying about what ifs! Look, everyone else in this village manages to make it work. Look at all the businesses there are here that depend on tourism. They earn enough during the main season to keep going through the winter months. I don't see why we shouldn't.'

'But locals still use the shops and the cafes and the pub out of season,' he explained in an annoyingly even tone. 'They're hardly going to want to visit a model village more than once, are they? Once their curiosity's been satisfied that'll be that, and then it really is down to us attracting enough tourists. I just don't see it happening, that's all.'

'So what are you suggesting?' I asked, my heart sinking at the prospect of him shutting the whole thing down. 'That we forget it?'

'No, of course not.' Jack took my hand and squeezed it. 'I can see you've got your heart set on this, love, and I don't want to take that away from you, but I think I should stick with my job on the trains. At least until we see how the land lies.'

'But you were looking forward to giving up your job! You said it would be great to be your own boss and work alongside me.'

'I know I did.' Jack sighed. 'It's just something you say though, isn't it? A pipe dream. I don't want to put that amount of pressure on us, that's all. We've got to think about this properly, love. We can't just jump in headfirst. Maybe if we give it a year, see how it goes...'

'You want me to work here by myself? How am I supposed to fit that around picking the kids up from school? And what about holidays and weekends, or if they're ill, or if they have to go to the dentist's?'

'Do you think,' Jack said carefully, 'that you're so keen to get back to work and, at the same time, have some back up with the kids, that you're maybe overlooking all the potential difficulties?'

I glared at him. 'For one thing,' I said coldly, 'the kids are as much your responsibility as mine. If I'm going to have to fit work around their school hours, I don't see why you shouldn't, too.'

Jack said nothing, but I saw his teeth nipping at his lower lip and knew he wanted to. I waited. Just let him say one more word, that was all.

It was okay for *him*, I reasoned. How was I ever supposed to get a job if I'd have to take a day off at the drop of a hat, should one of the boys become ill? Employers would take a dim view of that.

That's if I could even *find* a job. How did you explain that you'd had twelve whole years off work to look after children? There would be people far more appealing to employers than I'd be – people who felt at home in the workplace and had proved they could be trusted to stick at their jobs without having to juggle them around kids.

I could imagine the interviews – if I was lucky enough to get that far. The boss would probably ask me what childcare provision I had in place. I wasn't even sure if that was legal any longer, but would it stop them? They'd find a way, no doubt. People could be very sneaky. I'd bet fathers never had to worry about things like that.

I mentally shook my head at the injustice of it, then realised Jack was speaking after all.

'—when even running a Dyson over the carpet seems to be too much for you right now.'

I stopped dead. 'What did you say?'

Jack gave me a guilty look. 'I'm not criticising. I'm just worried, that's all.'

'Are you complaining about the state of the house?'

'No! I told you I'm not criticising. It's just...' He shrugged. 'It's not like you. You were always so houseproud, even when the boys were little. But lately—'

I blinked away angry tears. 'That sounds suspiciously like criticism to me,' I snapped. 'If you're so worried about the state of the house, why don't *you* pick up the Dyson once in a while?'

That wasn't fair, as Jack helped out around the house quite a lot, especially lately, but I was on a roll and fairness didn't come into it.

'Have you any idea how much hair that bloody dog sheds? You think I haven't cleaned up at least three times before you even get home? And then there are the boys, who come in like three mini tornadoes and destroy all my good work in minutes, and...'

I gulped down the tears, overwhelmed with emotion.

'Aw, love.' Jack pulled me into his arms, and I stiffened, not wanting to accept his apologies or his affection. 'I'm sorry. I wasn't having a go at you, honestly. I'm just so worried because you seem out of sorts all the time. You're worn out. You're falling asleep before Ashton's even gone to bed, and we never get the chance to watch the television together these days.' He hesitated. 'Let alone anything else.'

I shoved him away and glared at him. 'Are you seriously complaining that we don't have enough sex?'

He squirmed. 'Not complaining. Just, er, commenting.'

'Keep your bloody comments to yourself,' I snapped. 'Don't you think I've got enough to do without worrying about all that stuff?'

'"All that stuff"?' Jack sounded deeply hurt. 'I thought it was more than that to you.'

'You thought wrong then, didn't you? Honestly! Like I haven't got enough to deal with. You have no idea.'

'Well,' he said gently, 'tell me then.'

For a moment I was tempted to yell at him that he shouldn't need telling, but I saw the concern on his face, and I crumbled.

'I'm so tired,' I said, rubbing my eyes as if to prove it. 'I feel permanently exhausted, and my moods are all over the place.'

'Is that the whatchamacallit, perimenopause?' he asked.

'Yes, it bloody is. And I hate it. It's sapped my energy, scrambled my hormones, and made me so fat even my bloody coat doesn't fit. I'm fed up. I want my life back, and if you don't want to run this model village then I have no chance. Don't you get it? I can't do this without you! I need you to commit to it. I need you to say you'll work with me, and that you'll help me. I need *you*, Jack!'

Oh, lord, there I was blubbing again. Before I knew it my husband had me in his arms and I sobbed pathetically on his shoulder.

'It's all right,' he soothed. 'I'll help you, of course I will. We'll make it work.'

'Do you mean that?' I sniffed.

He handed me a tissue from his pocket, and I could only hope it was clean. Frankly, I had no option but to use it anyway.

'Course I mean it. Whatever you want, love. Promise.'

'Th-thank you.'

'But look, Clara, don't you think you should see the doctor again? This perimenopause lark has been going on for ages and you're only getting worse not better. There must be something they can give you, surely?'

'I told you; I don't want to take HRT. You know why!'

'What happened to your mum – there's no reason it should happen to you.'

Easy for him to say, though the doctors had told me the same thing. Mum had died of a blood clot, but they'd assured me that the risk of the same thing happening to me, even if I took HRT, was extremely low.

Mum had had other health factors that had made a clot more likely, not least that she smoked like a chimney.

I knew the facts, but it didn't stop me being terrified. It was the reason I'd come off the pill five years ago. I'd started to get terrible headaches, and the doctor suggested I go on the progesterone-only pill instead of the combined pill, but I wasn't taking any chances. Let Jack take responsibility for contraception for once.

My fear of going the same way Mum had meant I was desperate to avoid going on hormone replacement therapy, and I knew the doctor would only bring it up again if I went. It was easier to stay away and avoid the conversation.

'It's not fair,' I sobbed. 'I'm too young for all this. I'm only forty-one! I shouldn't be going through this for years.'

'But your gran did, didn't she?' he asked.

I was impressed he'd remembered what I'd told him when all this business started. Gran had been thirty-nine when she started the change of life, as she called it. My auntie had been forty-two. I guess it ran in the family.

'Well, it's still not fair,' I said.

'I know, love. I know.' Jack wiped my tears away and gave me a welcome cuddle. 'Come on, let's go back inside and I'll put the kettle on, eh? Make you a nice cuppa, and then how about after lunch we watch that film you wanted to see the other night. What do you think?'

'The boys—'

'Will be fine keeping themselves occupied for a couple of hours,' he said firmly. 'Come on. Inside.'

We headed back to the house, and I couldn't help thinking that, if Jack was so determined to keep the boys out of my way, it would be a wonderful opportunity to take a nap. Honestly, I'd prefer sleep to a film any day.

4

Lunch that day was a shambolic affair, with Freddie refusing to eat the tuna pasta I'd made him, even though he was the one who'd asked for it. Declan managed to drop his all over the carpet because he was too distracted by the television and failed to grasp the plate properly when I handed it to him, and Ashton didn't show up at all, having gone out with a school friend earlier and not bothering to return.

Jack took control, which was a good job because I was on the verge of meltdown.

'Freddie, if you don't eat that you'll get nothing else until dinner, and that's a promise. Declan, turn off the television and help me clean this mess up. From now on, you boys eat at the kitchen table, not in front of the telly. You understand?'

'Aw, Dad!' Declan began to protest but then his scowl turned to glee as Toby swooped in and ate the fallen pasta, clearing the area more effectively than even the Dyson would have managed. 'Ha, job done.'

'I don't think so,' Jack said firmly. 'That carpet will need scrubbing. It's tuna! Can you imagine…'

'Don't like sitting at the table,' Freddie wailed as I took his hand and led him into the kitchen.

'Well, the sooner you eat your lunch the sooner you can go back into the living room,' I told him.

'Not fair.' He climbed onto a chair and folded his arms, pouting.

'Whoever said life was?' I said, putting the plate in front of him. 'Now, eat it up.'

I gave Declan Ashton's meal, put cling film over what was left in the bowl, and put it in the fridge for my missing son, while Jack, bless him, scrubbed the carpet, and the two youngest boys sulkily ate their lunch.

I'd only just closed the fridge door when Ashton burst into the kitchen with a hearty cry of, 'Got anything to eat? I'm starving.'

Jack was just coming through from the living room with the bowl of soapy water and a cloth. He frowned as he tipped the dirty water down the sink.

'You're late.'

Ashton shrugged. 'Lost track of time.'

'It's past lunchtime.'

'Well,' Ashton said, nodding at his brothers, 'they're still eating so Mum can't have dished up that long ago.'

'They're still eating it,' I said, 'because Freddie refused his earlier and Declan dropped his on the floor and— Oh, never mind! Just wash your hands and sit down.'

'At the table?' he asked, wrinkling his nose.

'Yes,' Jack said firmly, 'at the table. From now on that's where all meals will be eaten. Honestly, it's like feeding time at the zoo with you lot.'

Ashton washed his hands and dropped into a chair, still grumbling. I handed him his lunch, passed all the boys a drink, and finally sat down, while my lovely husband made us a cup of tea. Jack and I had already decided we'd have a sandwich later while we watched television. Evidently the new rule about only eating in the kitchen didn't apply to us.

'Now,' Jack said at last, as he passed me a mug and joined us at the table, 'this afternoon your mum and I are going to watch a film in peace, so we want you lot to amuse yourselves.'

'I'm going out again anyway,' Ashton said, his cheeks bulging with pasta. 'I've only dropped in for something to eat. We're off to Rowan Farm to watch the ploughing. They're using Bonnie and Blossom.'

'What, when they've got that tractor?' Jack shook his head. 'Never understood why they still hang onto those two horses.'

'It's all part of the charm,' I reminded him. 'They're selling history there, aren't they? It's a Second World War farm and I reckon tourists are far more interested in seeing heavy horses do the work than an old tractor.'

'Speak for yourself,' Jack said. 'Besides, the use of tractors grew massively during the war. The farmers needed to feed a starving country, remember?'

'Maybe so, but horses were still used alongside them for long enough,' I said. 'Trouble with you is, you've got no soul. Horses are far nicer to look at than machines.'

'It's not *about* looking nice. Oh!' Jack gave up. 'Make sure you and those pals of yours don't get in Nick's way,' he told Ashton. 'Don't go causing any bother up there or I'll be having words.'

'We're not daft,' Ashton said scornfully. He chewed for a moment then said, 'Them market huts are going up, Mum. It's going to look great. You'll like that, won't you? You love a good market.'

I smiled fondly at him. 'I do, and this one is going to be amazing. They'll be selling all sorts of Christmassy stuff.'

'*I* want to see the market!' Freddie cried.

'It's not open yet, love. As soon as it does, we'll take you, promise.'

'Right, I'm off.' Ashton scraped back his chair. 'Thanks for that, Mum.'

'You're welcome. Be back at five.'

'Did that boy inhale his food?' Jack said, astonished. 'How can anyone eat so quickly?'

'*I* want to watch the horses on the farm with Ashton,' Freddie protested.

Ashton looked horrified. 'I'm not taking him with me!'

'Of course you're not,' Jack said. 'You get off. Me and your mum are going to watch a film and these two can occupy themselves with a game or something.'

'A game!' Declan pushed his plate away and gave me a pleading look. 'I'm not playing a game with *him*. How old do you think I am?'

'It'll only be for a couple of hours,' Jack told him. 'It won't hurt you to spend some time with your little brother.'

'If you'd let us have a telly in our bedrooms it wouldn't matter,' Declan pointed out, as Ashton took the opportunity to escape. 'But, oh no, we have to be the only kids in school who don't have one.'

'I know for a fact that's not true,' I said. 'Immi hasn't got one in her bedroom either.'

'Oh, her!' Declan said crossly. 'No, she just lives in a massive mansion and gets to talk with ghosts. Poor Immi.'

'Look,' Jack said, 'you've got plenty of board games upstairs. Why don't you play snakes and ladders with Freddie? Or Frustration. Something simple like that. It's not for long.'

'I want to go on my Nintendo Switch,' Declan said crossly.

'*I* want to play Lego,' Freddie said eagerly. 'Daddy, will you play Lego with me?'

'Yeah, *Daddy*. Why don't you play Lego with him?' Declan suggested.

'You know why! I've just told you, I'm watching a film with your mum, and—'

'It's okay,' I said. Honestly, I was worn out just listening to them, and totally past caring about watching TV with Jack. 'Declan, you go and play on your Nintendo Switch. Jack, you help Freddie with his Lego. I'll stick these pots in the dishwasher then I'll watch the film in peace.'

'But I was going to watch it with you,' Jack protested. 'We were going to have a couple of hours together. Just you and me for a change.'

'When the kids are in bed we'll have time then,' I said. 'You weren't that bothered about watching it anyway. We'll find something else we both like tonight.'

'You'll be asleep,' he mumbled, but I was too tired to argue, and he was clearly too smart. 'Okay, but I'll stack the dishwasher. You boys go upstairs, and I'll meet you up there in ten minutes.'

'Bring biscuits,' Freddie ordered as he scrambled down from the chair.

'Honestly, who do they think they are, issuing orders?' Jack demanded as the two boys rushed out of the kitchen.

I was already rustling through the cupboard. 'Here,' I said, putting a packet of custard creams on the worktop. 'Take them with you. Anything for a bit of peace.'

* * *

I really tried to watch the film but my mind kept wandering. I was tired, but not tired enough to doze off, and my levels of concentration were way too low to keep track of a heavily plotted, multi-character murder mystery.

I flicked through the channels, looking for something lighter that might interest me, but there was nothing. I sighed and switched off the television, then, on impulse, I went over to the sideboard and rummaged around in the bottom drawer. As I'd thought, my sketchbook and pencils were in there, and after a moment's hesitation I took them out.

Sitting on the sofa, I flicked through the drawings I'd done over the last few years. I hadn't touched the sketch pad for well over – well, I had no idea, really. I wasn't even sure if I'd drawn anything since Freddie was born.

I smiled wistfully as I gazed at the sketches I'd made. There was a drawing of Ashton and Declan, sitting together in an armchair, both fast asleep in their pyjamas. Ashton must have been around five years old, and Declan maybe two or three. Bless them. They looked like little cherubs.

I turned the page, and my heart fluttered in a way I thought it had forgotten how to do. There was a sketch of Jack, looking gorgeous in the jacket and trousers he wore for work.

He was a train driver, employed by the Harling Estate to drive the steam trains between the pretty Cotswold market town of Much Melton and Harling's Halt. Harling's Halt was part of the estate, and where many of the tourists to the living history village of Rowan Vale began their visit.

I'd been to Harling's Halt many times. It was wonderful to catch the steam train to Much Melton, for one thing. Travelling in one of those old carriages was a real treat, and the boys loved it.

But even without the train, the Harling's Halt experience was fun. With employees of the estate dressed in World War One uniforms and dresses, strolling up and down the platform or gathered together, for all the world as if they were saying goodbye to their sweethearts, there was an amazing atmosphere there.

Vintage bunting adorned the station, songs from the Great War played softly in the background, and propaganda posters were pinned to the noticeboards. There was also the most gorgeous little cafe, The Victory Tearooms, which I used to love going in before I had the boys. I never went in there now, though. It was far too elegant for me these days.

I smiled as I gazed at the drawing of Jack, drinking in every detail of that familiar face. He looked so handsome in his uniform, and I remembered how thrilling it had been to ride on the train, knowing he was driving it. It had been ages since I'd last done that. I couldn't even remember the last time I'd visited the station.

Sighing, I flicked through the drawings until I came to one I'd almost forgotten about. My fingers stilled and my heart beat a little faster as I gazed down at the portrait. Jack had once asked me who the man was, and I'd told him it was just some actor from the television who'd caught my attention. I'd hated having to lie to him.

Although hadn't I been lying to him right from the moment we met?

I felt a wave of shame and told myself, for the millionth time, that it hadn't been like that. That I hadn't used him. That my love for Jack was genuine.

Even so, I knew that if he ever found out the truth, he'd be so hurt our marriage might never recover from it. I should have been honest with him from that very first day...

5

SIXTEEN YEARS EARLIER

I'd had a wonderful holiday in Scotland and was utterly depressed that it was almost over, and I'd soon have to go home.

'That's what makes holidays so special,' my friend, Jenni, pointed out. 'The fact that they end. Chin up. We can always come back next year.'

I doubted it. This painting holiday had been relatively inexpensive, but given the way things were back home, who knew when I'd be able to put the money aside to return. If I could have afforded it, I'd have been back three or four times a year to paint the Highlands in all their different seasons. Unfortunately for me, I *couldn't* afford it. The future was way too uncertain, and I was already sick of the situation I'd found myself in.

'That's beautiful,' Jenni breathed as she peered over my shoulder at the canvas I was working on. 'You've really caught the atmosphere of Caerbrighde Castle. It looks – I don't know – haunting somehow.'

'I just painted what was there,' I said with a shrug.

'No, there's more to it than that. *I* painted what was there. You, on the other hand, added your own special magic to it. It looks amazing.'

I had to admit, I was quite pleased with it myself. I loved old buildings, and they seemed to bring out the best of my artistic talents. I was good at drawing figures and animals, but when it came to stately homes, castles, abbeys and the like, it was as if my brush had a life of its own.

Arriving back at the hotel later that afternoon, I'd showered and changed, ready and eager for dinner. It had been a long day. Jenni and I had gone out very early, taking only a few sandwiches and a thermos flask of coffee with us, so we were both hungry.

The hotel was pretty basic, but it was clean, and the food was tasty and filling, even if it had no chance of being awarded a Michelin star.

'You know what?' I said, as we settled at the table and perused the menu. 'I'm going to try the haggis, neeps and tatties.'

'You never are!' Jenni giggled. 'Are you insane? You know what they put in a haggis, right?'

'Well...' I hesitated. I wasn't 100 per cent certain to be honest, but I had a feeling it wasn't something I'd eat under any other circumstances. 'Not really, but—'

'Lamb's heart, lungs and liver,' came a voice behind me. 'All nicely mixed up with a bit of beef or lamb mince, some onion, oatmeal, suet, salt and pepper, spices like nutmeg, mace and coriander, and maybe an extra pinch of black pepper.'

I looked round to see a young man with dark hair and twinkly brown eyes smiling at me from the next table.

'All wrapped up and cooked in a sheep's stomach,' he finished cheerfully.

Jenni made a gagging sound, and he laughed.

A fair-haired man sitting opposite him shook his head. 'Fancy telling them! You should have let them eat it and *then* told them.'

'Well, aren't *you* charming?' Jenni said.

'I'd never be so cruel,' the dark-haired man said solemnly. He held out his hand. 'I'm Jack. My friend with the warped sense of humour is Richard.'

Hesitantly, I reached over and shook it. 'Clara, and that's my friend Jenni. You don't sound Scottish, but you seem to know a lot about haggis. Are you a chef?'

The two of them laughed.

'Him?' Richard whooped. 'He'd burn water, that one.'

'I just figured, if I was coming to Scotland, I should look these things up,' Jack explained.

'So have you tried haggis then?' Jenni asked doubtfully.

'Not yet,' he admitted. 'Trying to pluck up the courage.'

'Oh, come off it,' Richard said scornfully. 'You know perfectly well you won't touch it. None of us will, and who can blame us?'

'Well,' I said firmly, 'I'm *definitely* having it.' Who did he think he was, telling me what I would and wouldn't eat?

He raised an eyebrow. 'What, the full works or the vegetarian option?'

'There's a vegetarian option?' Jenni sounded relieved. 'Oh, thank God! I think I'd barf if I had to eat lamb's innards. I'll go for that.'

Jack and I looked at each other, each silently daring the other.

'There's the Balmoral Chicken,' Richard announced, studying the menu.

'What's that?' Jenni asked, as Jack and I continued to lock eyes in a challenge.

'Chicken breast, stuffed with haggis, wrapped in bacon and served with a whisky cream sauce.'

My mouth watered at the thought. It sounded so much nicer than haggis, neeps and tatties.

'No,' Jack said firmly. 'I'm going for the traditional dish.'

I tilted my chin. 'Me too.'

'Why don't you two wee lassies join us at our table?' Richard suggested, putting on a dreadful Scottish accent. 'Then we'll be able to keep a close eye on each other and see who throws it all up again first.'

'Deal,' Jenni said. We moved over to their table and duly placed our orders with a grinning waiter. He must have seen the fear in my eyes.

In the end, Richard went for the Balmoral Chicken, which really did look tasty, while Jenni – after all that fuss – chose scampi and chips. Jack and I were served our meals in long, shallow dishes with three compartments. One contained the neeps – mashed turnips – one the mashed potatoes, and one the dreaded haggis. We were also given a jug of what turned out to be the whisky and cream sauce, which we were expected to apply liberally to our meal.

Maybe, I thought hopefully, the sauce will hide the taste of the haggis.

Jenni and Richard were already eating, although I noticed Richard was tucking into his potatoes and avoiding the stuffed chicken breast for now.

I picked up my fork and let it hover uncertainly over the dish, not sure which compartment to dive into first.

'I dare you,' Jack murmured.

I narrowed my eyes and immediately dug my fork into the haggis. As I raised it to my lips, I realised all three of my companions were watching me in silence, and there was no going back now.

Trying not to think about what was in it, I shovelled it into my mouth and chewed valiantly. To my astonishment, it wasn't that bad.

'Well?' Jack asked.

'It's okay,' I told him. 'Sort of like a spicy mince.'

'Really?' Jenni asked suspiciously.

'Do you want to try a bit? Unless you're too scared.'

'Not scared,' she said wryly. 'I just have more sense than the rest of you. Mm, this scampi's fab!'

Richard and Jack immediately braved the haggis, and although Richard had technically taken the wimp's way out, all three of us congratulated ourselves as we finally put down our knives and forks and decided that, although we probably wouldn't make a habit of eating haggis, it hadn't been anywhere near as bad as we'd feared. Providing we didn't think about what it was, of course.

'I suppose,' Jack said thoughtfully, 'it's no worse than eating black pudding with your breakfast.'

'I would *never* eat black pudding,' I admitted. 'Just the thought of it makes me heave.'

Realising how ridiculous that sounded I couldn't help but laugh, and Jack joined in.

'Well, I think you did brilliantly,' he told me. 'Let me buy you a drink to celebrate your courage.'

I was about to tell him how patronising that sounded, but I was rapidly running out of money, and alcohol was an extra luxury I was having to ration, so I nodded and thanked him.

After that, the four of us hung out together in the bar. Richard and Jenni seemed to get along all right, but it was Jack and I who really clicked. He was funny, warm and kind, and – yeah, okay – seriously hot. We stayed up talking long after the other two had retired to their rooms for the night.

'So how long are you staying here?' he asked me, as we sipped whisky in the otherwise empty bar. He'd dared me to drink it, and after my bravado with the haggis I could hardly refuse, could I? I'd never tried it before and, to be honest, it was vile, though I had no intention of admitting it.

The hotel was all dark wood and tartan and clearly aimed at tourists. Even so, it was comfortable and had a nice atmosphere. I liked it, and wished I didn't have to leave so soon.

'Just another two days,' I said regretfully. 'How about you?'

'Only just arrived,' he said. 'That's a shame. It would have been nice to see more of you.'

I raised an eyebrow.

He blushed fiercely. 'I mean, more of your company. Not... Anyway, it's a shame. That's all.'

He was sweet, he really was. Surprisingly so, for someone so gorgeous.

'I guess there's no chance you could stay on a bit longer?' he asked, swirling the amber liquid round in his glass and eyeing me with a hopeful expression.

I shook my head. 'Afraid not. I've got to get back home.'

'Work?'

I sighed. 'If only.'

It was his turn to raise an eyebrow. 'You sound fed up.'

'I got made redundant a month ago,' I said. 'Not that it was a brilliant job anyway, but even so.'

'What did you do?'

'I worked in human resources for a paint manufacturer in Lancashire. Horrible company, but the pay wasn't bad. I got a bit of redundancy money, but it won't last long. I've signed up with a couple of employment agencies, but who knows how long it will be before I find another job?'

'Aw, sorry to hear that,' he said. He stared into his glass and pulled a face. 'You know what? This is bloody awful.'

I grinned, relieved he'd said it first. 'Isn't it just!'

'I could murder a beer. How about you?'

'Beer's fine by me,' I said.

He ordered us both a local beer which, thankfully, turned out to be much nicer than the whisky.

We spent the next hour chatting about my painting, and how I'd been lucky enough to find a work colleague like Jenni who was interested in art, too, and had been happy to come to Scotland with me instead of signing up for the package holiday in Lloret de Mar that some of our friends at the factory had arranged.

Jack told me how Richard had persuaded him to come up to the Highlands to do some hiking as his friend was, apparently, an outdoorsy type.

'Are you into hiking then?' I asked.

He pulled a face. 'You must be joking! This is my idea of hell really, but he's gone through all his other mates, and I was the only one left.' He laughed. 'Anyway, I had holiday owing, plus I needed to get away for a few days to give my parents some space, so I figured, why not?'

I wondered why his parents needed space but felt it would be insensitive to ask. Maybe they were going through a bad patch in their marriage? Although Jack didn't sound too worried. He had a twinkle in his eye and such a cheerful manner that I couldn't imagine anything getting him down. He was so relaxing to be around. And he had the most gorgeous smile...

'I suppose,' I said regretfully, 'we ought to be making a move. They'll be closing the bar in the minute.'

'I know.' He sighed. 'I've been trying to pretend I haven't seen the pleading looks they've been giving us, cos the truth is, I really don't want to say goodnight.'

My breath caught in my throat. The way he was looking at me...

'Well,' I said, trying not to sound too awkward or embarrassed, 'we don't *have* to say goodnight. Do we?'

I don't know what came over me that night. I really wasn't the sort of person to have a one-night stand, and I'd never done so before, but somehow, with Jack it was different.

We ended up in his hotel room, slightly the worse for wear with the bit of whisky and several beers we'd consumed, but nowhere near drunk enough to be unsure of what we were doing. Jack had been responsible enough to visit the gents and get a packet of condoms from the machine before we went upstairs, and he was very careful to check – multiple times – that this was what I really wanted.

By the time we'd taken each other's clothes off and tumbled into bed I was desperate for him to stop asking if I was sure and just get on with it.

Thankfully, my obvious passion finally reassured him that he'd no reason to worry, and he spent the next hour or so making very sure I had no cause to regret my impetuous behaviour.

'I don't make a habit of this, you know,' I said later, as we lay looking up at the ceiling, both of us a bit stunned by the unexpected events of the evening.

'Neither do I. I've never had a one-night stand before,' he admitted, sounding a bit ashamed of the fact.

'Neither have I,' I assured him. 'It's sort of exciting, isn't it? But I guess what happens in Scotland stays in Scotland, so no harm done.'

He turned over to face me, propping himself up on one elbow, so I did the same, and we gazed at each other a bit bashfully.

'Does it have to stay in Scotland, though?' he asked. 'Couldn't we keep in touch? Maybe meet up again.'

'I hardly know you,' I pointed out. 'You hardly know me. We might not even like each other.'

'Only one way to find out,' he said reasonably.

I shrugged. 'I guess... What do you do, anyway? I mean, I presume you have a job.'

'I do. I'm a fireman.'

As I gasped in admiration, he added hastily, 'Don't get any ideas! Not *that* sort of fireman. I work with heritage steam engines. It's my job to keep the hungry beast fed, among other things. I've been working there ever since I left school ten years ago, but soon I'll achieve my ambition to be a train driver.'

He sounded so proud of the fact that I laughed. 'Seriously?'

'Seriously,' he said, a bit huffily. 'And what's wrong with that?'

'Nothing at all. I don't think I've met *any* sort of fireman before, and I've certainly not met a train driver. Do you like working with steam engines then?'

'Love it,' he said. 'I never wanted to do anything else. My dad drove steam engines, too, and it was sort of understood that I'd follow him into the profession.'

'You're not one of those people who collects toy trains and has model railways running all through your house, are you?' I asked worriedly.

He hesitated, which didn't exactly fill me with confidence.

'Not through the house, no,' he said slowly.

'Oh, lord. Meaning what?'

'Well, we do have a model train station at home,' he admitted. 'But it's just part of a larger model village.'

'You have a model village?' Was he having me on?

'Yeah. In the paddock attached to our garden.'

My eyes widened. 'Blimey, get you. A paddock. Are you rich then?'

He laughed. 'Not at all. It's not our house. We rent it.'

'Who's we?' I asked. 'Oh, of course. You still live with your mum and dad.'

'For now. Pretty soon it will just be me. My parents are relocating to the Isle of Wight.'

'Random.'

'Not really. Dad retired last year and he always promised Mum they'd move there one day. She's from the island, you see. She still has family there and has always wanted to go back, so they made a deal they'd do so as soon as he stopped working. That's why I've come here out of the way. They're in the middle of packing and wanted me out from under their feet while they go through all their belongings.' He shrugged. 'To be honest, it's going to be weird living in Rowan Vale by myself, but they've bought somewhere and – are you okay?'

The shock must have shown on my face. 'Rowan Vale?'

He nodded. 'Yes. Do you know it?'

'Erm, think so. I haven't been there but isn't it that tourist village in the Cotswolds? The one that's like a living museum?'

'That's right,' he said. 'It's won awards. You ought to see it!'

'Rowan Vale... Yes, I've seen photos of it. It looks amazing. I've always wanted to visit there.'

He sat up, looking quite proud. 'Maybe you could visit one day.' He reached out and brushed back my wavy, red hair, which I suspected was even more of a tangled mess than usual, given my recent exertions. 'So, what do you think about staying in touch? I know we live quite some distance apart, but we could speak on the phone. See how it goes.'

I sat up, too, and hugged my knees, thinking.

I'd only just met this man, and okay, he looked and seemed to be lovely, and we'd certainly had a great time together. And there must be something special about him for me to go to bed with him the night I met him. I'd never done *anything* like that before. There *had* to be a reason. But – Rowan Vale...

I saw the hopeful look in his dark eyes and pushed away the warning voice in my head. 'Okay,' I said. 'I don't see why not.'

'Great! I'll give you my number. Well, later.' He pulled me to him and kissed me, igniting all sorts of passions that completely drove thoughts of exchanging phone numbers out of my mind for a satisfyingly lengthy amount of time.

But we *had* swapped numbers the following morning, and for months afterwards we'd chatted regularly on the phone, as Jack settled into life without his parents around and I tackled a succession of temping jobs.

On numerous occasions, Jack travelled up to Lancashire to spend the weekend at the flat I shared with Jenni and another girl. Nine months after our initial meeting, we even managed a package holiday in Spain, where we had a fabulous time, the bond between us deepening even more as we shared a hotel room for an entire fortnight and swam, sunbathed, went sightseeing and shopping together.

But I'd somehow managed to find an excuse not to visit him at Honeywell House, until one day he told me that his parents were returning to the village for a visit and would love to meet this mysterious woman their son had been dating all this time.

I couldn't think of a way out of it, and so a whole year after our fateful meeting in Scotland, I finally visited him at his home in Rowan Vale.

And I never left.

6

The knock at the door pulled me out of my mental excursion into the past, and I blinked, somehow surprised to find myself sitting in the living room of Honeywell House, and not in that dark wood and tartan bedroom back at the hotel in the Highlands.

Realising we had a visitor, I hastily closed the sketchbook and shoved it on the coffee table before rushing into the hallway.

'Who is it?' Jack called from upstairs.

'How should I know?' I called back. 'I'm not Madame Mariska, am I?'

'Who?' came his puzzled reply, and I rolled my eyes, wondering how Jack didn't recognise the name of the celebrity psychic and medium from the popular television show, *It's Haunted!* Then again, he rarely watched television apart from documentaries and the odd film he fancied.

I threw open the door and managed a smile as I found Callie and Brodie on the step. Part of me was pleased to see them, but the other part was frantically trying to remember how tidy the living room was, not to mention the kitchen, and if Jack had managed to get the smell of the tuna out of the carpet.

'Come in,' I said. 'Nice to see you both.'

'Who is it?' Jack called again.

'Callie and Brodie,' I called back, as I led them both into the living room.

'I'll be down in a minute,' he replied.

I heard a faint wail of, 'No, Daddy, not yet!' from Freddie and gave our guests an apologetic smile.

'He's helping Freddie with his Lego,' I explained.

'No need for him to leave it,' Callie said hastily. 'Honestly, it's just an informal visit. We've been out watching the huts go up and we thought we'd pop by and see how you were doing. Plus, we've got some big news.'

'Ooh,' I said. 'Are you two—?'

'It's not about us,' she said hastily. 'It's the Dickensian Weekend. We've got our star guest to open it. Cain Carmichael's said yes!'

Cain Carmichael had been a notorious rock star back in the dark, distant days of the 1970s. He'd had quite a few marital scrapes and some of his records had been banned, but in recent years he'd completely turned his life around and had become a model citizen and a pillar of society, residing in a Cotswolds mansion about a thirty-five-minute drive from Rowan Vale.

'Congratulations,' I said, although I had to wonder if they couldn't have found someone a bit more, well, relevant.

'It's one more thing ticked off the list,' Brodie said. 'Were you putting the kettle on by any chance, Clara?'

Callie nudged him in the ribs. 'Brodie!'

'What? You said you were desperate for a hot drink and it's bloody freezing out there.' He unzipped his coat and gave a sigh of pleasure. 'Your radiators are lovely and warm.'

'Here, I'll take your coats and make that drink,' I said.

'Are you sure?' Callie asked anxiously. 'You don't have to if you're busy. We wouldn't want to interrupt—'

'I wasn't doing anything,' I admitted. 'I was supposed to be watching a film, but I couldn't concentrate, so I might as well make a cuppa as just sit there.'

'Brain fog again?' Callie asked sympathetically, knowing all too well the struggles I'd been having lately.

I nodded, not wanting to talk about it. I was sick to the back teeth of the perimenopause, quite honestly. I was pretty sure there'd been a time when I'd talked about other things, but it was getting increasingly hard to remember it.

'Tea or coffee?' I asked, after I'd hung up their coats.

Brodie beamed at me. 'Coffee please. We brought you something to go with it.'

Callie rummaged in her handbag and brought out a paper bag.

'Lebkuchen,' she said.

'Bless you.'

Callie giggled. 'I know! It does sound a bit like a sneeze. It's German gingerbread. I got them from Mrs Herron's Teashop. Shona said Max has made them. They're celebrating Christmas with a whole selection of German desserts and bakes. I've tried some of them and, oh my word, they're absolutely yummy.'

Shona was the manager of the vintage teashop in the village, and Max was the German widower she'd recently started a relationship with. He was actually a teacher but loved making treats for the teashop. His baking was already legendary.

'I'd better stay well away then,' I said gloomily, patting my bloated stomach. 'I can't fit into most of my clothes as it is.'

'Well, if you don't want one...' Brodie said, grinning.

I took the bag from Callie's hands. 'I never said that,' I told him hurriedly. 'And it would be rude to say no since they're a gift.'

Jack came downstairs, trailing a reluctant Freddie.

'Look what we've got,' I said, knowing it would put a smile on my son's face. 'Gingerbread!'

Freddie's face brightened immediately.

'You'd never think,' said Jack, 'that he'd just wolfed down half a packet of custard creams. The kid's a walking dustbin.'

I handed the bag of lebkuchen to Jack and went to make drinks, declining his offer to make them instead.

Ten minutes later we were all sitting in the living room, drinking coffee (or milk in Freddie's case) and munching the lebkuchen. They were so tasty. Soft, chewy and spicy, and not at all as I'd expected. Freddie decided he didn't like them after all, but Toby happily finished what he'd started, while our youngest – clearly bored with all the grown-up chat – closed his eyes and fell asleep.

'Thank goodness for that,' Jack said, nodding at our sleeping angel who was curled up in the armchair. 'I thought I'd never get a break.'

'Welcome to my world,' I said grimly.

'Ooh,' Callie said suddenly, 'is that a sketchbook? Who's the artist?'

'No one,' I said quickly. 'It's just some doodling, that's all.'

'Doodling?' Jack laughed. 'Don't be so modest. Not to put too fine a point on it, she's brilliant. Has she never shown you her drawings, Callie?'

Callie shook her head and gave me a reproachful look. 'I didn't even know you could draw! Why didn't you tell me?'

'Honestly, they're just amateur scribblings,' I said desperately. 'Nothing worth showing you.'

Before I could stop him, Jack reached over, grabbed the sketchbook from the coffee table, and handed it to Callie. 'See what you think,' he said, before turning to me. 'I haven't seen you with that for a long time, love. Are you thinking of starting again?'

'I was just looking for something in the sideboard,' I lied. 'It was in the drawer. I'd forgotten all about it.'

'But, Clara, these are really good!' Callie showed Brodie the drawing she was looking at and his eyes widened.

'Wow, that's brilliant. You've got Jack to a tee.'

'Ooh, is that the one of me in my uniform?' Jack winked at me. 'You were particularly fond of that as I recall.'

'Shut up,' I said, blushing.

'He does look handsome,' Callie said. 'I can see why you like it. Aw, and look at this one. It's Toby!' She waved the drawing in front of our dog, who looked suitably impressed. 'See, it's you, you gorgeous, gorgeous boy.'

'Are you sure you're not still talking about the one of me?' Jack said, laughing.

Callie rolled her eyes. 'You're so talented,' she told me. 'Look, Brodie. It's your grandfather!'

She must have reached the one of Lawrie, sitting on the bench outside All Souls' church. That meant...

I jumped up and snatched the sketchbook from her hand. Callie looked startled, as well she might.

'Sorry,' I said, 'but I find it all a bit embarrassing.'

'But why would you?' Brodie asked, sounding confused. 'If I could draw like that, I'd be showing my sketches to everyone.'

'Well, I'm not you,' I said, shoving the sketchbook back in the drawer and slamming it shut. Realising that sounded rude I added, 'But thanks for being so nice about them. How's the market coming on? You said the huts are going up?'

Callie and Brodie exchanged puzzled glances but kindly didn't push me.

'Really well,' said Callie. 'The huts look so cute. The village green's been transformed, and there's a line of them along Victoria Walk, too. We've got some brilliant traders lined up. The fairy lights will be installed over the next few days, and the Christmas tree will be arriving and put in place by early next week, so it should be all systems go for the big switch-on next Friday.'

'The boys are really excited about it,' Jack said. 'It's going to be a long two weeks for them until the lights go on. Mind you, I'm pretty excited about it, too. We've never had a Christmas market in Rowan Vale before, at least as long as I've been alive. It's going to be amazing.'

'I'm looking forward to the Dickens-themed weekend,' Brodie admitted. 'I can't wait to get all dressed up as Inspector Bucket from *Bleak House*, although I really wanted to be Ebenezer Scrooge.'

'You're far too generous and nice to be Scrooge,' Callie said, laughing. 'Bad enough that you're going to be dressed entirely in black. It was good of Jasper to tell us where he gets his costumes from. Our own designer would have been swamped.'

Jasper Edgecumbe was the photographer who worked in a studio on the green, taking photographs of customers who had hired Victorian costumes from him. He produced the most amazing sepia photographs which looked startlingly authentic and did a good trade all year round. He'd no doubt make a killing from this Dickensian weekend.

He had kindly given Callie the name of his supplier, as – like she'd said – the designer who provided most of the costumes for the actors employed for the living museum would never have coped with so much demand in such a short space of time, especially so close to Christmas when there was a huge surge in fancy dress parties and events. The one Jasper used not only made and sold costumes, but sourced and hired them from other suppliers around the country on their customers' behalf.

'What about the station?' Jack asked eagerly. 'Did you decide about what's going to happen there? Are you still going to include *The Signal-Man*?'

'Yes,' Callie said. 'We're going to have actors playing the parts, and a narrator. But only when it gets dark so it's a bit spookier and there won't be any small children around.'

'We're also going to be selling copies of the book and other Dickens novels in The Victory Tearooms,' Brodie said. 'We've come to an arrangement with the bookshop in Chipping Royston. We won't make anything from it, but it adds to the atmosphere, and it's a good way to build a relationship with our neighbours.'

'You never know when we'll need their help,' Callie agreed. 'In return, the bookshop is putting posters up advertising our event. And, of course, lovely Pippa is covering it for *The Cotswolds Courier*,' she added, referring to Shona from the teashop's youngest daughter, who was a local reporter. 'With our star guest we might even be able to get the local television news interested.'

'Star guest?' asked Jack hopefully.

'Cain Carmichael,' she said proudly.

Jack visibly slumped. 'Oh, really?'

'Sounds like you've got it all under control,' I said hastily. 'You're a whizz at this stuff, Callie. Look how quickly you organised the 1940s weekend in the summer! I'd never have believed it possible.'

'Oh, that wasn't down to me,' she said modestly. 'I had so much help. Everyone was brilliant, pulling together the way they did.' She tilted her head, thinking. 'Hey, you know what you could do, Clara? You could draw scenes from the market and the Dickensian Weekend! We could get the sketches printed and sell them, or make them into Christmas cards, or...'

'We wouldn't have time to make them into Christmas cards,' Brodie said gently.

'For next year!' Callie said excitedly.

'She doesn't just draw, you know,' Jack told her proudly. 'You should see her paintings. She's especially good at old buildings. Show them that one you did of the castle in Scotland, love. And that one of the ruins of Hailes Abbey.'

'Seriously?' Callie looked thrilled. 'Hey, Clara, what about painting Harling Hall?' She looked at Brodie. 'It's your grandfather's birthday in February. He'd love a painting of the Hall, wouldn't he? What do you think?'

'Would you be able to paint it by February?' Brodie asked me doubtfully.

'She painted the castle in less than a week,' Jack said. 'In fact, she painted it in a day, but she wanted to perfect it. February wouldn't pose any sort of challenge, would it?'

'Thanks for deciding for me,' I said, feeling a flutter of panic at the thought. 'Thanks, Callie, but honestly I'm not up to the job.'

'You've just lost your confidence, that's all,' Jack soothed.

'I'm not good enough!' I insisted.

'Well, look, why don't you two come to dinner tomorrow night and we'll chat about it a bit then?' Callie suggested. 'You can have a look around and see what you think. You've only been to Harling Hall once, so you're long overdue a visit.'

Jack and I exchanged glances.

To my shame, I'd turned down all Callie's previous invitations. I'd always had an excuse – I wasn't feeling well, the kids had to be somewhere, Jack had already made plans...

'But the thing is, I mean, we'd never get a babysitter at such short notice.'

'That wouldn't be a problem,' Callie said. 'I'm sure Mia would look after the boys for you, and if not, you could bring them with you.'

'How about it?' Jack asked me hopefully. 'They'd love that, wouldn't they? They've always wanted a look inside the big house.'

I gave a half-laugh, feeling increasingly trapped.

'I could hardly focus on looking at the house with those three to keep an eye on.'

'Don't worry about that. Immi will keep them occupied,' Callie promised.

'And we've got our spies anyway,' Brodie added, with a laugh. 'Agnes and Aubrey will make sure they don't get up to anything they shouldn't, and Florrie will love to grass on them if they do.'

Callie laughed, too. 'Ooh yes, she'd love that. So, you'll come then? How about sevenish?'

I closed my eyes. 'No, sorry!'

There was a silence, and I opened my eyes, feeling sick with dread. Jack gave me a slight shake of the head. Callie and Brodie looked stunned.

'Is there – is there something you're not telling me?' Callie asked nervously. 'Only, you've turned down so many invitations to the Hall, and I'd really love you to pop by one day. It doesn't have to be anything formal, you know. And if you don't want to paint the house, that's fine. I'd still love you both to come to dinner.'

I gave Jack a pleading look and he sighed.

'You're going to have to tell them, love,' he said.

'Tell us what?' asked Brodie.

Jack looked at me. When I didn't speak, he said, 'Fact is, she's scared to go to Harling Hall. She's afraid of ghosts.'

There was a long silence as Callie and Brodie absorbed that information. I could only imagine what they must be thinking. Callie had only just accepted her ability to see all ghosts after years of denial, and poor Brodie had lost his inheritance because, unlike his grandfather, he didn't have that ability.

Callie's gift had led to her becoming the new owner of the Harling Estate, whereas Brodie's lack of it had meant he'd lost his claim to his inheritance. Ghosts were a big deal in both their lives for different reasons, but I don't think someone having a fear of ghosts had ever entered their heads – particularly not someone living in Rowan Vale, of all places.

'Well,' Brodie said at last, 'you moved to the wrong village then, didn't you?' He tried to make a joke of it, but I wasn't in the mood for laughing.

'But you came to the Hall for the ball at the end of the 1940s weekend,' Callie said, puzzled. 'Although,' she admitted slowly, 'you were a bit hyped up, as I recall. On edge. But I thought that was just your hormones.'

'Not hormones for once,' I joked feebly. 'Nerves. I didn't want to let you down when you'd gone to so much effort, and Jack really wanted to be there.'

'Right...' Callie seemed dazed by my confession. 'But as for the Hall's ghosts, you wouldn't even know they were there. You must know that from the ball.'

'The ball that ended with you being whisked away by the spirit of a Roman centurion?' I asked dryly.

She looked sheepish. 'Yes, well, that was unexpected. But look, *you* wouldn't see them. You can't even hear them. They won't bother you at all and you can just pretend they don't exist.'

'But they *do* exist!' I said desperately. 'And it gives me the creeps, knowing they might be watching me. Sorry but I just can't do it.'

'Well...' Callie shrugged helplessly. 'What if I explained the situation and asked them to stay upstairs? I'm sure—'

'No!' Even I realised how abrupt that had sounded, and I held up my hands in an apology. 'I'm sorry. I don't mean to be rude. It's very kind of you and all that, but can we just drop it? I don't want to go to Harling Hall. The whole situation makes me feel queasy to be honest.'

Callie must have known that I had no such problems going to The Quicken Tree for the pub quiz, even knowing that the ghost of a former landlord hung around there. Or that it was very probable that I passed ghosts in the street every time I ventured out. Even so, she very nobly didn't point that out.

Instead, like the true friend she was, she said, 'Of course. I'm so sorry if I've upset you. It's not a problem. Let's forget it, shall we?'

Tears pricked my eyes as I nodded.

'Anyway,' she said brightly, 'to change the subject a little, remember we're collecting our costumes on Monday. You *are* still coming with me, aren't you?'

'Of course,' I said. 'I'm long overdue a trip to Much Melton. I'm looking forward to it.'

'I thought,' Callie said eagerly, 'that we'd leave the car and go on the train. What do you think?'

I looked at my handsome, loyal husband, who was smiling at me without a trace of annoyance, despite my weird behaviour. He'd be driving. It had been a long time since I'd travelled on his beloved steam train.

I nodded with genuine enthusiasm. 'That sounds brilliant, Callie. I can't wait.'

7
AUBREY

'Them little sheds are all over the place,' Florence announced as she skipped into the drawing room in the Wyndhams' upstairs suite. 'All round the edge of the green, and down Victoria Walk. It looks proper smashing. Immi reckons there's gonna be lights 'anging up everywhere, an' all. It's gonna look like fairyland.'

Aubrey stifled a smile as Agnes rolled her eyes, in evident despair at Florence's failure to pronounce her aitches, despite the poor woman's endless elocution lessons.

'I'm sure it will look splendid when it's all done,' he told his little girl, ruffling her hair with affection.

'Immi says there's gonna be a Father Christmas, an' all,' Florence told him eagerly. 'And there's gonna be loads of food on sale. We'll be able to smell it all! Immi says—'

'Oh, for goodness' sake, child!' Agnes could obviously bear it no longer.

Florence stared at her. 'What's rattled your cage?'

'It's going to, not gonna! And if I hear you say, "Immi says" one more time I shall scream.'

Florence dropped onto the sofa and leaned towards Aubrey. 'What's up with Mother?' she whispered.

'I'm sure it's nothing, dear,' he assured her. 'Don't take it personally.'

He was fairly certain he knew exactly what was up with Agnes. When she was frightened, she could be quite bolshy, and it was very clear to him that she was frightened now – frightened that Florence was about to ask her the impossible, and not for the first time.

'All this talk of a Christmas market. What nonsense it all is,' Agnes muttered. 'The festivities shouldn't start until Christmas Eve. I've said it once and I'll say it again. This is not a time for putting up little sheds and gaudy lights and expecting people to spend far too much money on silly fripperies. What happened to reverence? That's what I'd like to know.'

Florence frowned. 'Reverends? You mean like that old goat, Reverend Alexander?'

Agnes stiffened at the very mention of his name, and Aubrey said hastily, 'No, my dear. She said reverence. That means having a deep respect for something sacred. Christmas is, after all, about the birth of Our Lord.'

'Hmm.' Florence didn't sound too impressed. 'Anyway, that reminds me, I saw the old goat today. 'E was walking up and down the green, muttering to 'imself and shaking 'is fist the way 'e does. I think 'e's a bit barmy.'

'You mustn't say such things,' Aubrey said gently. 'The Reverend Alexander is a—'

'Monster,' Agnes said abruptly. 'A nasty, spiteful man who you should keep well away from. Florence, I forbid you to go anywhere near him.'

Florence blinked. 'Why the 'eck would I *want* to go anywhere near 'im? I'm just saying I saw 'im when I was out and about, that's all.' She turned back to Aubrey. '*Is* 'e a monster, Poppa?'

'Not at all,' Aubrey assured her. 'He's a God-fearing old gentleman with very strong personal views. That doesn't make him a monster. It just makes him – difficult.'

'Oh. Well anyway, Immi—' She corrected herself as Agnes glared at her. '*I* was wondering, are you two gonna come to the village one day? I really want you to see them little sheds when the lights go up. And there's gonna be lights all over the village, you know. And quite a few Christmas trees, from what I 'ear! It's gonna be lovely. And, Poppa,' she added, wrapping her thin little arms around his, 'it's all Victorian. You know, like what it was when you was alive. You wouldn't want to miss that, would you?'

Aubrey swallowed as he looked down at her earnest little face. He felt such a rush of love for this child, who had come into his afterlife completely unexpectedly when she'd arrived at Harling Hall as a wartime evacuee, only to tumble to her death down the stairs. Since then, he and Agnes had taken care of her and treated her like their own child. Indeed, in their eyes she *was* their own child.

It still humbled him that she'd accepted them as her parents and evidently loved them almost as much as they loved her.

Yet here they were, about to let her down once again. He lifted his gaze to Agnes, an appeal in his eyes. She quickly turned away from him.

'I wonder if we shall have snow this Christmas?' she said, gazing out of the window over the drive.

There was a short silence. Aubrey knew Agnes too well. She was, no doubt, hoping to change the subject, knowing how excited Florence normally got by the arrival of snow. This time, though, their daughter wasn't biting.

'Well?' she demanded, turning to her mother. 'What about it?'

Agnes didn't reply, still facing the other way.

'Agnes,' Aubrey said gently, 'Florence is speaking to you.'

'She is?' Agnes spun round reluctantly, feigning surprise. 'I'm sorry, I was miles away.'

Florence sighed. 'I was saying, will you come to the village for the Christmas market? It's gonna be ever so much fun, and it ain't fair.'

'I'm sorry,' Agnes mumbled. 'I know it's unfair to you, Florence, really I do—'

'I ain't on about me!' Florence cried. 'I mean it ain't fair on you two. You always miss out on everything, and it makes me sad. I want you to 'ave a bit of fun. All the other ghosts will be going. You'll see the Roman stomping around, keeping an eye on everything. 'E's a proper sight for sore eyes! And I'll bet even the old goat will 'ave a good nosy round, 'owever much 'e complains.'

Aubrey mentally shook his head, realising that Florence, by her mention of Silas Alexander, had just said the one thing guaranteed to make sure he and Agnes went nowhere near the village.

He looked over to where his wife was standing and gave her a pleading look. She straightened but looked away, clearly unable to meet his gaze.

'We shall see,' was all she could manage. 'Now, are you in for the foreseeable future, Florence? Because if you are, I think we have time for an elocution lesson. What do you say?'

'I say, no bloomin' fear,' Florence said, scrambling off the sofa. 'I'm off to the kitchen to see Mia and Brian. I'll see you later.'

'You won't go outside, will you? It's getting dark now,' Agnes cautioned her.

'No. I'll stay in, honest.'

Florence skipped out of the suite and Agnes joined Aubrey on the sofa, heaving a sigh of relief.

'Well played,' he said, rather more abruptly than he'd intended.

She looked at him in surprise. 'I have no idea what you mean.'

'The one thing guaranteed to send Florence scuttling from this room was to suggest a lesson, as well you know.'

'I find that suggestion quite offensive,' she said indignantly.

'Agnes, we must discuss this situation once and for all. It can't go on. Why, do you realise we haven't been outside the grounds of this house for...' He tilted his head, trying to remember. 'Well, I don't even know how long it's been,' he admitted in the end, 'but it's certainly many years. Don't you miss the village? Don't you miss the sights and sounds and smells of Rowan Vale? Wouldn't you like to stroll by the river? Maybe even venture further afield to visit the stones?'

'We have everything we need here,' she said with a sniff.

'But we don't have companionship,' he pointed out heavily.

She turned to him with astonishment in her eyes. 'What *can* you mean, Mr Wyndham? We have Lawrie and Brodie, and Callie and Imogen, and Mia, and Brian—'

'Brian is a kitten,' Aubrey said, trying not to lose patience.

'And the cleaners, and the gardeners. We have more than enough companionship, I should think.'

'Only three of those people can see us! And what about the other ghosts?'

'Fiddlesticks to the other ghosts! A motley collection of souls if ever there was one.'

'That's hardly fair, Agnes. Anyway, you used to like conversing with Mr Swain. You always said he was a most genial and respectful chap.'

'Hmm. And you used to like conversing with that dreadful Isaac Grace,' she reminded him. 'You said he was quite a character.'

'So he is.'

'That's one word for it.'

'Oh, Agnes, for heaven's sake!'

It wasn't like him to raise his voice, and he regretted it immediately when he saw the look of fear in her eyes.

Mortified, he clasped her hand in his. 'I'm sorry, my dear. I didn't mean to be so sharp with you. You know I would never hurt you, don't you?'

'Of... of course,' Agnes mumbled.

'I just... Agnes, I feel increasingly restless within these walls.'

'But we have the grounds, too.'

'I want to go to the village. I want to visit Isaac in The Quicken Tree. Callie and Brodie go to some event there each week, you know. A quiz of some sort. I'd like to go with them and see what happens there.'

'I can imagine all too well what happens there,' she said shakily.

'I'd like to go to Midnight Mass at Christmas,' he said quietly. 'Wouldn't you?'

Agnes was silent for a very long time. Aubrey was about to ask the question again when she said finally, 'You know we can't go to the church, Mr Wyndham. And you know why.'

Aubrey rubbed his forehead, feeling increasingly frustrated. 'But we can't let one man stop us from living our afterlives, Agnes! I don't understand why you're so against this. We used to frequent the village and yes, Silas may have said some things, but we ignored him, didn't we?'

'You may have done,' she said. 'I did not. He wounded me deeply. The things he said! The insults he hurled! The terrible aspersions he cast on us, in full view of all the ghosts. It is not to be borne, Mr Wyndham!'

'I know, my dear, but—'

'Did you not hear him that night when Callie invited all the ghosts round? He was outside the gates, warning them not to enter this den of iniquity! *Den of iniquity!* He was referring to us and our – arrangement! Oh, I'll bet they had a good chortle about that at our expense,' she finished bitterly.

'I don't really care if they did,' Aubrey said. 'What I care about is Florence. She wants her parents with her. It's not right that she must always visit the village alone. We couldn't go to the 1940s weekend with her, and can you imagine how much that would have meant to her, given her personal history? Now, here we are, letting her down again. I do *not* want to let my child down, Agnes. Can't you understand that?'

'Of course. Of course I can. I... I—'

To his horror, her eyes filled with tears, and she began to shake uncontrollably. He hadn't seen her in such a state since the evening of the 1940s ball, when her panic had ensured he'd had to stay with her in their suite and miss the entire event. He still regretted not meeting Quintus Severus, but of course Agnes came first, always.

'Agnes?' He was filled with remorse and pulled her into an embrace, holding her fiercely as she quivered against him. 'I'm so sorry, my dear. So very sorry. I wouldn't distress you for the world.'

'I can't – I can't cope with it all, Mr Wyndham,' she managed.

'I know, I know. I understand. Really, I do. We shall speak no more about it,' he promised her.

'But – but Florence—'

'Florence has Imogen and Callie. She can go with them. I'm sure she'll enjoy herself just as much without us two old fuddy-duddies bothering her.'

Agnes sniffed. 'Are you quite sure?'

'Of course I'm sure. Now, are you quite yourself again? Let's have no more of this unpleasant talk. We still have Christmas to look forward to at Harling Hall, and I'm quite sure the Davenports and Callie and Mia have lots of wonderful things planned within these walls.'

She nodded. 'I'm sure they have,' she agreed. 'Thank you, Mr Wyndham. I'm afraid I have one of my headaches coming on.'

'It's the stress,' he told her kindly. 'That was my fault, and I can only apologise once again. Why don't you go and lie down, my dear? When you wake up the whole subject will be forgotten, as if it was never discussed.'

Agnes smiled and kissed him gently on the cheek. 'Thank you, Mr Wyndham.'

'Think nothing of it,' he said.

She headed into her room, head clutched in her hands as if she was in great pain.

Aubrey sat back on the sofa and sighed. Had he really expected a different outcome? Not really, but it still hurt.

Ah well, so long as Agnes was all right, he would make sure Florence understood the situation, and that their Christmas would be as perfect as it possibly could be in the circumstances. A wonderful family Christmas.

They were, after all, the only family he had left.

8

Having dropped the two younger boys off at school, I ignored the pull of Auntie Pat's Pasties and headed straight back to Rowan Vale, where I was meeting Callie.

It was Monday morning and, sadly, it was pouring with rain. The sky was drab and grey, and the landscape – which usually had the capacity to lift my spirits at any time – just seemed to reflect the dullness I felt inside.

Even the prospect of travelling on the steam train to Much Melton had lost its excitement. I wasn't in the mood. I had backache, I felt bloated, and I was too tired to look forward to the trek to the costume shop, which was a good twenty- or thirty-minute walk from the station.

Callie's enthusiasm was obvious, though.

'Isn't this fabulous?' she cried, as we began our journey by hailing the little vintage Leyland bus from outside the Hall. 'Brodie's dead jealous. He wanted to come with us, but I told him no way. This is a girly day out and we're going to have fun.'

I tried to smile, not wanting to spoil things for her. She was still new enough in the village to find everything thrilling. The ride on the vintage bus clearly still filled her with excitement, as she was practically bouncing up and down on the seat like a child, exchanging jolly gossip with Stan, the conductor, or 'clippie'. I just wanted to cry, and I hated myself for it.

'Shall we get something to eat in Much Melton?' Callie asked. 'Or would you rather we wait and visit The Victory Tearooms when we get back? My treat,' she added. 'I think we deserve afternoon tea, don't you? I've been dreaming of scones with jam and clotted cream for weeks.'

My stomach lurched and I put a hand on it, feeling embarrassed. I'd had an increase in, er, shall we say, *digestive disorders* recently, and I knew it was my own fault. I was clearly eating too much. Or the wrong things. Or both. It was all right for thirty-year-old Callie, sitting there looking impossibly pretty, with her shoulder-length dark auburn hair, large hazel eyes and her size twelve figure, rabbiting on about clotted cream.

I, on the other hand, was forty-one, fat, a bit spotty (yep, another thing to thank the perimenopause for), with red hair that had a mind of its own, and now a stomach that liked to play pogo. The only possible chance I had of reversing the situation was to put myself on a strict diet and possibly shave my head.

Poor Jack, I thought wistfully. Look what he'd got himself involved with. Sixteen years ago, he'd bagged himself a twenty-five-year-old hottie, full of confidence, and quite willing and able to squeeze herself into size twelve jeans. Now he was married to an obese old woman with acne, who lumbered around in jogging bottoms and trainers. And at forty-two he looked more handsome than ever! How was that even fair?

Luckily, Callie didn't seem to be waiting for an answer. She rabbited on about Brodie, and how much she was looking forward to seeing him in his costume for the Dickensian weekend, and how she couldn't wait to try on her dress, until all I wanted to do was leap off the bus and make my way back to the safety of Honeywell House.

I wasn't fit to be seen in public. People would stare at me. I could imagine the shop assistants' faces when I walked in with Callie. We looked like Laurel and Hardy.

'Are you okay, Clara? You're very quiet,' Callie said at last. She sounded a bit subdued, and I was angry with myself for pulling her down, when she'd clearly been looking forward to this excursion.

'I'm fine,' I said. 'Just looking at the rain and thinking I should have brought an umbrella.'

And thinking how soaked I was going to get, since I couldn't even zip my coat up any longer. Why hadn't I bought another one? I'd have to go shopping for a new one before winter really set in, despite the expense. Maybe I'd get a cheap one today while I was in Much Melton. It might cheer me up.

'If you like,' Callie said hesitantly, 'we can get a taxi from the station to the costume shop?'

I thought of my aching back and nodded. 'Might be best.'

The platform at Harling's Halt didn't look anywhere near as cheery as I remembered it. Out of season, and with the rain bouncing on the roof, the actors who normally paraded around in costume were nowhere to be seen. The soggy bunting fluttered half-heartedly, and the sound of 'Pack Up Your Troubles' playing over the speakers seemed like a sarcastic comment rather than a morale booster.

The train was waiting, though Callie and I were the only people on the platform. Peering through the windows I could see a couple of others on board, but the train was mostly empty. A far cry from high season when you'd have trouble getting a seat unless you'd booked ahead.

Callie said she'd get the tickets from the booking office, so, ignoring the rain, I hurried along the platform to the end of the train and found Jack and his fireman, Tom, in the cab. They were wearing heavy navy-blue jackets and trousers, but I knew they'd have been in boilersuits earlier on when they did the hard, dirty work of getting the engine ready. The day for them started early. By six o'clock they'd have arrived at Much Melton to join the rest of the staff. Safety checks, loading up the coal, firing up the boiler... There was so much to do before the train was ready to leave the station on its first journey.

Tom was a lovely man in his late twenties, and Jack was very fond of him. He always said that Tom was the real hero of the railways. Having been a fireman himself before becoming a driver, he was all too aware of how hard Tom worked, and that his job was far more skilful than most people realised.

'All right, Mrs Milsom?' Tom called cheerfully. 'Long time no see. Heard you were going on an excursion. Lovely weather for it, eh?'

'Isn't it just?' I wrinkled my nose and looked up at the sky. 'All ready?'

'If we're not, we never will be,' Jack said.

Only one engine ran out of season, as it wasn't financially viable otherwise. Not that the railway made money. It barely broke even, especially the way the price of coal had gone up. If it wasn't for all the wonderful volunteers, Jack often said he doubted the Davenports would have kept it going.

Although Sir Edward Davenport had purchased the line, the rolling stock, and the station itself after it was closed by the government in the sixties, following the Beeching report, where British railways were reshaped, he'd quickly come to realise that managing the heritage railway was too much for him.

A manager had been put in place who worked closely with the staff at Much Melton and the wider rail network, and the owner of the Harling Estate – in other words, Callie now – oversaw the station and its staff, while Harling Heritage Railway took care of the trains themselves, along with the lines.

Jack and Tom were employed by the Harling Estate, but it was the Harling Heritage Railway management committee who'd interviewed, hired, and trained them, and they spent far more time at Much Melton than they did at Harling's Halt.

I noticed Jack looking me up and down, and squirmed with embarrassment, feeling incredibly scruffy.

'You're soaked,' he said. 'Why haven't you got your coat fastened?'

I blushed. 'I'm fine,' I lied. 'A bit of rain never hurt anyone.'

'Don't hang around out here,' he said. 'Get on board and make yourself comfortable. Where's Callie?'

'Just getting the tickets.' I glanced round and noticed her standing on the platform, talking to thin air. I sighed. 'She's got them, I think. I'll leave you to it then.'

'Enjoy the journey,' Tom said cheerfully.

'Have a good day, love,' Jack said. He blew me a kiss and I smiled and blew him one back, making Tom groan in mock horror at the soppiness of it all.

Callie looked awkward as I made my way towards her. I heard her muttering something then she turned to me and said, 'All done? Jack okay?'

'You don't have to pretend,' I said. 'I take it we're in the presence of those two soldiers who are always fighting?'

Callie gave a quick glance sideways. 'Er, actually no. They're in the waiting room, arguing, naturally. I was just talking to Perks – I mean, Mr Swain. He's the porter. *Was* the porter. *Is* the porter. Oh heck, shall we get on the train?'

Giving an apologetic look to what, to me at least, seemed an empty space, she bundled me on board, and we entered the first compartment.

Within a few minutes we were on our way to Much Melton. Derek, a retired bank clerk who now volunteered as a guard, popped into our compartment to check on our tickets, giving an embarrassed laugh when he realised who Callie was. He seemed to take her friendly response as an invitation to stay and chat for ages, and we were nearly in Much Melton before he finally pushed off to check the other tickets.

'Wow.' I didn't know what else I could say.

She laughed. 'Chatty, isn't he? I hope he's not like that with all the passengers!'

'I suspect you're a special case, being the lady of the manor,' I said.

Callie frowned. 'Are you sure you're okay? You just don't seem yourself today.'

'I'm fine,' I assured her. 'And look, you don't have to feel bad about talking to the ghost on the platform. I saw the look on your face, and I felt awful about it. I know what Rowan Vale is. I know how it all works. I'm not expecting you to pretend they're not there.'

'I just don't want to scare you,' she admitted.

'I'm not that much of a wimp!' I shook my head. 'Look, it's just... Well, it's knowing they're in the house with me. That's what would freak me out. It's fine if we're outdoors. It's like I have an escape route there, whereas inside... I know, I know. It sounds stupid.'

'No it doesn't,' she said. 'I'm just the same with spiders.'

I couldn't help but laugh. 'Well, I'm not scared of those.'

She shuddered. 'You're braver than I am then. I'd rather face a hundred ghosts than one of those eight-legged monsters. Well, if you're sure you don't mind? Mr Swain was just telling me that the ghosts have decided they don't want to be left out of this Dickensian weekend, so they're staging their own production of *A Christmas Carol*. Can you imagine? They wanted Silas Alexander to be Ebenezer Scrooge and Perks said he was apoplectic when they asked him!'

Her eyes sparkled with glee, and I chuckled despite everything, having heard all about the grouchy vicar. I decided that I'd wallowed enough for one day and that I was going to make sure Callie and I had a good time, despite the weather.

We caught a taxi from the station and headed to Bradwell's Creative Costumes, noticing hopefully that the rain was finally dying down and we might be able to get from the car to the shop without getting drenched.

We'd visited Bradwell's back in early October, when Callie had first mooted the idea of having a Dickensian weekend.

Jack's uniform was being made by Garrett's, the estate's usual costume provider. He and Tom were to wear dark blue trousers, white shirts, and black neckcloths. They were also being given peaked navy-blue caps.

Brodie had apparently visited Bradwell's online and had chosen what he wanted to wear from the website.

'I'm not so sure about him being Inspector Bucket, you know, but apparently *Bleak House* is his favourite Dickens novel. I've never read it, but he told me all about it, which is why I'm going as Lady Dedlock. I wanted him to dress more like Aubrey. He looks so elegant. Did I tell you we've recently found his portrait in the Hall?' Callie asked as we travelled in the taxi. 'It was in one of the many unused rooms in the attics. Lawrie thinks he remembers his father storing it up there when they were decorating the bedrooms, and it just never came back down for some reason. We also found a portrait of Agnes's late husband, but she wouldn't let us hang that back up and I suppose I can understand why, given her current living arrangements.'

I didn't want to hear about Aubrey and Agnes, so I said, 'I'm hoping my dress still fits. Maybe I should have ordered a bigger size.'

Callie frowned. 'Don't be daft. You only ordered it, what, six, seven weeks ago?'

'The rate I'm expanding that means nothing,' I said, only half-joking. God, what if it didn't do up? I'd be mortified!

The taxi pulled up outside Bradwell's, and Callie leaned over and paid the driver, refusing my offer to pay as she'd bought the train tickets.

'You can buy me a sticky bun or something,' she said. 'Or we can go halves on that afternoon tea if you fancy it?'

'Let's see how we feel after we've tried these dresses on,' I suggested, my heart sinking as I wrestled with the very real fear that I was about to be thoroughly humiliated.

Bradwell's was far from the usual fancy dress shop, being what I'd have termed swanky. They didn't just have costumes in the shop but were able to source them from around the country and even had dressmakers to make them from scratch if you wanted to own your outfit and were willing to pay for it. They had provided period clothes for various film, television, and theatre productions, and there were signed photographs of actors and actresses in Bradwell's costumes dotted around the walls.

The shop assistants couldn't have been more welcoming, which wasn't surprising given the big order they'd had from the Harling Estate, and how much money they must have been making from it.

'Miss Chase and Mrs Milsom,' said a blonde woman with black-rimmed glasses and an impossibly tiny waist, as she scanned a computer screen for information on our order. 'Ah yes. They came in last Wednesday. I'll fetch them to you, and you can try them on, then we'll see if everything's to your satisfaction.'

'Ooh,' Callie said, her eyes bright with excitement, 'this is going to be brilliant! I can't wait to see how I look as Lady Dedlock.' She scooped up her hair and held it against the back of her head. 'I'll need an updo,' she mused. 'I'll have to see if Ingrid at the salon will do it for me, although Mia's pretty good at that sort of thing. Did I tell you she's going as Nancy from *Oliver Twist*?'

Mia, the housekeeper, cook, admin assistant, and general Girl Friday at Harling Hall was good at everything, so it didn't surprise me she could style hair too. She was also incredibly attractive. I'd bet she'd look stunning, even dressed in the sort of thing poor Nancy, the thief and prostitute, would have worn.

The elegant blonde assistant arrived back carrying the two dresses in zipped costume bags over her arm. 'If you'd care to follow me.'

She led us to the back of the shop where a row of changing rooms stood and checked our names before handing each of us our dress. Callie gave me an excited thumbs-up before disappearing inside her cubicle and drawing the curtain shut. I looked ruefully at the bag over my arm and headed into my own cubicle. I made very sure that the curtain was fully drawn and that there wasn't even an inch at either side where anyone might see me.

There was a full-length mirror in the cubicle, but I didn't want to look at that. One quick glance as I'd walked in had been enough to give me the horrors.

I hung up the dress, shrugged off my coat and kicked off my trainers, then slowly and reluctantly I removed my jumper and jogging bottoms, my back firmly to the mirror. At last, dressed only in my underwear, I reached for the costume bag and unzipped the cover, carefully removing the dress.

'If you need any help just let me know,' the assistant said, sounding frighteningly close. I eyed the curtain suspiciously but there was no movement.

Heart thudding, I stepped into my costume and began to pull it up. I'd chosen a mid-Victorian dress without a hoop which, frankly, was so generic I could have been any character. I'd decided, if asked, to say I was Bob Cratchit's wife from *A Christmas Carol*. I'd said no to a corset. God help me trying to lace one of those up!

'How are you getting on?' Callie called.

'Er, nearly done,' I said, putting my arms through the sleeves and tugging the dress up over my shoulders. 'How about you?'

'Ready to show you.'

'Okay, hold on a minute.'

Frantically, I smoothed down the dress then reached round to do up the zip. It was impossible. There was no way I could manage that on my own.

'Callie,' I said at last. 'Can you come in? I need help with this zip.'

Callie pulled aside the curtain and just about managed to squeeze inside the cubicle with me. She looked lovely. Her dress was a striped dark green, with a bateau neckline, and long sleeves, though I had to admit I'd never have known she was Lady Dedlock.

'Shut the curtain,' I begged her, not wanting to attract the attention of the assistant who was no doubt still hovering somewhere close by.

She managed to shut it, with some difficulty, given how little space there was and how voluminous our dresses were, even without the crinolines.

'Right,' she said. 'Turn round and I'll do you up.'

I groaned inwardly, knowing that to turn round meant I had to face the mirror.

Callie began to slide the zip up, but she hadn't got far before I realised she was having difficulty.

'Er, Clara,' she whispered, 'are you sure you ordered the right size?'

I knew it! Hadn't I guessed that I'd put too much weight on for this dress to fit me, even though it had only been a few weeks ago that I'd ordered it?

'It should be,' I said weakly. 'What size does it say on the label?'

She had a look and read it out to me.

'Well,' I said, 'that *was* my dress size. Evidently, it's not now.'

'I'm sorry,' she said, as if any of this was her fault. 'Look, slip it off and get dressed, and we'll see if we can order one in a bigger size.'

'I don't want to order one in a bigger size,' I said, on the verge of tears. 'I don't think I'll bother. Sorry, but I'm not going to get a costume after all.'

'But – but I'm sure there'll be—'

'No, Callie, honestly! It's too uncomfortable anyway. My stomach's permanently bloated and my back aches and I really don't want to be squashed into a dress when I feel like this.' The tears were spilling down my cheeks now, and I didn't think it was possible to feel any worse than I did at that moment.

I wrestled my arms free of the sleeves and, past caring, I pushed the dress down to my ankles.

I heard a gasp from Callie and looked up, seeing her shocked expression as she eyed my reflection in the mirror. Well, thanks for that. As if I didn't already know I looked...

My mouth fell open and I stared at my own reflection, hardly able to believe my eyes.

'Clara...'

'No!'

'Turn to the side,' she said gently.

In a daze, I did as she said, staring in horror at the mirror.

'Didn't you know?' she whispered, at my shocked expression.

'I can't be! It's not possible. I'm going through the perimenopause!'

'Maybe you are,' she said, squeezing my shoulders sympathetically, 'but unless we're both very much mistaken, I think you're also pregnant.'

9

It was a long wait until Thursday morning, when I'd finally managed to wangle an appointment with the doctor. I'd somehow managed to keep my secret from Jack, still dazed enough with my own thoughts. The last thing I needed was him chipping in with his, confusing me even more.

Callie had promised to come with me, and, in fact, she drove me to Kingsford Wold, where the surgery was, insisting that, if her suspicions were confirmed, I'd be in no fit state to drive myself home.

I felt pretty bad about it, as I knew she had enough on her plate. The village was being decorated with fairy lights even as we left, and she'd no doubt want to be on hand to make sure everything was going to plan.

'Mia and Brodie are on it,' she reassured me as I voiced my concern. 'They'll manage just fine. This is more important.'

'I'm not pregnant,' I told her for probably the hundredth time, as we parked up in the health centre car park. 'It's not possible.'

As soon as I'd got home from Much Melton, I'd dug out one of the pregnancy tests I'd bought after missing a period when the perimenopause started. It was negative. And so was the one I did the following day. Whatever this was, it wasn't a baby, and the alternatives scared me to death.

'Have you really had no symptoms?' she asked, turning off the engine and facing me, a puzzled look in her eyes. 'I mean, you've had three kids. You must have realised...'

'No! I've told you, I'm not pregnant. It's something else.'

'Like what?' she asked doubtfully.

'I don't know.' Truthfully, I had my own thoughts on the matter, but it was too terrifying to put into words. Let's just say I'd googled Mary Tudor a lot over the last few days. 'Wind?' I suggested faintly. Hadn't Mary died not long after her second phantom pregnancy?

'Well,' she said, opening the door, 'if it *is* wind, I hope I'm standing far, far away when it finally blows. You look like you've swallowed a beach ball.'

'Cheers.'

But it was true, and the thing I couldn't understand was how I hadn't noticed. I'd just assumed I was getting fat. Overeating junk food, I'd thought. That and the middle-aged spread that seemed inevitable when women hit the perimenopause.

I'd read loads of articles about it over the last year. A thickening of the waist was par for the course, according to the women's magazines. I'd just bought trousers with elasticated waists and tried not to think about it. I shouldn't have avoided the mirrors at home. What if I'd left it too late? What if this huge lump was something...

'I feel sick,' I groaned, on the verge of tears.

'Morning sickness?'

'Hardly! How many times? I'm not pregnant. It's got to be something else. I just hope they can sort it out.'

Callie said nothing, but she hooked her arm through mine as we headed towards the surgery. 'Well, we'll soon find out.'

Dr Allam was brisk and no-nonsense. He listened to my tale of woe and my assertions that, however large my stomach looked in the mirror, I couldn't possibly be growing a baby in there because the pregnancy tests said so, and anyway, I'd *know*, then said, 'Well, let's see, shall we?'

I climbed onto the examination table and pulled my jogging bottoms down under my stomach. Dr Allam gently prodded and pushed, his face kept carefully neutral so I couldn't read his expression.

'Mm.' Was all he said. Then, 'Okay, you can come and sit down now.'

He washed his hands and sat at his desk as I shakily took the seat opposite him, bracing myself for bad news.

'Well,' he said, 'despite your earlier diagnosis, it's not wind.'

'Okay,' I said jokily. 'Relief all round, right?'

'I hope so,' he said. His expression softened and he said kindly, 'You are most definitely pregnant, Mrs Milsom. Did you really have no idea?'

I gaped at him. 'But – but you said I was experiencing the perimenopause!'

'It's perfectly possible to get pregnant during the perimenopause,' he said. 'Not as likely, but certainly possible.'

'But...' I couldn't take it in. 'But the pregnancy tests...'

'When exactly did you buy them?'

'When I first skipped a period.' I thought about it. It was hard to remember. My menstrual cycle had been all over the place for so long now. 'About eighteen months ago, maybe.'

'There are expiry dates on these things, you know. A year from the manufacturing date, some of them. Three years at best. If yours was out of date it wouldn't be accurate.'

I rubbed my forehead, finding it hard to process. 'How far along am I, exactly?'

'Prepare yourself for a shock. You're well into the third trimester. What I need to do is to book you in for an ultrasound,' he said, reaching for his pen. 'That must be a priority. You've missed out on antenatal care so far, so we need to get this sorted as soon as possible. That will tell you your due date, and make sure that everything's progressing as it should, given that you claim not to have felt the baby moving. Now, while you're here, I'll do a quick blood pressure check, and do you think you'd be able to fill a sample bottle? I'd like to check your urine.'

I just couldn't take it in. How could I have had three babies and not recognised that I was carrying this one? And – hang on! Had he just said *third trimester*?

Bloody hell!

How on earth was I going to explain this to Jack?

* * *

'I still think you should have told him,' Callie muttered as we headed into the ultrasound department at the nearest hospital the following Tuesday. 'Jack's your husband. He's the baby's father. He has a right to know.'

'And he will,' I said. 'Once I'm sure there's a baby in there.'

Callie stared at me. 'Clara! The doctor did a physical examination and confirmed it. You did two new pregnancy tests when you got home – both positive. You look like you're about to pop at any moment. What more proof do you need?'

'An ultrasound,' I said firmly. 'I want to see an actual baby in there and then I'll believe it.'

Because I still couldn't. I knew I'd been a bit absent-minded in recent months, but even I couldn't be so ditsy that I wouldn't notice I was pregnant. I just couldn't.

'Do you want me to come in with you?' Callie asked gently. She must have seen the sheer bewilderment on my face. 'I'd be happy to if it would help.'

I shook my head. 'It's okay. It wouldn't be fair if you saw the baby before Jack.' *Or anything else they might discover, for that matter.* 'If,' I added quickly, 'there really is a baby in there.'

'Fair enough, but I'll be right out here if you need me,' she assured me, taking a seat as I was led into the dimly lit ultrasound room by the sonographer, a tiny woman with dark hair and a beaming smile.

As instructed, I lay down and lifted my jumper, pushing my leggings down a little so the sonographer could prepare me for the procedure. I was desperate for the loo, having been warned to drink plenty of fluid before the scan. I just hoped this wouldn't take too long.

'Is no one with you?' she enquired.

'My husband's at work,' I explained. 'My friend's waiting outside but I wanted to do this alone.'

'It's your first scan, is that right?' She raised an eyebrow as she tucked tissue paper into my turned-down waistband. 'Well, for this pregnancy at any rate. Looks like you're quite far along.'

'I think it's all been a terrible mistake,' I said shakily. 'When I had my other children, you could see I was pregnant. No mistaking it. I looked like I had a rugby ball stuffed under my T-shirt. But this,' I said, glancing down at the hillock she was currently spreading cold gel on, 'is just big and round...'

I mean, I was a few pounds heavier than I had been the last time I was pregnant. Well, more than a few. But surely it didn't make that much difference?

Now that the moment of truth was here, I felt as if my heart was about to burst out of my chest. What if the scan did reveal something sinister, as I feared?

She smiled kindly as she sat down in front of a monitor and picked up the probe. 'Let's see, shall we?'

I barely heard her. My mind was running away with me. I'd heard of false positive pregnancy tests before, caused by some sort of fatal illness. Hadn't I? I was sure I'd seen it on a soap once. If I was honest, it was why I hadn't wanted Jack to come with me. I had to know what I was dealing with before I broke it to him in the gentlest way possible.

The sonographer gently passed the probe over my stomach, peering intently at the monitor as she did so. It was facing away from me so I couldn't see anything, and it seemed like forever as she glided the probe up and down, backwards and forwards, repeatedly checking the monitor and adjusting the images.

I turned away and gazed up at the ceiling, blinking away tears of fear. It was taking far longer than I remembered. I waited for her to tell me she was going to have to speak to a doctor. I imagined the doctor arriving back with her, his face grave with sorrow. I imagined him gently telling me that my GP had been mistaken. I wasn't pregnant, and they were really very sorry but there was nothing they could do...

The Christmas tree had arrived in the village that morning. It would be decorated soon. On Friday there was to be the big switch-on. The boys were so excited about it. Would I be able to go with them to see the lights go on? Or would I be in hospital, facing goodness knows what? Would I even make Christmas?

How, I wondered tearfully, would they cope without me?

'Well,' said a cheerful voice beside me, 'everything looks absolutely fine here.'

I blinked, my attention snapping back to the sonographer. 'I'm sorry?'

She beamed at me. 'Baby's doing really well, by the looks of things. I'll turn the monitor round so you can see.'

Before I could catch my breath, she turned the thing round and, there on the screen was...

'It's a baby,' I breathed.

She laughed. 'Sure is. Listen.'

The room was flooded with the most reassuring sound in the world. A baby's heartbeat, tootling along like a miniature steam train. It reminded me of the times I'd first heard my boys' hearts beating inside of me. I burst into tears.

'Aw, bless you,' she said sympathetically. 'Have you been very worried?'

'I didn't believe it,' I said, wiping my eyes with the sleeve of my jumper. 'I don't understand any of this. How can I be pregnant and not know it? I've had three healthy boys. I knew I was pregnant with Freddie – my youngest – before I'd even missed a period, because I just *felt* it. I was so sick, too. I've had no symptoms with this one. Nothing.'

'Hmm.' She tilted her head, thinking. 'It's what we call a cryptic pregnancy. They're rare but they do happen. Are you sure you've had no symptoms? Nothing at all?'

'Well...' I tried desperately to think. 'Obviously my periods were erratic and light. But I *did* have them,' I added, as if defending myself from accusations of sheer stupidity. 'I mean, I missed a few, but that was just part of the peri-menopause. And yes, I felt tired, and my moods have been all over the place, but I thought it was the same thing. You know.'

She nodded. 'I take it you were using contraception?'

'Always,' I said fiercely. 'Like I said, we've got three boys, so we were very careful about that, believe me. I just can't understand it.'

'Well,' she said cheerfully, 'however it happened, it definitely happened. I see you can't be certain about the date of your last period, but I would say baby's due date is around the eleventh of January.' She whistled. 'You'd better start shopping for a pram.'

'Just for starters,' I said weakly. *And how were we going to afford all that?*

What was Jack going to say about this? What would the boys think? What about the model village? We didn't even have a spare room so two of the boys would have to share a bedroom. Oh, they'd hate that...

I gasped suddenly as her words sank in. 'The eleventh of *January*? You mean, I'm already eight months' pregnant?'

'Would you like me to fetch your friend?' she asked gently. 'You look like you've had a shock.'

'That's one way of putting it,' I said, feeling utterly dazed. 'I just can't take this in. Oh no!'

I gave her an anguished look as guilt kicked in. 'I've been drinking! I mean, once a week, every week, just about. A couple of glasses of wine at the pub quiz. What if I've done something to him? Or her?'

'Like I said, everything looks fine. Now we know baby is here we'll make sure you get regular antenatal care. I really wouldn't worry, although maybe say no to the wine from now on.' She lifted an eyebrow. 'Would you like to know the baby's sex?'

'Can you tell?'

She glanced back at the monitor and nodded. 'Oh yes. I can tell.'

I was almost bursting to know, but I knew it wouldn't be fair on Jack. I'd already kept him in the dark enough. Regretfully, I shook my head. 'No. It can be a surprise.'

'Seems like it's the day for it,' she said, wiping the gel off my stomach with the tissue paper. 'Would you like a scan photograph?'

'Oh, yes please,' I said gratefully. 'At least that way I'll really believe it. And to be honest, I think I'm going to need photographic evidence to convince my husband.'

'He had his doubts, too, then?'

I gave her a sheepish look. 'I haven't told him. I wanted to make sure that everything was okay first.'

'Ah, well.' She nodded at me as I sat up and pulled down my jumper. 'If I were you, I'd make sure he's sitting down before you break it to him. My word, I'd like to be a fly on the wall in your house tonight!'

10

I'd heard that people's faces could go grey with shock, but I'd never really believed it. That was, until I saw Jack's face when I told him our news and presented him with the scan photo.

We'd got the house to ourselves for the first time in forever. Callie and Brodie had taken the boys, along with Immi, to the cinema in Much Melton. It had been Callie's idea.

'You need time alone to break the news to Jack,' she'd said kindly. 'We'll pick the kids up about five and take them for a burger as a treat before we see the film.'

'Are you sure?' I'd asked doubtfully. 'They can be a heck of a handful, you know.'

'Of course I'm sure,' she said, waving away my concerns. 'Brodie and I will manage them between us. It will be fun.'

'And – and you won't take them back to the Hall?' I asked hesitantly. It seemed really ungrateful, but I had to be sure of that.

She'd looked a bit sad. 'Not if you don't want us to. We'll be about three hours, all told. Will that be long enough for you and Jack?'

I wasn't sure three *months* would be enough time for me and Jack to wrap our heads around all this, but I'd nodded. 'That's great, Callie. Thanks so much.'

Jack had been stunned to come home from work and find only Toby and me in the house, but he'd whooped with delight when he'd discovered that the kids were out.

'And just what,' he'd said, wrapping his arms around my non-existent waist and pulling me to him as I'd tried to serve him his dinner at the table, 'do you have planned while they're out? I hope it involves you having your wicked way with me.'

He'd given me a hopeful look, and I'd tried to smile but failed dismally.

Instead, I'd dropped into the chair next to him and stared at him in mute terror.

His smile had died immediately. 'What's up? You look like you've seen a ghost.'

I was too distracted to dwell on that comment, let alone make any sarcastic retort. 'Jack,' I said weakly, 'there's something I have to tell you. Show you. Both.'

Five minutes later we were sitting there, staring at the scan photograph, which lay on the table between our forgotten plates of sausage casserole.

'But – but how?' Jack asked dazedly.

'You want me to remind you?' I asked. 'Has it been so long you've forgotten how babies are made?'

'Well, yes, it has really,' he said bluntly. 'But I mean, joking aside, we're always so careful.'

'I know,' I said. 'I can't understand it either.'

'The eleventh of January,' he said faintly. 'Though it could come earlier, couldn't it? That doesn't give us long to get everything sorted, does it? I mean – bloody hell, Clara! This is serious.'

'I know.' Didn't I just! I hardly needed him to point out the obvious.

He shook his head and picked up the photo again, staring at it intently.

'So, it would have been some time in April when you got pregnant? Early or mid-April? Around then?'

I shrugged. 'Somewhere around then.'

He narrowed his eyes, thinking.

I picked up my fork and prodded a sausage, before pushing it away in disgust. Maybe I'd make a slice of toast later, instead.

'Clara,' Jack said slowly, 'Mum and Dad visited in early April. Remember?'

I frowned. 'I thought that was May?'

'No, definitely April, because if you recall, they brought the boys' Easter eggs early because they were going away in mid-April for two weeks and wouldn't be able to visit over Easter.'

'Oh yes,' I said, nodding. 'But so what?'

'Mum and Dad took the boys out alone,' Jack said heavily. 'I'd taken the week off work to spend time with my parents, but they said we should have some time to ourselves, and they'd take the kids to the water park for the day.'

I stared at him. 'Uh-oh.'

'It was warm and sunny. We went for that picnic, remember? Just you and me.'

'And got a bit carried away.'

'A *lot* carried away. We hadn't had a day like that since—'

'Yeah, all right,' I said indignantly, trying not to feel annoyed as I realised how proud of himself he sounded. 'But we were careful!'

'The *first* time we were careful. But the second time...'

There was a gleam in his eyes as he remembered. I supposed it *had* been quite an event. Thinking about it, it had probably been the first time we'd managed sex more than once for years. It had taken us both by surprise.

Jack had only brought one condom, and he admitted later that he hadn't even expected to use that, but maybe it had been the scenery, or the peace and quiet, or just the sheer exhilaration of having no kids around for once.

Whatever the reason, we'd thrown caution to the wind that second time, and thinking about it some more, I was convinced it had probably been the last time we'd had sex at all.

'Wow,' Jack breathed. 'To think I thought that was such a great day. Well, we're really paying for it now.'

'Don't say that,' I said miserably. 'What do we do?'

'What *can* we do?' Jack pushed his plate away, clearly as revolted by the sight as I was. 'This baby's going to be here in a few weeks, and there's no stopping that. We're just going to have to get on with it.'

'But...' I didn't know where to start. There were so many reasons why this was all wrong, and I wasn't sure how to put my fears into words.

Jack rubbed his forehead and stared at the photo again. 'Why didn't you tell me? I should have been with you for the scan.'

'I didn't believe it could possibly be true,' I told him, not wanting to admit I'd dreaded I was about to be told I was going to die. 'I thought it was a waste of time.'

'But how did you not know?' He sounded thoroughly confused. 'You've carried three kids. Surely you know the signs? Didn't you feel it moving around?' He shook his head. 'We used to watch the boys kicking, remember? You used to put my hand on your stomach so I could feel it. And you could see your bump moving around by the time you got to this stage. I don't understand how you didn't know.'

I had felt *some* movement, but nothing like I'd had with the boys. I'd honestly thought I had digestive problems. Maybe when you've totally ruled out pregnancy your mind invents other reasons for what's happening to your body? I really didn't know, but I didn't like being attacked as if I'd done this deliberately.

'Did *you* know?' I demanded. 'You sleep next to me every night. Did you notice anything?'

'Well, no,' he admitted. 'But you've been wearing baggy clothes for ages, and you've taken to covering up in bed. And it's not like we get that close any more, so...'

'So it's my fault?' Tears sprang into my eyes.

'God, no! That's not what I'm saying. I'm just confused,' Jack said. He put his arm around me. 'I'm sorry. I'm not having a go at you, love. I just don't understand.'

'Well, join the club. The sonographer told me it's called a cryptic pregnancy. I've been reading about it online. Apparently, some women don't realise they're pregnant until they go into labour. At least I won't have that shock to deal with. Can you imagine?'

The tears began to roll down my cheeks. 'Oh, Jack! I don't want to go through all that again. I thought I was done with it.'

Jack seemed to have no words of reassurance. He looked almost as horrified as I felt.

'Sleepless nights,' I continued. 'All that crying, and having to get up to feed the baby, and feeling like a zombie, and nappy changes, and teething, and the terrible twos and—'

'You're really not selling this to me,' he said, clearly attempting to joke about it.

'How do you think the boys are going to take it?' I said, as the thought struck me.

'All three of the boys are at school,' he said glumly. 'We were going to set up the model village. I guess that's off now anyway.'

'What? Why?'

'Oh, come on! You can't possibly take on such a huge project when you're only weeks from giving birth! And let's face it, you're going to be at home for ages, taking care of a newborn. It has to be a no-go.'

I could feel all my plans and dreams for the future slipping away from me. I'd been so close to finding the old me again; to having some sort of life outside this family. Now it was moving away, out of reach.

'I don't want this, Jack,' I murmured. Even as I said the words, guilt and shame seared through me. What kind of mother would say such things? But I didn't feel like a mother at that moment. This baby didn't feel real. And all I felt was trapped and hopeless.

Jack squeezed my hand. 'It's just the shock, love. Once we get our heads around it, we'll be fine.'

He pushed the scan photo towards me. 'I wish you'd let me go with you. And they definitely said everything seemed okay?'

I nodded. 'Baby seems fine,' I said sarkily. 'Mother in terminal shock, but never mind, eh?'

Jack's expression softened. 'But look, it's a baby. A healthy little baby with a beating heart. And it's going to be with us very soon. It's not all bad, is it? In fact,' he said with a smile, 'maybe it's a good thing.'

'In what version of reality can this possibly be a good thing?' I demanded tearfully. 'Do you remember what I went through having Freddie? I said then, never again!'

'I know it wasn't an easy birth,' Jack said, in what he no doubt imagined was a soothing voice. 'But that doesn't mean it will be as bad this time around. And look at the positives! You've been moaning about the weight you've put on. Well, once you've had the baby, you'll probably be a stone lighter at least! And maybe it was pregnancy that made you so weepy and moody, not the periwhatsit. Your hormones might settle down after it's over.'

'Or I might get post-natal depression and feel even worse,' I snapped. 'Or have you forgotten how bad I felt after Freddie?'

Hell, I'd ended up on antidepressants. I didn't want to go through that again. I just couldn't.

'It was different then,' Jack said. 'You still had Declan at home, and Ashton was very young, and I was doing a lot of overtime for extra money.'

'Because we had another mouth to feed,' I reminded him. 'So tell me how it's going to be different this time?'

'I'll take time off,' he promised. 'I swear it. I'll stay home and help you. The kids are my responsibility, too. I'm sorry I let you down before—'

'We needed the money,' I said dully. 'It wasn't your fault.'

But I couldn't see how he could possibly take time off work this time around either. If anything, we'd need the money more. Unlike with Freddie, I had nothing for this baby. I'd given everything away. We'd need to start from scratch with a pram, a cot, baby clothes and everything else. It was going to cost a fortune.

And we were already struggling. Everything had gone up in price. The water rates, the gas and electricity, the council tax, the broadband, the weekly shop... The Harling Estate had kept our rents low but even so, now was definitely not a good time to add in another mouth to feed.

I rubbed the tears from my eyes, feeling completely overwhelmed.

Jack put his arm around my shoulders. 'It'll all be fine, love. You'll see. We'll manage somehow. We always do. And at the end of the day, this is our child. Who knows? This time we might even get a little girl.' He smiled down at the photo. 'Whatever it is, we'll love it just as much as we love our boys.'

He sounded so sure of that. I could see the affection in his gaze as he studied the photo, and suddenly I felt even more panicked.

Jack was warming to the idea of a new baby already, but I felt only dread and fear and – yes – resentment.

What if I never loved this baby? What kind of life would either of us have then?

11

AGNES

'Mother, Poppa, come quickly! You 'ave to stop 'er!'

At Florence's anguished cry, Agnes and Aubrey – who'd been sitting in the drawing room in their suite for three hours now, working their way through the first series of *The Crown,* which Callie had kindly found for them on Netflix – exchanged startled looks and jumped to their feet.

'Whatever can have happened?' Agnes's fingers clutched the ribbons at the top of her bed jacket, as they always did when she was anxious.

Aubrey was already running out of the room, and she followed him, relieved to see Florence halfway up the stairs on her way to meet them.

'Whatever is the matter, child?' Aubrey crouched down and wrapped his arms around their daughter, who was sobbing noisily by now.

'She's... she's leaving, and you've got to stop 'er!'

'Who's leaving, Florence?' Agnes joined Aubrey on the step and stared down at the little girl in alarm. Clearly, whatever had happened had thoroughly distressed her.

'Florrie! There you are.'

Mia began to run up the stairs, quickly followed by Callie.

'Whatever has happened?' Aubrey asked. 'The poor child's an emotional wreck.'

'I'm afraid Florrie was eavesdropping again,' Callie explained. 'She overheard a conversation that wasn't for her ears and misunderstood.'

'I didn't misunderstand nuffink,' Florence said fiercely, through her tears. 'I 'eard 'em both, plain as day, Poppa. Mia's leaving. She's 'ad enough of this place and she's off.'

'Is this true?' Agnes demanded. 'Is she really planning to abandon the child? Of all the heartless—'

'That's not what she said at all, Agnes,' Callie said firmly. 'Look, let's sit down and chat about this, shall we? And I'll explain everything.'

'Mia, too?' Florence said.

Mia smiled. 'Of course. Please don't get so upset, Florrie. I'm not abandoning you, I promise.'

'I should think not indeed,' Agnes muttered as they headed upstairs and into the Wyndhams' suite.

'Please, do take a seat,' Aubrey said politely.

'Poppa says to sit down right next to me,' Florence told Mia, dropping onto the sofa.

'He didn't say it quite like that,' Callie assured Mia with a wry grin. She picked up the remote and paused *The Crown*.

'Thank you, Callie,' Aubrey said. 'I have to say, we were rather enjoying that, weren't we, my dear?'

'Yes, yes, but what's this about Mia leaving?' Agnes had to admit, if only to herself, that just a few short months ago she'd have been delighted if that had been the case.

When she'd discovered that Mia was Florence's great-niece, and their blood connection meant she could see Florence, Agnes had been horrified, and desperate that her daughter shouldn't learn the truth. She'd been afraid that Florence would see Mia as her real family and wouldn't want to know Agnes and Aubrey any longer, even though they'd taken care of her ever since she was killed in an accident on the stairs in 1941.

As it turned out, although Mia and Florence had become very close, Florence's relationship with her adopted parents had only deepened and strengthened, and Mia had been no threat to their little family at all. Agnes had rather regretted keeping her little girl and Mia apart for so long. Now she wondered if she'd been wrong after all, if Mia was about to leave and break Florence's heart.

'Well,' Callie said, 'she's not exactly leaving, Agnes. This is what I mean about Florrie misunderstanding. What we were discussing was Mia leaving her job as housekeeper at Harling Hall.'

'What? But why?' Agnes couldn't understand it. To hold such a position in a household like this was an honour. What more could any single woman ask for?

'I don't want 'er to leave,' Florence wailed. 'I won't let 'er go!'

'Now, Florence dear, please let Callie and Mia explain properly,' Aubrey chided. 'I'm sure it's not as bad as you fear.'

'Thank you, Aubrey,' Callie said. 'Mia, would you like to explain? This is your idea, after all.'

Mia cleared her throat. 'It's a bit odd, having a conversation with two people I can't see or hear, but if you think I should be the one to tell them...'

'I won't never speak to you again if you go,' Florence warned her, folding her arms and pouting.

Agnes rolled her eyes. 'My dear girl, that is utterly ridiculous. It's, I won't *ever* speak to you again, not *never*. That's a double negative. One cancels out the other. How many times do I have to—?'

'Agnes, perhaps now isn't the time or place,' Aubrey said gently, and as an oblivious Mia had already begun her explanation, Agnes had to agree.

'So now Callie's here,' Mia was saying, 'things have changed a lot. She, quite rightly, likes to cook for Immi and herself, and lately she's also been cooking for Brodie, too. They like to eat in the kitchen, more informally, and now Lawrie has taken to joining them.'

'It's no reflection on Mia's cooking,' Callie explained hastily. 'I love her cooking and still prefer her Sunday roasts to mine. It's just, I never felt comfortable eating in that big dining room, and to be honest, I don't feel comfortable with Mia cooking for me either. And Immi's *my* responsibility. I want to look after her. I certainly don't want Mia doing our washing and ironing, and we've already got a team of cleaners as you know. In short, I don't really feel we need a housekeeper.'

'Very shortsighted of you if you don't mind me saying so,' Agnes said with a sniff. 'A woman in your position should always employ a housekeeper. You have far better things to do with your time.'

'Yes,' Callie said. 'And so does Mia.'

'You mean, the administration for the estate?' Aubrey asked. 'Yes, well. Obviously, Brodie may still need a bit of help, but surely—'

Callie quickly repeated what the Wyndhams had said to Mia, who laughed. 'I'd like to think I've given Brodie more than a *bit* of help,' she said. 'But either way, I think he's got things under control now. Since he became estate manager and stopped doing all the things he had no need to do, such as unblocking gutters and mowing lawns, he's really cracked on with the administration. These days he probably just needs someone to do basic clerical work, and that's not me. I want to get my teeth into something new and exciting. And Callie has just the job for me.'

'Oh?' Agnes was curious. 'And what's that?'

'It's been pointed out to me,' Callie said, 'that Rowan Vale needs another eating establishment of some sort. The queues at Mrs Herron's teashop are crazy in high season and although we have The Victory Tearooms, they're quite out of the way at the station, and we need somewhere in the village itself to stop hungry tourists from going elsewhere.'

'Wait,' Agnes said, frowning. 'Are you saying that Mia is going to run a cafe, of all things?'

'Not exactly a cafe,' Callie said cheerfully. 'An Italian trattoria. At least, that's the plan.'

'An Italian...' Words failed Agnes.

'I say!' Aubrey said, wrinkling his nose. 'Italian food? In Rowan Vale?'

Callie laughed.

'I take it they're not too enthusiastic about the idea,' Mia said wryly.

'I think they just need time to adjust,' Callie assured her.

'What's an Italian tattyoria?' Florence asked, sounding confused.

'Trattoria!' Mia giggled. 'It's a sort of restaurant, but less formal. I'll be serving pizzas and pastas and risottos. Lasagne. Bolognese. Fresh fish dishes. Ooh, and gelato! That's ice cream to you and me, Florrie.'

'I ain't never 'ad pizza,' Florence admitted. 'I've seen Immi and Callie eating it, though.'

'That was frozen pizza from the supermarket,' Callie explained, somewhat embarrassed. 'The pizza Mia serves will be made from scratch.'

'All fresh ingredients,' Mia added. 'And I'm hoping to get a licence to serve wine, too. Italian, of course.'

'What on earth is this obsession with Italy? What's wrong with good, plain English food?' Agnes wanted to know.

'Nothing's wrong with English food,' Callie said. 'Just, we already have two tearooms on the estate, not to mention a fish and chip shop and a pub selling traditional dishes. When Mia suggested something different, I thought it was a great idea. Personally, I can't wait to try it.'

'I've travelled extensively with my parents,' Mia added. 'Italy's long been my favourite place to visit, and I absolutely adore Italian food. I've done cookery courses in Rome, Florence and Sorrento, and another one with a top Italian chef in London. Italian cuisine is the one thing I've really missed while I've been living here. There was never any call for it at Harling Hall. Bit too exotic for Lawrie.'

'But you'll definitely stay in Rowan Vale?' Florence checked. 'You're not moving away?'

'Of course I'm not.' Mia gave her an affectionate smile. 'I'd never leave you, Florrie. I'm only just getting to know you properly. Although…'

Florrie straightened. 'Although what?' she asked suspiciously.

Callie and Mia exchanged glances.

'Although, there may come a point when I move out of the Hall,' Mia admitted.

'What? But why?' Florence wailed.

'I'll still be close by,' Mia said quickly. 'Callie and I have been talking about this. I really feel that there's going to come a point when I want a bit of independence. I've loved being at Harling Hall, but although I don't want to move away from the village, I do feel ready to find my own space – especially now I'm hoping to run my own business.'

'But you can't leave,' Florence whispered. 'You're the only family I've got left.'

Agnes barely had time to register the words before the girl added quickly, 'I mean, the only *living* family I've got left.'

She gave her adopted parents sheepish smiles. Aubrey ruffled her hair and said, 'We knew what you meant, poppet. Never fear.'

How, Agnes wondered, could he be so confident of their daughter's love? It never ceased to amaze her how relaxed he was about these things, especially given the sort of life he'd led. She wished she had the same gift.

'You can come and visit any time you like,' Mia told Florence. 'I won't move over the estate boundaries, I promise. Anyway, all this is theoretical. We have no idea where we can fit a new eating establishment so it could be months or years before it happens.'

'And right now, there are no vacant cottages in Rowan Vale either,' Callie added. 'But as soon as one comes up, you'll have first dibs on it, Mia.'

'And I'll have your photograph framed and take it with me,' Mia assured Florence.

'The one of her with the other evacuee children when they arrived at the Hall?' Aubrey enquired.

'Aubrey wants to know if it's the one Lawrie had of the evacuees,' Callie explained.

Mia shook her head. 'No. The one my gran had of her before she was sent here. It was taken in the back yard of their old house in Poplar. Have Aubrey and Agnes never seen it? I'll show it to them if they like.'

'Oh,' Agnes sighed. 'I would love to see that. Thank you, Mia.'

'Most kind of you,' Aubrey agreed.

'They'd love to see it,' Callie said.

'Tell you what,' Mia said brightly, speaking to where she assumed the ghosts were sitting, 'why don't I get you a copy? I'll put it in a frame, and you can put it on your bedside table. Then you can both wake up to her smiling face every morning.'

Agnes and Aubrey glanced at each other.

'Two copies, perhaps?' suggested Aubrey.

'If it's not too much trouble,' Agnes added.

'Two copies?' Callie frowned. 'What for?'

Florence laughed. 'Well, one for Poppa's bedroom and one for Mother's, of course!'

Agnes watched as Callie's face turned a rather common shade of pink. Really, blushing was so vulgar.

'Oh, I see... Sorry, I just assumed you shared a room,' Mia said. 'No worries, I'll get you both a copy.'

'*Shared a room?*' Agnes hardly knew where to put herself.

Aubrey was staring fixedly at the floor, as if he wished it would open up and swallow him whole.

'Well, I sort of did, too,' Callie said awkwardly. 'I mean you are... kind of... *married.*'

'What do you mean, *kind of* married?' Florrie wanted to know. "Course they're married. Aren't you, Mother? Poppa?'

Agnes felt quite faint.

'We are very much a family,' Aubrey said firmly. He cleared his throat. 'I think that settles that.'

Callie glanced at Mia. 'Well, I er, think that's all sorted out now,' she said. 'No need to fuss at all, was there, Florrie?'

'Easy for you to say,' Florence said. 'Not your family moving out, is it? But wherever you end up, I'll definitely come and visit,' she told Mia. 'Don't think I won't, cos I will.'

'I'd expect nothing less,' Mia said, laughing. 'And you could even stay the night sometimes – if your parents approve, of course.'

Agnes gave her an appreciative nod. It was good of the woman to acknowledge their parental rights – even if she had made the most terrible blunder about the photograph.

'Right, well I'm off to rehearsals then,' Florence announced, jumping to her feet.

'Rehearsals?' Aubrey and Agnes chorused.

'Rehearsals for what?' Agnes demanded.

'Didn't Florrie tell you?' Callie asked. 'The ghosts in the village are putting on a production of *A Christmas Carol*. Florrie, John and Robert are playing Cratchit children. Little Robert is going to be Tiny Tim.'

'Why didn't you tell us, Florence?' Aubrey asked, sounding rather hurt.

Florence shrugged. 'Didn't seem much point. You ain't gonna see me in it anyway, are you? See you later.'

She skipped out of the room like the whole drama surrounding Mia's plans had bored her, and as if none of it had been brought about by her overreaction to something she should never have heard in the first place.

'You will keep us informed?' Aubrey asked, as he showed Callie and Mia to the door of their suite, ever the polite gentleman. 'About the cafe situation, I mean.'

'Trattoria,' Callie corrected him.

'Yes, quite. You will let us know of any developments? Just so we can prepare Florence, you understand.'

'Of course we will,' Callie assured him. 'And I'm sorry for the misunderstanding – about the bedroom situation.'

Aubrey glanced round at Agnes, and she saw him visibly swallow.

'Well, let's say no more about it,' he said faintly.

Agnes sucked in her cheeks and turned her head away as Callie gave her an apologetic look. Really, it was not to be borne! This young woman might be the lady of the house, but she had no class or breeding. To bring up such a subject, and not just once but several times! It simply wasn't to be tolerated.

Callie and Mia took their leave, closing the door behind them, and Aubrey returned to the sofa.

'Well, er, that was...'

'Indeed it was, Mr Wyndham,' Agnes said crossly. 'I have never...'

'Yes. Quite. I think we should draw a veil over that conversation, my dear. Or at least parts of it.'

'Indeed.'

There was an uncomfortable silence, then Aubrey ventured, 'So Florence is going to be in a play. *A Christmas Carol*. Sounds like fun, doesn't it?'

'It depends on your definition of fun, I suppose,' she said flatly. The last thing she wanted was to be drawn into another conversation about visiting the village.

'I suppose it does,' he mumbled.

In desperation, they both turned and stared hopefully at the television screen.

'Oh drat,' Aubrey exclaimed. 'Callie didn't take *The Crown* off pause.'

12

'I'm going to have to go into town tomorrow,' I announced, putting the ironing board away after working my way through what felt like every item of clothing we owned.

Jack, who was unloading the dishwasher, raised an eyebrow. 'Town? You mean Much Melton?'

'May as well,' I said. 'I need to make a start on the shopping.'

His face brightened. 'For the baby?'

'Shh!' I gave him a stricken look. 'The boys are only upstairs! And no, not for the baby. In case it had escaped your notice it's only a fortnight to Christmas, and we haven't bought a thing for the kids yet.'

'Not true,' Jack said, shutting the dishwasher door and straightening. 'I've ordered them all Liverpool football shirts online. They'll be arriving any day now.'

'Liverpool football shirts?' I rolled my eyes. 'Why?'

'Why not? Liverpool's our team. Stands to reason the boys will want their latest strips.'

'Liverpool's *your* team,' I pointed out. 'Though I have no idea why. You've never even been to Liverpool.'

He looked aghast. 'What's that got to do with it? Anyway, you're wrong. I've been to Anfield twice.'

'I stand corrected,' I said sarkily. 'Doesn't mean the boys are remotely interested.'

'Ashton's a proper fan these days,' he assured me. 'And it won't be long until Declan's just the same. And I can't leave Freddie out, can I? Besides, think how cute they'll look in them.'

'Liverpool wear red, don't they? It will clash with their hair,' I groaned. 'Honestly, the price of them, too. Couldn't you have bought them something more sensible?'

'It's Christmas! Sensible doesn't come into it. Besides, I'd already ordered them before I knew about... Anyway, when it comes to football, money's no object.' He put his arm around me. 'Hey, you look done in. Come and sit down. I want to talk to you.'

'What about?' I asked suspiciously. 'If you want a Liverpool football shirt, too, you can whistle for it. I'm not made of money.'

'It's not about Christmas,' he said quietly. 'It's about the baby.'

'Oh, Jack! Not again.' I ran a hand through my hair, sick of hearing it all. 'What else is there to say? It's done now and I'm just going to have to live with it.'

'We haven't even scraped the surface,' he said. 'I'm worried about you, Clara.'

'You should be,' I told him. 'I'm forty-one and knackered, and I'm about to push something the size of a beach ball out of my body when I haven't even got the energy to take a shower some mornings. I'll tell you one thing; it's a vasectomy for you or you're never touching me again.'

'I'm serious,' he said.

I glared at him. 'You think I'm not?'

'I think it's time we told the boys.'

'No way.' I shook my head and strode into the living room. I wasn't having this conversation again.

Jack, however, was clearly not going to give up so easily this time. 'It makes no sense not to,' he said, sounding snappy for the first time. 'Think about it.' He waved a hand at me and said, 'The baby's due in just a few weeks. It's becoming more obvious by the day, and it's only a matter of time before one of them notices. And they have a right to know.' He hesitated. 'Especially since even Callie knows.'

I knew it was a sore subject. He'd not reacted well when I'd admitted Callie had come with me to the doctor's and the scan. In fact, he'd been quite annoyed and obviously hurt.

'She won't say anything. I'll bet even Brodie doesn't know,' I mumbled.

'That's not the bloody point! For God's sake, what's the problem?'

'Are you honestly asking me that? I mean, where do I even start?'

'I mean with telling the boys. Oh!' Jack threw up his hands in frustration. 'I don't know how to get through to you. You're so bloody stubborn!'

'Fine!' I glared at him as I plonked myself in an armchair and folded my arms over my bump. 'Whatever. Have it your way.'

I'd honestly expected him to back down, but to my horror he went straight into the hallway and yelled up the stairs. 'Boys! Come down here. We've got something to tell you.'

'Now?' I said, panicked. 'They've been at school all day. It's not fair to—'

'Coming!'

There was the sound of heavy footsteps as three boys raced down the stairs. Three expectant faces turned to us.

I gulped.

'Sit down,' Jack said quietly. 'Your mum and I have something important to say.'

'Are you getting a divorce?' Ashton asked, not sounding too worried about the possibility.

'What's a divorce?' enquired Freddie.

'When a mum and dad decide they hate each other's guts and split up,' Declan explained. 'There are a few people in my class whose parents are divorced. They get trips out every weekend and double Christmas presents.'

'Would *we* get double Christmas presents?' Freddie asked, clearly interested.

'We're not getting divorced,' Jack said hastily. 'Far from it, in fact. This family isn't splitting up. It's er...'

He looked at me, but I said nothing. I merely returned his look with cold indifference.

'Getting bigger,' he said lamely.

'Like me,' I added bitterly.

'What do you mean?' Declan asked. 'How is it getting bigger?' His face brightened. 'Are we getting a puppy for Christmas?'

'A dog is for life, not just for Christmas,' Ashton pointed out primly.

'Are you kidding me?' I gasped. 'Don't you think we've got enough to do with Toby?' I glanced over to where our Bernese mountain dog was lying on the rug, nose on paws, snoring like an old man.

'It would be nice for him to have a friend,' Declan said.

'*I* want a puppy!' Freddie announced. 'Can I have a puppy for Christmas?'

'No, you blooming can't,' Jack said. 'This isn't about a puppy. It's...'

He swallowed and Ashton groaned.

'Oh no! Don't tell me. Not again! You're not having *another* kid, are you?'

I realised my face was burning with embarrassment. Ashton was old enough to know how babies were made. He'd never look at me and his dad in the same way again.

'Yes,' Jack said. 'We are.'

There was a stunned silence.

'That,' Ashton said at last, 'is truly disgusting.'

'Thanks for that,' I said.

'Nothing disgusting about it,' Jack said sternly. He smiled at Freddie. 'What do you think? A baby brother or sister!'

'I'd rather have a puppy,' Freddie said. 'Can we swap it?'

'Afraid it doesn't work like that,' I told him.

'How am I ever going to show my face at school now?' Ashton groaned. 'They're going to kill themselves laughing at me.'

'I don't see why,' Jack said indignantly.

'Are you joking? You're *old*. Now they'll know my parents still do it. At your age! It's gross.'

'Do what?' Declan asked.

'Put orders in with the stork,' Jack said.

'What stork?'

'Look, can we concentrate on what's important here?' Jack pleaded. 'Your mum and I are going to have a baby in January. You'll have a new brother or sister and—'

'January?' Ashton cried. 'Whoa! Took your time telling us, didn't you?'

'We didn't know,' I admitted. 'We've only just found out ourselves. I just thought I was getting fat.'

'Yeah, I thought you were getting fat, too,' Declan agreed. 'So that's a baby in there?' He stared at my bump with interest. 'And you don't know if it's a boy or a girl?'

'No. It will be a nice surprise,' I said, trying to sound as if I meant it.

'Where's it going to sleep?' Ashton said suspiciously. 'We only have four bedrooms. One each. I'm not giving my room up for it.'

'It can sleep in my room with me,' Freddie offered excitedly.

'I don't think that's such a good idea,' Jack told him. Knowing how boisterous and impulsive Freddie could be, I dreaded to think what would happen if we left a helpless baby within his grasp all night.

'While it's very little it will sleep in a cot in our room,' I explained. God, wouldn't it just. All those sleepless nights. I could feel my wrinkles deepening and my eye bags swelling just at the thought of it. 'After that, we'll probably put it in its own room for a while. Two of you will have to share.'

'Which two?' Ashton asked immediately. 'I can't give up *my* room. I'm at high school! It would be humiliating to share a room with my kid brother.'

'I'm not a kid,' Declan said angrily. 'I'm nine!'

'That's what I said. A kid. You can share with Freddie.'

'That's not fair!' Declan protested. 'Either I'll have to share with Freddie, or I'll have to share with Ashton. No matter who you pick I lose my bedroom, don't I?'

He was right. And it wasn't fair.

'I don't know what else we can do,' Jack said. 'I'm sorry, Declan. The fact is, at some point this baby is going to need a bedroom of its own and two of you are going to have to share. And yes, you will be one of them.'

'Bagsy my own room,' Ashton said immediately. 'He can share with Freddie, like I said. Freddie will love it.'

'I don't want to share with Declan,' Freddie said. 'Can I share with Ashton?'

'No!' Ashton cried, outraged. 'Tell him, Dad! I'm too old to share a room.'

'For God's sake,' Jack said. 'Can't you three just have a bit of consideration for your mum? This has been a big shock to her, and it's your mum who's got the biggest change ahead of her. She's carrying this baby. She'll have to give birth to it. She'll be the one looking after it more than any of us. The last thing she needs is you three arguing and bickering about bedrooms. Stop being so selfish.'

'You're the selfish one,' Ashton said. 'We didn't ask you to have another baby, did we? But it's us three who are going to have to make the sacrifices. Not to mention the embarrassment when everyone finds out at school.'

'Don't tell them then,' I said bleakly.

'Immi will tell them,' he wailed. 'She'll know soon enough. You can't keep anything a secret in Rowan Vale.'

'You'd be surprised,' I muttered.

'We don't have to decide anything just now,' Jack said, trying to calm the situation. 'We've still got weeks before the baby arrives, and then it will be another year before we have to move it into its own room. Right now, I just want you to think about the fact that you're going to have a new family member. Whatever you might think right now, it's an exciting event. A new brother or sister! Maybe you can start to think of names for it.'

'How about Cuckoo?' suggested Ashton.

'Can we call it Bluey?' Freddie asked.

'Definitely not.'

'Spiderman?' he asked hopefully.

'Sorry.'

'Paddington?'

'Why don't you just think about it for a while,' I suggested. 'A long while. We've got ages yet.'

'Is that it then?' Ashton asked.

'Yes, that's it for now,' Jack said. 'We just wanted you to be aware of the situation, that's all.'

'Right. I've got homework to do,' Ashton said. He headed back up the stairs without another word.

Declan shrugged. 'Okay, well I'll finish my game then.'

He followed his brother upstairs, leaving Freddie standing alone, his head tilted to one side as he considered me thoughtfully.

'Does it hurt to grow a baby in your tummy?' he asked at last.

'No,' I said. 'Not at all.' *It's the pushing it out that's the killer.*

'I hope it's a girl,' he said.

Jack smiled. 'Why's that?'

'Mummy needs a girl in the house. There are too many boys already and it's not fair.'

I held out my arms and he climbed onto my knee, hugging me tightly and burying his face in my hair.

'Love you,' he mumbled, and I kissed his cheek and stroked his red hair and inhaled the scent of him.

'I love you, too,' I said fiercely. 'Always and forever.'

'Even when you have a little baby to look after?'

'Even then. You'll always be my baby. Even when you're twenty-one.'

His eyes widened. 'Twenty-one! That's real old. I won't be a baby then.'

'No,' I said sadly. 'I suppose not. But I'll love you just the same.'

'If you like,' he said, 'it can have my room. I don't mind sharing with Declan. Not really.'

'You're a good boy,' Jack said, as I was too overcome with emotion to respond. 'Now, it's almost bathtime, so let's you and I go upstairs, shall we, and I'll run the bath, then make you some supper.'

Freddie clambered off my knee and reached for his dad's hand.

'I'll make the supper,' I began as I started to heave myself out of the chair, but Jack gently pushed me back.

'I'll make it. You sit there and chill out. You've just done the ironing. Besides, busy day for you tomorrow, remember?'

I nodded. Christmas shopping. Usually, it was something I looked forward to. Now it was just another chore. I'd never felt less Christmassy in my life.

13

I had to admit, there was the faintest flicker of excitement as I waited with Jack and the kids for the Christmas lights to be switched on. At least it wasn't raining, but it was freezing cold, and I could see the mist from my breath hanging in the darkness of the December night air. I shivered, glad that I'd finally bought a new bigger coat at Jack's insistence. One that I could actually zip up!

We were standing on the grassy verge in front of the river, just across the road from All Souls' church. We'd decided to take the boys to that particular spot because it was there that the Christmas tree had been placed.

Usually, the tree stood on the village green, but this year the market stalls were there, so another location had been selected, and as there was a wide grassy area in front of the church, Callie and Brodie had chosen to place it there, just to our right of the lychgate.

Rowan Vale had been transformed, with fairy lights strung along all the main streets and in the shop windows. Many of the cottages had also decorated their windows, and some had placed smaller Christmas trees in their front gardens or in large pots by their front doors.

I couldn't help feeling guilty as we hadn't even dragged the decorations for Honeywell House out of the loft yet, let alone bought a Christmas tree. I hadn't so much as written a Christmas card. With only two weeks to go until the big day I needed to get my act together, and fast. The trouble was, I had no headspace for it. I think I was still in shock about the baby and couldn't focus on anything else.

Even my shopping trip had been a waste of time. I'd become completely overwhelmed as I'd trawled the shops, looking for ideas for Christmas presents for the boys.

They'd written their lists, but half the stuff was either sold out, not available in Much Melton, or out of the question. There was no way I was getting Freddie a pet donkey, for a start. And Declan had no chance of the top-of-the-range gaming computer he'd requested.

Funnily enough, it was Ashton who'd surprised me the most. He'd barely written anything on his list, and when I pushed him to add a few more things to it, he'd shrugged and mumbled, 'I don't really need anything, and babies cost a lot of money.'

Sometimes, my kids amazed me. To be honest, I was desperately worried about our finances, but even so, there was no way I wanted the boys to go without anything just because Jack and I had been so reckless. The credit card would just have to take the beating. I'd worry about it in the new year.

I felt Jack's arm go around my shoulders and I snuggled into him, glad to have a leaning post more than anything. My back was aching, and I was tired out. Even so, I wouldn't have missed the Christmas lights switch-on for the world.

I must have missed the signal, but suddenly all the villagers who were lined up along Church Lane began to chant a countdown, and my boys joined in enthusiastically – even Ashton, who'd had to be persuaded to join us because he felt that twelve was far too old to be excited about a Christmas tree.

Jack was louder than all the boys put together, and I glanced at him, seeing the sparkle in his dark eyes and remembering all the times he'd decorated our own tree and been so excited about it that the boys had told *him* to calm down.

I was so lucky to have him.

'Jack,' I said impulsively, 'I really do love you, you know.'

He didn't hear me, because at that moment the countdown reached its climax and there was a collective cheer as the Christmas tree lights lit up and the rest of Rowan Vale along with it.

Church Lane was flooded with Christmas. I looked up, tears pricking my eyes as I saw the streams of fairy lights crisscrossing the street. The lights had gone on around the gates of The Quicken Tree Inn, and I could see more of them draped along the banks of the River Faran, leading all the way past the green and up to the mill.

'Oh wow,' Declan breathed. 'It's fantastic!'

'When's Father Christmas coming, Mummy?' Freddie asked, tugging at my hand.

I looked down into his big blue eyes and felt such a rush of love for my family that I could barely speak. 'Not long now,' I told him, ruffling his red hair. 'Not long at all.'

'Isn't it gorgeous?'

I looked round, smiling as I saw Shona and Max standing nearby, their arms around each other. Next to them stood Shona's eldest daughter, Christie, along with her husband Scott and their two young children.

'I think this is the best display we've ever had,' Shona continued. 'We're going to have a wander up to the market in a minute – check out the competition at the food stalls.' She laughed. 'And we have the Dickensian weekend to look forward to, still. It's going to be fantastic.'

'You're right there,' Jack said. 'Callie and Brodie have really done us proud.'

'Our Pippa's out and about somewhere reporting on this,' Shona said proudly. 'You'll have to pop into the teashop, Clara. Max has made some gorgeous Christmassy German desserts and if the customers aren't quick, I'll have scoffed them all before they get the chance.'

'We had some of the lebkuchen,' I told Max. 'They were delicious.'

'Thank you,' he said, smiling. 'I'll be glad when school term finishes. All that teaching is getting in the way of my baking!'

I'd completely forgotten he was Head of Languages at the Chipping Royston Academy. I glanced round and noticed Ashton trying to hide behind Jack. I grinned. Nothing more embarrassing for a child than to bump into his teacher off duty!

As Max and Shona moved off to talk to our vicar, Amelia Davies, who was standing by the lychgate chatting animatedly with her partner, Tully, Christie scooped up little Maddie, who was yawning and rubbing her eyes.

'I think this one's ready for bed,' she said, kissing her youngest daughter's forehead.

'How old is she now?' Jack asked.

I glanced round at him and saw the big smile on his face.

'Nineteen months,' Christie said. 'She'll be two before I know it. Honestly, it goes by so quickly, doesn't it? It seems only days ago that she was a tiny baby and now look at her. Little madam's always up to mischief.'

'They keep you young, don't they?' Jack said affectionately.

'Or age you!' Christie laughed. 'But I wouldn't be without them. Autumn's so excited about Christmas now she's just turned four, and it's making Scott and me really excited, too. One thing about kids, they do remind you what the Christmas spirit's all about, don't they?'

'Mm,' I mumbled.

'Well, we'd better take them home,' she said with a sigh. 'It's past Maddie's bedtime. Lovely to see you all again.'

As she and her little family headed over to say goodbye to Shona and Max, Jack squeezed me.

'Makes you feel all warm and happy inside, doesn't it?'

'Does it?' I gasped suddenly and my eyes widened. 'Oh blimey!'

'What is it, love?' Jack's brow creased with anxiety. 'Are you all right? It's not the baby, is it?'

'Yes,' I said, feeling dazed. 'But don't worry. It's nothing bad. It just kicked, Jack. It's the first time... I mean, I've felt these weird movements before but that – that was a proper kick. Ow! There's another one!'

Jack scooped me into his arms. 'Aw, that's amazing! We're going to be all right, aren't we? You'll see.'

I unzipped my coat and put my hand on my stomach, feeling it suddenly jerk again.

'Yes, of course,' I murmured. 'We're going to be fine.'

This baby was real. I'd struggled to come to terms with that fact, even when I'd seen the scan and heard the heartbeat, but this was something I could feel. Something I could touch and even see.

I was going to be a mum again, and it wasn't the baby's fault, so how could I possibly resent it? It had all been down to the irresponsibility of Jack and me, so there was no way I could blame this tiny life. I wouldn't let it suffer because of our actions, any more than I'd let the boys suffer. These children – our children – were going to have the best life we could possibly give them.

Christmas was just the start.

14

AUBREY

Aubrey was standing by the window of the drawing room, looking out over Rowan Vale. He could sense the excitement in the air, and closed his eyes for a moment, imagining the bustling scene playing out in the streets beyond the Hall.

For many years, he, Agnes and Florence had accompanied Lawrie into the village to witness the great Christmas lights switch-on, until Agnes had put a stop to their visits. From what he understood, this year the tree had been moved to the front of All Souls, as market huts had been placed on the green. He tried to imagine what it would look like.

Callie had told him that they'd added even more lights to the village display this year, with some of the side streets like Victoria Walk being included in the illuminations. He thought it must look marvellous.

She'd very kindly opened the window for him before she left so he could lean out and get a better look. In the distance he could hear chanting, which he recognised as the countdown. Moments later he saw a flood of lights, heading all the way from All Souls down towards Harling Hall.

'Splendid,' he murmured. 'How wonderful.'

He wished he could see them up close. Somewhere down there, Florence would be enjoying the festivities. She and Immi had gone with Callie and Brodie, and Aubrey was grateful that his little girl had made such a good friend in Callie's eleven-year-old daughter.

After an initially rocky start, they'd become inseparable in recent months, going everywhere together. It was incredibly fortunate that Immi shared her mother's gift of seeing all the ghosts on the Harling Estate. It didn't always happen that way.

His thoughts strayed to his own childhood, when his inability to see the ghosts had caused his parents such distress. They'd been desperate for him to take over the estate and took his failure to inherit his father's ability as a personal insult – as if he'd done it on purpose.

And when his own son had also failed to inherit the gift, the Wyndhams' fate was sealed. His mother had never forgiven him. As for Elspeth...

The sadness that he tried so hard to keep at bay – usually with great success – overwhelmed him suddenly as he turned away from the window. Even after all this time, the memory of how he'd felt back then could still return with a bitterness that stung so sharply it could have been yesterday.

He remembered those dark days of utter wretchedness. The loneliness. The shame. The confusion. He'd never thought to find happiness in his life, and it was fair to say he hadn't. But his afterlife was another matter. He still couldn't believe what joy he'd found after passing on, all thanks to one wonderful woman who'd given him hope and strength and shown him what true love really felt like.

As if his thoughts had summoned her, Agnes's voice came to him, gentle and full of affection and warmth.

'Are you all right, Mr Wyndham? You're looking very pensive.'

He lifted his head, breaking into a smile as she hurried towards him.

'I was just thinking how very lucky I am to have found you, my dear.'

Agnes beamed at him, looking suddenly far younger than her forty-five years – give or take a couple of centuries.

'It is I who was lucky to find you,' she assured him. 'I count my blessings every single day.'

He had the sudden overwhelming urge to pull her into a fierce hug and kiss her passionately, but Agnes was a lady, and one simply didn't do these things. Especially given the circumstances. It would be highly inappropriate.

Instead, fighting his embarrassing surge of desire, he turned quickly back to the window and waved his arm, encompassing the whole of Rowan Vale in one dramatic gesture.

'Look, my dear. Isn't it splendid? The Christmas lights have been switched on, and the whole village is illuminated. What a joyous sight it is to behold, is it not?'

Agnes came to his side and peered out. Her hand flew to her chest, and she nodded. 'Quite beautiful indeed,' she said softly. 'I hope Florence is behaving herself.'

Aubrey hesitantly slipped his arm around her shoulders, and she gave him a look of surprise but didn't shrug him off, which he found encouraging.

'I'm sure she's having a wonderful time. I understand the market stalls have opened for a short time this evening, and Florence was most excited about all the food that is to be served. She's looking forward to smelling all sorts of delicious festive fare.'

'I just hope she doesn't overdo it,' Agnes said firmly. 'She'll be dreaming of food tonight, and that can lead to no good. You know how angry she gets when she wants something she can't have.'

'Well...' Aubrey sighed heavily. 'I suppose we all must learn to accept that there are some things we can never have.'

'Is this about going into the village again?' She moved away from him, leaving him feeling strangely bereft.

He hadn't been thinking of that at all. He'd had something far more intimate in mind, but he could hardly express that to her, could he? Besides, she had a point.

'It would be nice to see the display at close quarters,' he said wistfully. 'I haven't been to the Christmas market in the village for many, many years.'

'It hasn't *run* for many, many years,' she reminded him.

'No, but now it's returned, and it would be good to visit, don't you think? Surely it couldn't harm to have a stroll down to the green, Agnes? Wouldn't you like to—?'

'Mr Wyndham, we've had this discussion!'

Now she sounded exasperated, and he knew he'd disappointed her. A feeling of gloom settled on him as his hopes and happiness evaporated. He hated letting her down.

'I'm sorry,' he told her. 'I just feel that it's wrong to let someone like Silas Alexander win. Why should his opinion of our – er – living arrangements dictate how we live our afterlives?'

'He is the vicar of All Souls, Mr Wyndham,' she reminded him primly. 'His opinions exert much influence on the villagers.'

'Actually, my dear, he *was* the vicar of All Souls. He hasn't been in that position for over a century. As for his opinions – I would venture to suggest that none of the villagers pay heed to those. He exerts no influence over them any longer. I fail to see why *we* give his wretched ramblings credence.'

'He is a man of the cloth!' She sounded shocked, as if she'd completely forgotten that it wasn't so long ago that she'd called him a monster. 'Whatever we may think of him, nevertheless, he deserves our respect. Besides...'

Her voice trailed off and she turned away and headed over to the sofa.

He watched as she sat down, noting the fumbling with the ribbons on her bed jacket, and the nervous trembling of her fingers. His eyes narrowed and he went to sit beside her.

'Agnes, you don't give his utterances any validity, surely? The man is a zealot! He was insufferable even when he was alive, but in the afterlife he has proved to be quite insane.'

'Not insane, Mr Wyndham. Merely a man of principle.'

'Principle!' Aubrey stared at her. 'You're not saying – you can't mean that you actually agree with him?'

Agnes twisted the ribbons so tightly that, had she been alive, she'd probably have choked herself. Aubrey gently took her hands and lowered them, gazing into her eyes with deep concern.

'The fact is, Mr Wyndham, whatever we say to the contrary, he does have a point, doesn't he?' She gave him an anxious look. 'The truth is, we *are* married, but not to each other. And I suppose, looked at from the outside, that *does* make Harling Hall a den of iniquity.'

Luckily, Aubrey managed to smother the shout of bitter laughter and the cry of, 'Chance would be a fine thing!'

Conscious of Agnes's sensibilities, he took her hands between his own and said calmly, 'It is hardly that, my dear. We have separate rooms. We have never—'

Seeing her eyes widen in horror he said hastily, 'That is, we have always behaved with propriety. That other people make more of it than it is, cannot be blamed on us.'

'But we share a suite of rooms, Mr Wyndham,' she whispered. 'And we refer to each other as husband and wife.'

'Because I think of you as my wife, and I hope that you think of me as your husband,' he said, hoping the hurt he was feeling didn't come across in his tone of voice.

'I do,' she said. 'Indeed, you are far more of a husband to me than Cyril Ashcroft ever was, even without all that ghastly business taking place.'

It was as close as Agnes had ever come to discussing marital relations, and evidently she realised it, for she turned away from him, obviously too embarrassed to face him.

Aubrey sighed. *Ghastly business.* It could be so much more than that. At least, that's what he'd always believed. He didn't suppose he'd ever get the chance to find out and, clearly, Agnes had no desire to test the theory.

'However,' she continued, still facing away from him, 'the fact remains, you are not my husband, and I am not your wife. We made vows to other people.'

'Till death us do part,' Aubrey said, refusing to let go of her hands even though she went to pull them away. 'There are no rules about the afterlife, are there?'

'We can have no way of knowing that.' He saw her tremble and swallowed. She looked so fragile. So utterly beautiful. His own hand shook slightly as he lifted it to her face and gently stroked her cheek.

'Mr Wyndham…' Agnes's voice trailed off, and encouraged, he turned her face to his and leaned forward, his lips lightly touching hers.

It was the first time he'd kissed her mouth and the effect it had on them both was startling. Aubrey felt the shoots of desire springing to life and coursing through him like blood through his veins – if only he'd had blood coursing through his veins.

Agnes's palms rested on his chest and, daring to hope, he cupped her face and kissed her again, the pressure increasing slightly on her lips as he reminded himself to be careful, that she was a lady of refinement and high morals, and he simply couldn't overstep the mark.

No really, he simply couldn't…

But her lips were soft and yielding, and her hands were firm on his chest, and she was so close to him, so irresistibly close, that he quite forgot himself and, overcome with a sudden, urgent need for her, his hand strayed from her face to her neck, where it lingered for a moment before moving even lower, his trembling fingers tracing a line along her breastbone…

Agnes gave a strangled cry and pushed him away before leaping to her feet.

'I have a headache,' she announced, and without so much as glancing in his direction, she rushed into her bedroom.

Aubrey sank back in the sofa and stared at the closed door, feeling stunned, foolish, and – worst of all – rejected.

Elspeth's voice came to him as clearly as if she was standing beside him. 'You have had your way, and I have done my duty. Now, leave me alone! I have no desire to lie with you again. I would thank you to remember that you were born a gentleman and should behave like one, not a common gamekeeper like your father.'

It was all his fault. He'd let his working-class urges overwhelm him and now he'd repulsed Agnes, the woman who had given him so much happiness after so much pain. How could he ever earn her forgiveness? And would she ever trust him again?

15

On Monday, Callie and Brodie were due to come over to Honeywell House for a business meeting.

Jack had swapped his Saturday off for the Monday so he could be present at the meeting without us having the boys running riot as we tried to talk, which is what would most likely have happened if we'd met at the weekend.

We'd all agreed that we should discuss the model village before the schools broke up for the Christmas holidays, as we were anxious to put some firm plans into place.

There was tension in the air even before Callie and Brodie arrived at our home. Jack and I had a bit of a row because he tried to help me by putting a wash load in and somehow managed to slip my favourite woollen cardigan into a hot wash, with the result that it came out looking as if it would fit our new baby when it arrived.

Not only that, but I had to vacuum the carpet yet again, as Toby had done an epic moult, and to top it all, just half an hour before Callie and Brodie were due to arrive, I discovered that the boys had left the bathroom in a terrible state and I'd had to frantically set to work cleaning and scrubbing, as well as collecting the inevitable wet towels from the floor.

'If we had a separate toilet, it wouldn't matter so much,' I grumbled, as I gathered the cleaning cloths, disinfectant spray, and cream cleanser from the cupboard under the kitchen sink. 'What kind of four-bedroomed house only has one toilet in it, anyway? What if they need the loo while they're here? I'd die of shame if they saw the state that bathroom is in right now.'

'What does it matter?' Jack asked wearily, as he shoved the clothes in the tumble dryer. 'They're our friends and they know we have three boys. I'm sure—'

'What the hell are you doing?' I gasped.

He paused, looking puzzled. 'Putting the clothes in the dryer.'

'Do you think we're made of money? Have you any idea how much electricity the tumble dryer uses? You ought to look at that little gizmo we got from the energy company, that'll open your eyes.'

'Well, what have we got a tumble dryer for if we're not going to use it?' he demanded.

'It's strictly for emergencies only,' I snapped. 'If you bothered to look at the fuel bills once in a while instead of burying your head in the sand and leaving it all to me, you'd know that.'

'Fine!' Jack slammed the dryer door shut. 'I'll put them on the radiators then.'

He began to drape various items of clothing on the kitchen radiator.

'Are you deliberately trying to wind me up?' I snatched them back off and stuffed them in the laundry basket. 'We have guests coming.'

'Only Callie and Brodie!'

'I don't want them to see our wet clothes drying on the radiators,' I said, exasperated. 'What kind of impression will that make?'

'Well, what the hell do you want me to do with them then? I can't exactly hang them outside. They're not going to dry in this weather.'

'I don't see why not. It's not raining or damp. Hang them on the line and then we can bring them in and air them on the radiators when Callie and Brodie have gone.'

'Bloody hell!' Jack looked thoroughly fed up, but he did as I asked, while I frantically cleaned the bathroom. At least, I thought, Toby never ventured upstairs, despite the boys frequently urging him to. He didn't like stairs, and it was a good job because I wasn't in the mood to vacuum the stair carpet on top of everything else.

By the time Callie and Brodie arrived I was hot, red-faced and thoroughly fed up, and feeling quite irritated by Jack who was smiling from ear to ear, looking all handsome and acting as if nothing in the least bit stressful had happened.

Between us we made them both welcome, and we all relaxed for twenty minutes or so over a cup of tea and the few dodgy-looking biscuits that the kids had left us – most of which ended up being fed to a blissfully grateful Toby.

Callie carefully brought up the subject of the baby by asking how I was feeling, while casting a nervous look at Jack. To my relief, he appeared to have got over his grudge and even thanked her for being there for me and accompanying me to the health centre and the hospital. I had to admit, he was a lot more forgiving than I'd have been in his situation, and Callie looked as relieved as I was that he wasn't still annoyed about it.

Brodie congratulated us both on the news, and we had a short discussion about how well the Christmas lights switch-on had gone, and how busy the market had been over the weekend.

Callie told us that rehearsals for the ghosts' version of *A Christmas Carol* were going as chaotically as she'd expected, with plenty of artistic differences coming to a head.

'They really wanted Harmony to be in it, but she's said she'll be too busy elsewhere,' she told us. 'I can't imagine what she's doing but it doesn't surprise me she's not going to be involved. Anyway, they've got Isaac from The Quicken Tree as the Ghost of Christmas Present, Millie as the Ghost of Christmas Past, and Quintus Severus as the Ghost of Christmas Yet to Come.'

'Quintus Severus!' Jack whistled. 'Never thought he'd agree to take part.'

'He finally did when he found out he wouldn't have to speak, just stand there looking threatening and point a bit.' Callie laughed. 'Old Perks is playing Fezziwig, Polly and Ray are the Cratchits, and Pillory Pete is Jacob Marley, while Danny and Brooke are playing Scrooge's nephew Fred and his wife.'

'And who's the star turn?' I asked, intrigued. 'Surely the vicar didn't agree?'

She laughed. 'Well, no, but luckily, they had someone more than eager to take the leading role. Walter! Should be fun.'

'I wish I could see it,' Brodie admitted, as we finally headed outside to look at the model village. 'You'll have to tell me all about it.'

'They're arguing so much about who has the most lines that I think if they weren't already dead, they'd have killed each other,' Callie confessed. 'Right, let's have a think about this prospective new tourist attraction, shall we?'

We gazed around the paddock at the jumble of cottages, shops, and other buildings that were such a beautiful representation of the Harling Estate.

'The issue,' Brodie said, 'is obviously how we get the tourists into the paddock while encroaching as little as possible on your privacy.'

'Maybe,' Callie suggested, 'we could put up dividing walls in the central outbuilding and create a corridor so they could go through that without seeing what's in your outbuildings?'

'It would have to be a pretty wide corridor in peak times,' Brodie said. 'There'd be a big queue in the courtyard otherwise, which isn't ideal. Plus, they'd still have to go through the garden to get to the paddock.'

'We were thinking we'd have to put up a six-foot fence,' I said, 'creating a path at the side of the garden directly to the paddock.'

'Six-foot fencing all round your garden, I'd have thought,' Callie said, rubbing her chin. 'Otherwise, the tourists will be able to see everything going on in your garden and you don't want that.'

'I don't want the views blocking either,' Jack said grumpily. 'I mean, look at what we'd be giving up if we went ahead with the fencing.'

We all stared out across the landscape of farmland with the woodland in the distance. I could make out Nick or one of the 'POWs' ploughing one of the far fields. They were using the vintage tractor today by the looks of things, rather than Bonnie and Blossom. It would be hard to give those views up, I had to admit.

'We'll be able to see it from the bedroom windows, though,' I pointed out feebly.

Jack gave me a withering look. 'And by putting in a pathway we're losing another slice of the garden. As you can see, it's not that big to begin with. I'm not happy about it, especially with four kids and a dog to accommodate.'

'And there's the ticket office,' Callie said suddenly. 'We'd have to find room for that.'

'Surely one of the outbuildings would be the best place for that?' Brodie said, frowning. 'There's plenty of room in those, after all.'

'Not as much as you'd think,' Jack said. 'There are decades of junk in there. Stuff my dad and grandad left behind. Not to mention the kids' bikes and outdoor toys.'

'Time we had a declutter anyway,' I said.

'And you've got time to do it, have you?' Jack asked, sounding quite irritated. 'Cos I'm not sure I have.'

'Well, when you give up your job…'

'Give up your job?' Both Callie and Brodie stared at Jack. 'You're quitting the trains? Since when?'

'I told you this,' I said to Callie.

'You told me you were thinking about it,' she said, shaking her head, 'but I thought it was just an idle comment. I never thought you were serious.'

'Well, I am. He's going to work with me at the model village,' I explained. 'We're going to run it as a partnership. He'll oversee the maintenance, obviously, and we'll both work selling tickets, while I'll also do the promotional stuff. I've already had ideas for some posters and a website.'

'That's…' Brodie shook his head. 'A big step. You have a decent job there, Jack. It's a bit premature to think about quitting it to go self-employed, don't you think?'

'Yes,' Jack said flatly. 'I do think. Try telling *her* that.'

I glared at him. 'We've been through all this! I can't do it on my own and this was supposed to be our passion project. Something we could do together. Our own slice of the village.'

I turned to Callie, pleading with her to understand. 'We don't own this house. Everything in this village belongs to the Harland Estate. But this model village is ours. Jack's great-grandfather designed and built it, and Jack's worked on it ever since he was little, helping to keep it in good condition. This is something we can pass onto our kids. We really want to make it work, but I can't do it alone. I need Jack.'

'And you need money even more,' he said. 'Or have you forgotten our recent conversation about not turning on the tumble dryer? You can't moan about the cost of living one minute and expect me to give up a perfectly secure job the next – especially now, with a new baby on the way.'

'You're just making excuses,' I snapped. 'You never wanted to do this really, did you? Just admit it.'

'It was a pipe dream,' he said, clearly past caring about pretence. 'A nice one, but we must be realistic. There won't be enough demand to make this work all year round. It's a summer attraction, that's all. Ask them!' he added, waving a hand at our guests. 'They'll tell you. Go on,' he said to an awkward-looking Callie and Brodie, 'explain it to her. She won't listen to me.'

'I think Jack's got a point, Clara,' Brodie said, sounding apologetic. 'When we envisioned opening the model village we weren't thinking of it as a year-round attraction. I honestly don't see how it will earn enough money for you to make it a full-time career for both of you, and I certainly wouldn't advise Jack to give up a secure, well-paid job on the railway to become self-employed at such a precarious business.'

'And to be honest,' Jack said, 'I don't see that all the disruption to our lives will be worth it for a seasonal attraction. Losing more of the garden, losing our views, our privacy, the messing about with the outbuildings. No.' He shook his head firmly. 'The whole thing's a non-starter. I'm sorry to have wasted your time.'

'You haven't wasted our time,' Callie said quietly. 'It was our idea anyway, and I still think opening the model village to the public would be a good idea, but maybe now's not the best time to discuss it. You two obviously have a lot going on in your lives, and perhaps we'd be better to leave it for now and revisit the idea in a year or two.'

'I agree,' Jack said, and Brodie nodded his assent.

'So, I don't get any say in the matter?' I asked tearfully. 'What about me? This was supposed to be my return to work. You know I'm going to find it difficult to get a job that works around the kids. This was the perfect opportunity for me to get back into employment while building something we can leave to the boys. Making our own stamp on Rowan Vale. Something of ours that doesn't belong to the Davenports or the Chases.'

I wiped the tears from my cheeks, aware that Callie, Jack, and Brodie were all staring at me as if I'd suddenly grown two heads.

'I didn't realise that mattered so much to you,' Callie admitted.

'Well,' I said, 'it does. Living here – it's not like anywhere else, is it? No opportunity to buy our own home. Nothing to pass on to our children. It's not fair.'

'But that's the deal with Rowan Vale,' Jack said. 'You knew that when you moved here.'

'When I moved here, I didn't have any kids,' I reminded him. 'I didn't think about things like that then.'

'Well…' He rubbed the back of his neck. 'It's just the way it is. We're lucky. We'd never be able to afford to buy a four-bedroomed house in the Cotswolds on my wages. And the estate keeps our rent low, too. Imagine if we had to pay market price. You'd have to get a full-time job then. As it is, there's no rush for you to go back to work, is there? You'll have your hands full with the new baby. Like Callie said, we can revisit this in a year or two. See how things stand then.'

'I can tell you exactly how they'll stand,' I said bitterly. 'The only difference between then and now is that I won't be pregnant. I'll have a two-year-old taking up all my time and energy instead, and then you'll say it's too much for me to start working on our own business, and why don't I wait until the little one starts nursery. And then school. And then it'll be, why don't you just get a part-time job in a shop or something?'

'That's not what I'm saying at all,' he protested. 'But you're not thinking straight. If you'd just be reasonable!'

But I was beyond being reasonable. I stamped back through the garden and headed into the house, slamming the kitchen door behind me.

Let them think of me what they liked. I was past caring.

16

Sometimes, living in Rowan Vale was as awkward as hell. Not only could we not buy our own house on the Harling Estate, but delivery vans weren't allowed to drive into the village.

I'd given up all hope of doing the Christmas shopping in town, or even at the market, and realising how close to the big day we were, I'd gone into full panic mode. I'd quickly written a list of presents to get the kids, Jack's parents, Callie, Brodie, Immi, and the kids' teachers, as well as a few bits and bobs for Jack, and had placed a huge order with an online retailer, courtesy of my already groaning credit card. I'd even, as an afterthought, bought a few baby vests and sleepsuits for our forthcoming arrival. In for a penny, in for a pound.

It had all been delivered within a couple of days, but as was the case with all deliveries to Rowan Vale, it had been left at the drop-off point not far from Harling Hall.

This particular piece of land, down a lane close to the village boundary, was also home to the garage, the taxi firm, the shop where you could hire mobility scooters and wheelchairs, the villagers' car park, and the overnight storage depot for the vintage buses.

It made sense and I understood the reasons why we weren't allowed to park our cars in the village, and why modern delivery vans couldn't sail back and forth through our streets. After all, this was a living history village, and the sight of modern vehicles would really break the illusion that visitors had stepped into the past.

The only vehicles allowed to move freely through the village – apart from the emergency services and any vehicles needed for building materials – were the vintage buses, a couple of taxis with wheelchair access, and a Fordson Thames delivery van from 1940, driven by a local man called Eric Edwards who, for a few quid, would collect your deliveries from the drop-off point and bring them to your door.

It had never bothered me much before. Yes, on rainy days, having to trawl all the way to Hall Lane to pick up the car was infuriating, but it was something you had to accept if you wanted to live here. Part of the deal.

In exchange, we were charged low rents, and repairs and maintenance were done quickly and for free on our homes. Plus, we got to live in this stunning village. Jack was right. We'd never have been able to afford to buy somewhere like Honeywell House. Cotswold prices had shot up with an influx of celebrities and London commuters, not to mention holiday homeowners. People like us didn't stand a chance.

I knew all that, and deep down I was grateful, but there was still a part of me that seethed with resentment as I took delivery of all the parcels from Eric that Thursday afternoon, all too aware that the news of my splurge would be all round the village within the hour.

No doubt people would shake their heads and condemn me for not supporting the local shops and businesses.

Well, I thought as I directed Eric to one of the outbuildings so the parcels could be dumped in there until Jack could get them safely upstairs out of the way of the boys, *they can criticise me all they want. I don't have the headspace, or the physical energy to go Christmas shopping again this year.*

The good mood that had come over me when I watched the Christmas lights being switched on had evaporated, leaving me as low as I'd ever felt.

With the model village – and my life – on hold for at least two years and potentially forever, I couldn't see a way forward. The future held nothing but nappies and toddler groups and more money worries.

I'd barely purchased a thing for the baby and told myself I'd deal with all that in the new year, but at the back of my mind the fear nagged away at me. How was I going to buy all the things we'd need when I'd pretty much maxed out our credit cards on Christmas?

I didn't even like to think about how I was going to pay them off as it was. And now winter was here the fuel bills would only increase.

I thanked Eric and paid him, then headed into the house. In the kitchen, Toby greeted me with hopeful eyes and an encouraging nudge. The hope turned to reproach when he realised I had no treats for him. As he sloped into the living room, I sat at the table, resting my head in my hands in despair.

Reluctantly, I had to accept that my low mood was partly caused by knowing that Jack was right. It *would* be stupid for him to leave his job on the railways. It was the only security we had, and walking out on a regular wage to set up a new and – being honest – seasonal business would have made things ten times worse, only adding to our stress rather than lowering it.

I knew that. I just didn't want to admit it. I'd wanted so much to believe that we could run our own business, work together, have a stake in Rowan Vale...

My mind drifted back to one weekend, fifteen years earlier, when we'd discussed my forthcoming first visit to the estate.

'Rowan Vale sounds like something out of a fairytale,' I'd told him, as we'd sat together in my bed, eating our breakfast of bacon sandwiches. 'A steam railway, no modern vehicles allowed, people wearing period costume to work.'

Jack had eyed me nervously. 'It's not for everyone,' he'd said cautiously. 'But it's definitely an, er, special place.'

'I'm sure it is,' I said. 'I can't wait to see it.'

He'd hooked his arm around me, and I'd snuggled against him, my mind full of thoughts of this stunning Cotswolds village that I'd heard so much about and had longed to visit ever since I could remember.

Now I finally had the chance. I just had to be very careful and keep my wits about me...

I mentally shook my head, not wanting to go back to those days. Knowing how I'd behaved still filled me with shame. I could only hope Jack never found out. Although, as the years went on, it seemed less and less likely that he would. Which was a good thing, naturally. Except, I sometimes felt that Jack knowing my secret would be worth it. I was tired of keeping it.

As if compelled by some mystical force, I got up and ventured into the living room, where I quickly located the sketchbook I'd hidden under piles of old takeaway menus, shopping lists, out-of-date bills and everything else we'd casually tossed into the 'junk drawer'.

I lifted it out and went back into the kitchen, placing it on the table while I made myself a cup of tea. Maybe, I thought, I *should* take up sketching again. Art had always soothed me. It gave me something to focus my mind on. Maybe that was what was missing from my life?

Finally settled, I was just about to pick up the book to leaf through it again when there was a knock on the door.

It was Callie. She looked a bit pensive as I greeted her, as if she wasn't entirely sure what mood I'd be in. I could hardly blame her, given how up and down I'd been recently, not to mention that the last time I'd seen her I'd stormed off and hadn't even said goodbye.

'Brought you these,' she said, waving a bag in front of my nose. 'Peace offering.'

'You don't need a peace offering,' I said, smiling in spite of myself. 'What's in there?'

'Churros,' she said. 'Hot and crunchy and utterly yummy. I may have eaten one on my way here.'

'Only one? Well done.'

I stepped aside and ushered her in.

'I'm sorry about the other day,' I told her, feeling embarrassed as I led her into the living room. 'I should never have left like that. It was childish.'

'You were upset,' she said, sitting on the sofa. 'We understood. All of us. Let's just forget it for now, shall we? I haven't come here to go over all that again. Actually, I was wondering how you got on at the antenatal appointment. It was yesterday, wasn't it? Did Jack go with you?'

I nodded. 'Yeah. Wild horses wouldn't have kept him away.'

'You two have made up then?'

I blushed. 'I apologised to him, too. And he apologised to me. We're both under a lot of pressure right now, what with finances, and lack of space, and the shock of a new baby. I know he was just trying to be practical, and he knows I'm disappointed. It is what it is, I guess.'

'And the appointment?'

'Everything's progressing well. My blood pressure's fine, though God knows how. Of course, there were some amused comments about me not realising I was pregnant. All very tactful, naturally, but I felt an idiot. As if it's not bad enough that I'm referred to as a geriatric mother.'

Callie laughed. 'The main thing is you're healthy, and everything seems to be going well with the pregnancy. And at least you've got a few weeks to get your head around everything. I was going to organise a baby shower for the new year, but it might be cutting it a bit fine. What do you think?'

I rolled my eyes. 'Believe me, that's the last thing I need. I've got enough to worry about.' I nodded at the bag of churros. 'We should eat those before they get cold. I'll put them on plates. Would you like a cup of tea to go with them?'

'Love one,' she said, beaming. I left her in the living room, while I quickly made her a cup of tea and fished out two plates for the churros.

Opening the bag, I was met with the most divine smell, and my mouth watered in anticipation of the taste and texture. Crunchy cinnamon sugar coating, a fluffy centre, all drizzled with chocolate. I could hardly wait.

I made the tea and divided the churros up onto two plates, then reached for the tray to put everything on. As I lifted it and turned to take it into the living room, I nearly dropped it in horror.

Callie was in the kitchen. I hadn't heard her come in. And she was browsing through my sketchbook!

'What – what are you doing?'

She gave me an apologetic look. 'Sorry. I came to see if you needed any help, and I just couldn't resist when I saw it lying there. Your drawings are so good, Clara. They really are. This one of Lawrie is amazing!'

Before I could stop her, she'd flipped the page over and I watched, unable to move or speak as her eyes narrowed in confusion. Then they widened and her mouth fell open as she slowly lifted her head to look at me.

'I don't... I mean, how?'

I put the tray down and leaned against the worktop, taking a deep breath. I knew my face was burning and that I had no way of avoiding what was coming. No explanation would satisfy Callie. I knew that. It was obvious that I'd have to come clean, and that, if I handled this badly, it could be the end of everything for me.

'It's – it's not what it looks like,' I murmured, my heart thumping in alarm.

'Well,' she said, clearly perplexed, 'it couldn't be, could it? Because what it looks like is a sketch of Aubrey Wyndham. And that's just not possible, is it?'

* * *

Callie carried the tray into the living room and settled it on the coffee table while I followed her, clutching the sketchbook in one of my shaking hands, and my tea in the other.

'Okay,' she said, as we settled onto the sofa. 'So how come you've managed to sketch one of our resident ghosts?'

I swallowed. 'I think I saw his portrait when I first moved here. I can't remember where.'

Callie shook her head. 'There's only one portrait of Aubrey that I know of, and it's in Harling Hall. And before you tell me you saw it on the night of the ball, remember it was only discovered very recently, as I told you.'

'Maybe there was a picture of him in a library book,' I said desperately. 'I did look up the history of this place when I moved here, you know. Yes, now I think about it, that's where I saw it. I must have copied it from that.'

'Lawrie told me the portrait we have is the only one of Aubrey that's known about. If there was another one that had been used in a book, I'm sure we'd have heard about it,' she said suspiciously. 'What's going on, Clara?'

My eyes filled with tears. I had nowhere left to hide, and I was terrified.

'Please, Callie. Can you just drop it?'

She bit into a churro, surveying me as she chewed, her mind obviously ticking over as she tried to work out what was going on.

'You can see him, can't you? Aubrey, I mean.'

I opened my mouth to deny it, but the words wouldn't come. I lowered my head, nodding miserably.

'Is he the only one, or can you see others?'

'Only Aubrey,' I whispered.

'And the reason for that is…?'

I took a deep breath. 'And the reason for that is, we're related. I'm his great-great-great-great-granddaughter.'

Callie stared at me. 'You're a Wyndham?'

'Descended from his son James,' I said. 'Callie please, *please* don't say anything.'

'I don't understand,' she admitted. 'I thought the Wyndhams had left the area. Lawrie said—'

'They did,' I said desperately. 'It's just me. I came back. And it was purely accidental.'

She said nothing, simply staring at me, and I suppressed a sob. 'Okay,' I admitted eventually, 'it wasn't *purely* accidental. But please, hear me out. It really isn't as bad as it sounds.'

'Okay,' she said, taking a sip of tea. 'I'm all ears.'

'I guess I'd better go back to the beginning,' I said slowly. 'It all really started when I met Jack.'

17

FIFTEEN YEARS EARLIER

The train journey to Harling's Halt had been amazing. I'd thoroughly enjoyed travelling on the steam train, and when I alighted at the railway station and looked around, seeing all the characters in their Great War costumes parading up and down the platform, and hearing the distant refrain of 'Goodbye-ee' over the speakers, I could hardly contain my excitement.

Jack met me, his face lit up with happiness.

'You're here at last! I thought the day would never come.'

'I know. I can hardly believe it myself.'

We exchanged hugs, and I hoped he couldn't sense how nervous I was about being here on the Harling Estate.

We caught the vintage bus from the station to the village, alighting at All Souls' church. I gazed at it in awe.

'It's just as beautiful as I knew it would be,' I breathed.

'You've been looking it up?' Jack asked and I blushed.

'Yes. Thought I'd better see what I was getting myself into.'

'And what did you think?' I could tell he was desperate for me to like the place, and I wasn't going to disappoint him.

'I think,' I said honestly, 'that it's absolutely stunning, and I'm so glad to be here.' Terrified but glad. A strange combination of emotions. No wonder I was trembling.

His smile couldn't have grown any wider, and there was a definite spring in his step as he led me down the lane that ran alongside the river, past the inn and the library, and various stunning cottages, until we turned off down another lane and within minutes found ourselves entering the courtyard at Honeywell House.

I stared up at the square, golden stone building, my stomach churning as I remembered that I was about to meet Jack's parents.

I glanced at him for reassurance, and he nodded, smiling. 'They can't wait to meet you. Don't worry. They'll love you just as much as I do.'

If he'd realised that he'd just declared his love for me, he didn't show it. In the year we'd been together we hadn't said those exact words to each other. I wondered if it had been a throwaway remark, and decided it was best if I pretended I hadn't heard him. I had enough to think about as I braced myself to meet the parents.

In the event, Jack's mum and dad, Carole and Alex were lovely and couldn't have been more welcoming.

'We'd given up hope of him getting serious enough about a girl to introduce her to us,' Alex told me cheerfully, causing poor Jack to groan and bury his hand in his hands, 'and now here you are at last. We've heard so much about you. Trust Jack to finally meet someone just as we were moving away!'

'I expect Jack's told you we live on the Isle of Wight now,' Carole explained, patting my hand as if we'd known each other for ages. 'It's where I'm from originally and I'd always wanted to go back there, as much as I love this place. What about you?'

'What about me?'

'You're from somewhere up north, aren't you? I know you two met in Scotland, but Jack said…'

'Yes, I'm a northerner.' I smiled. 'I'm from Lancashire, actually.'

'How lovely. I've heard there are some very nice places round there,' she said. 'Well, I've made up the guest bedroom for you so I'll show it to you now, shall I, and then we can all have a nice little chat over tea and cake.'

Really, I couldn't have asked for a warmer welcome, and as I settled into my room that night (evidently, it hadn't occurred to Jack's mum that I'd expected to share his!) I said a silent prayer of thanks that they were such lovely people, along with another prayer that they wouldn't ask too many questions, and I wouldn't slip up.

I was supposed to be staying in Rowan Vale for two weeks. The first couple of days were a hectic whirl as Jack's parents – who would be returning to the Isle of Wight two days after my arrival – gave me guided tours of the estate. His dad was particularly keen to show me the railway station in greater depth, and his mum was passionately fond of the Wyrd Stones, and insisted on taking me to see them so she could explain all about their history and the mythology that surrounded them.

The night before they left Rowan Vale, they insisted on treating us all to dinner at The Quicken Tree, and Carole took me to one side and told me how happy she and Alex were that Jack had found such a wonderful girl.

'I'm so glad we got to meet you at last,' she said. 'I was a bit worried about you two having a long-distance relationship, and I wasn't sure it would work, but I was wrong. You've lasted a whole year, and I can sense that you're made for each other. My Jack's such a lovely man, and I want the best for him, but you're lovely, too. You've got such a kind, honest face. I know I can trust you to be good to him.'

I'd never felt more ashamed in my life.

For the rest of that week, Jack and I spent every moment together, and with his parents gone I soon moved into his bedroom, where we were free to make as much noise as we wanted, which was very handy. We did some sightseeing, but it's a fact that we spent more of our time in Honeywell House, where I got to see most of the rooms in the place from some very funny angles.

After the first week, though, Jack had to go back to work.

'Are you sure you don't mind being here on your own during the day?' he asked worriedly. 'I could maybe call in sick...'

If I'd known, back then, how conscientious and responsible Jack was, I'd have realised what a huge deal it was for him to even suggest that. But I didn't really know him, so I just laughed and told him not to be silly.

'I'll be fine,' I said. 'There's loads to explore in the village, and I'll probably visit the Ashcroft Mill and have a look around the museum. Honestly, don't worry about me. And I'll have your tea on the table ready for you when you get home.'

'Like a good little wife?' he asked, his eyebrows shooting up in astonishment.

We stared at each other, both slightly pink in the face.

'Anyway,' Jack said hastily, 'I'd better get to bed. Up and out of here by five-thirty tomorrow morning.'

'Seriously?' I'd groaned in horror at the thought of it.

'Don't worry,' he said. 'I won't wake you. I'll be really quiet.'

'You certainly will wake me!' I said indignantly. 'I want to send you off to work with a smile on your face.'

He looked as if he wasn't sure if I was joking or not, but I wasn't. And I definitely sent him to work with a smile on his face, which wasn't just down to the breakfast I made him when we finally tumbled downstairs.

When he'd managed to drag himself away and head off to work, I washed the breakfast dishes, then wondered what to do with myself. I wasn't so sure a visit to a museum was something I fancied any longer, since the sun was shining and it seemed a shame to be indoors.

I decided to pay a return visit to the Victorian shops clustered around the village green. Jack and I had done a quick tour of the area, but I hadn't really taken it all in. Left alone to have a good look around, I really wanted to absorb the sights and sounds of Rowan Vale for myself. I'd waited a long time, after all.

The green was just across the river from Honeywell Lane. Luckily, there were several little stone footbridges across the water, so I didn't have to do much of a detour to get over to the Victorian shops.

There was a well in the centre of the green, which I knew had stood there for centuries. The shops were housed in sweet little buildings made of honey-coloured Cotswold stone, and there was also a cottage that had been decorated and furnished exactly as it would have been in Victorian times.

I strolled along the path, nodding and smiling at dozens of tourists, and the 'Victorian' gentlemen and ladies – actors employed by the estate – who were moving from shop to shop, peering in at the windows as if they were genuinely about to make some purchases.

This place really was something else!

With an old-fashioned sweetshop, a chemist's, a photography studio, a grocer's shop, a butcher's and a curiosity shop just like something from a Charles Dickens book, it was enchanting, and I lingered far longer than I'd expected to, even treating myself to some sugar sticks and a quarter of bullseyes for Jack from the sweetshop.

As I left the shop, I noticed a rather distinguished-looking man in elegant clothes that looked superior to the other characters' costumes. He was walking along the path, and I drew back into the shop doorway, feeling a bit wary when I realised he was talking to himself.

Unless, I thought suddenly, he had an earpiece in. Maybe that was how the staff stayed in touch? Maybe there was a tiny microphone pinned to their clothes that they could communicate through. Although, that would be a pretty expensive operation. Or maybe he was on the phone, hands free? Which wasn't really appropriate, given he was in costume and was supposed to be selling the idea that we were in Victorian England.

Then I blinked and stared around me in astonishment. Goosebumps sprang up on my arms and I shivered. No way!

I'd seen him, plain as day, walk through the closed door of the photography studio.

But that wasn't possible. Was it?

My hand flew to my mouth as realisation dawned. Everything my dad had told me about this place was true. There really were ghosts here! I'd half believed it, of course, but there'd always been that small element of doubt.

Now I looked wildly around me, not sure what to do or say. It felt as if something so momentous should be obvious to everyone, but people were carrying on with their browsing and chatting as if nothing was out of the ordinary at all.

Not sure what to do for the best, I told myself I should go back to Honeywell House and think this through. I could be putting myself in grave danger. Yet, somehow, I couldn't drag myself away.

A moment later, and the gentleman walked out of the photographer's and began to head up the path back towards the church.

I couldn't help myself. I had to follow him. I could see him nodding and waving his hand now and then, and from the way his left arm was positioned I guessed he was arm in arm with someone I couldn't see.

I'd always known I didn't possess *the gift*, but the fact that I could clearly see this one ghost meant I had to be related to him. The question was, who was he? There were only two real options, and I wished I'd studied period costume – as well as my family tree – a bit harder so I could make a more educated guess.

The man continued on his way, and I crept along at some distance behind him. At one point he seemed to let go of his companion and hurried over to some roses that were hanging over a garden wall.

I saw him lean over and sniff them, his eyes closed and a look of bliss on his face. I hung back, squeezing myself against the wall, hoping he wouldn't spot me, but he seemed oblivious to my presence.

Eventually, he reached a pair of double iron gates and walked directly through them, heading up a long drive.

I hurried over to the gates and peered through them, watching him curiously. He was strolling towards a big country house, and I knew, even before I noticed the sign on the wall beside the gatepost, that this was Harling Hall.

Howling Hall!

How many times had my dad mentioned this place to me? It had featured in so many of the bedtime stories he'd told me and had taken on an almost fairy-tale quality.

This was the beautiful Elizabethan house I'd heard so much about.

This was the place where magical things happened.

This was my ancestral home.

I waited until the man had vanished through the huge front door, then I turned and trudged back to Honeywell House, deep in thought.

Was I even safe here any more? Maybe I should pack my bags and leave before I was found out. Yet I couldn't bring myself to do it. I wanted to know more about the man whose ghost I could see as plainly as if he was made of flesh and blood.

Besides, I didn't want to leave Jack. Every moment I spent with him was precious. He was kind and gentle and funny, and, quite honestly, good in bed. The truth was, over the course of the last year, I'd fallen for him and if I left here now without a plausible explanation it could ruin things between us.

No, I just had to be careful, that was all. If I kept my wits about me, no one need ever know who I was.

18

FIFTEEN YEARS EARLIER

It was two days later when there was a knock on the door, and I opened it to find an elderly man standing on the step.

'Good day to you,' he said, smiling pleasantly as he held out his hand for me to shake. 'Sir Lawrence Davenport, owner of the Harling Estate. It's very good to meet you, Miss, er...'

I stared at him in amazement. Did the owner of the estate introduce himself to every visitor to the village? Then alarm bells started ringing. He was the *owner*. I had to be doubly careful around him.

Tentatively I shook his hand and told him it was nice to meet him, too.

'I'm afraid Jack's at work,' I said shakily. 'And his parents have gone back to the island, so if you wanted—'

'Actually,' he said, 'it's you I've come to see. Would you mind if I came in?'

I could hardly say no, could I? This man owned Honeywell House, for one thing, and the last thing I wanted to do was be impolite to Jack's landlord. Besides, he was getting on. It would be rude not to offer him a seat or a drink of some sort, especially if he'd walked all the way from Harling Hall.

Even so, I could hardly control my anxiety as I led him into the living room and invited him to make himself comfortable.

'Would you like something to drink?' I enquired politely.

He shook his head. 'Nothing for me, dear girl,' he said. 'Would you sit down please? I really think you and I need to talk.'

I almost fell into the armchair and gulped as I stared at him in dread.

'Well,' he said. *'I've* introduced myself. Perhaps you'd like to tell me who *you* are?'

I'd been so scared I'd quite forgotten to give him my name.

'Clara,' I said, hoping I sounded casual. 'Clara Walker.'

'Walker, eh?' He considered the information. 'And I gather you're here as a guest of Jack.'

'That's right,' I said. 'That's allowed, isn't it? I mean, I know you own the house, but he's allowed to have visitors stay over, isn't he?'

Sir Lawrence laughed. 'Of course. And Jack is such a good young man. I'm very fond of him. His family have lived in this village for generations, you know.'

'I know,' I managed. 'He showed me the model village that his great-grandfather built back in the 1930s. It's amazing.'

'It certainly is,' he agreed. 'So much history in this village. So many stories that could be told, if only we could listen.'

'Mm.' I was sweating now; I was sure of it. I fidgeted restlessly in my chair, half-hoping he'd get to the point and half-dreading it.

'So, Clara Walker, I've been hearing some interesting things about you.'

'Me?' I squeaked. 'Nothing interesting about me at all.'

'I believe you're from Lancashire,' he said pleasantly. 'Beautiful part of the country. And you met Jack in Scotland, I understand. A painting holiday, wasn't it? How delightful.'

I gaped at him. Wow, he was well informed!

'That's right,' I said, glancing at the clock and wondering how long he intended to stay.

He followed my gaze. 'I shan't keep you long,' he assured me. 'I just wanted to introduce myself. It seems we have a mutual acquaintance.'

'We do?' I frowned. 'Well, yes, Jack.'

'No, not Jack,' he said, still smiling. 'I was referring to Aubrey Wyndham. The former owner of this estate, back in the mid-nineteenth century.'

I stared at him in horror, while a part of me was thinking, *so it was Aubrey, not his father, Thomas*. That brought him one generation closer to me at any rate, but given the choice I'd have picked Thomas.

'I d-don't know what you mean,' I stammered.

'I'm afraid you were spotted following him the other day. It was quite clear that you could see him. No mistake.'

'Spotted by whom?' I said indignantly. I'd been very careful, and I hadn't seen anyone around who'd been taking any notice of me.

'Aubrey wasn't alone,' he explained kindly. 'He was walking with his, er, companion, and she was watching you. She said you couldn't take your eyes off him.'

I groaned inwardly. How could I have been so stupid? It was obvious that Aubrey was walking with someone, yet I'd given no thought to the fact that his unseen companion could be watching me.

'I'm so sorry,' I said miserably.

'No need to look so glum, but I am interested. Am I to take it that you are a descendant or a relative of Aubrey?'

I nodded. 'He's my great-great-great-great-grandfather,' I explained.

'I rather suspected as much,' he said, leaning back on the sofa and surveying me with interest. 'How fascinating. I expect you know that James Wyndham was the last of the family to own the estate but had to sell it on some time after his father, Aubrey's, death. After James left here there is no record of what happened to him. That's the way it is in Rowan Vale, you see. When the previous owners of the estate leave, there is no contact, and they are never heard of again. Mainly, it must be said, because the new owners never try to find them. I suspect it might prove more difficult in the future, now we have the internet.'

'I know,' I said dully. 'My dad told me. And I know I'm not supposed to be here. I'm sorry.'

'Yet you still came here, even knowing the rules?'

'It wasn't intentional,' I burst out. 'Meeting Jack was a total coincidence. When I found out where he was from, I couldn't believe it. I've put off coming here for a whole year now, but he wanted me to meet his parents, and I just couldn't resist the opportunity. I wanted to see where my family once lived. Is that so hard to understand?'

'Not at all,' Sir Lawrence said, shaking his head. 'Unfortunately, that doesn't make it right, does it? Rules are in place for a reason. As a Wyndham, you should never have come near the village.'

'But I wanted to be with Jack,' I whispered.

'Does Jack know?'

I shook my head. 'No. I haven't said a word.'

'So you've lied to him already? That doesn't bode well for the future of your relationship, does it?'

'It's not like that!' I cried. 'I genuinely like him. A lot. I bumped into Aubrey accidentally outside the Victorian shops, and when I saw him walk through the closed door, I just couldn't help myself. I had to follow him. He's family!'

'You said your father told you about the rules? I take it then that it's the paternal line that connects you to the Wyndhams?'

'Yes. James had a daughter, who had a son, who had a daughter, who had a son. That son was my dad.'

It wasn't difficult to remember that information. I'd been teased long enough that if I ever had a child, it was bound to be a boy, as ever since James's day the line had gone boy, girl, boy, girl, boy, girl.

'You know, I expect, that Aubrey and James were not close.'

I shrugged. 'I gathered there was no love lost, but I don't know the details. My dad always suspected that Aubrey was some stern, authoritarian Victorian father who probably bullied James. I know James adored his mother.'

'Elspeth.'

'Yes,' I said, surprised he knew even *her* name. 'That's right. Elspeth Wyndham. We had a miniature portrait of her with Aubrey. Even though they were young, he looks quite stern and serious. She looks thoroughly miserable.'

'Indeed?' Lawrie raised an eyebrow. 'Interesting interpretation. Well anyway, the point is that I have spoken to Aubrey about you, and he is adamant that he doesn't want to meet you.'

I hadn't been expecting that! For one thing, I hadn't dreamed about meeting him face to face anyway. For another, the fact that he'd been so rude blew my mind. He didn't even know me.

'But, why not?'

'As I said, Aubrey and James were not close. Aubrey has no wish to meet any of James's descendants. He would appreciate it if you would leave him alone.'

I swallowed. I couldn't deny, that hurt a bit. Even though I'd always known Aubrey Wyndham was probably a nasty piece of work, I'd still have liked to talk to him, now there was the opportunity right in front of me. It seemed harsh to be dismissed so casually.

'Well,' I said with a sad shrug, 'I guess I'll be leaving soon anyway.'

'Really?' Sir Lawrence sounded suspiciously relieved. 'Well, it's been nice to meet you, but perhaps it's for the best.'

His attitude rankled, and I snapped, 'Or maybe not. Who knows how things will work out with Jack?'

He lifted his chin and gazed at me steadily.

'You do, of course, know the rules. No members of the former owners' families are to return to the Harling Estate. The rule has stood for hundreds of years, yet here you are.'

'It seems a stupid rule to me,' I muttered.

'Nevertheless, I think you'd probably find that Jack would be appalled if he knew who he'd brought to Rowan Vale. I should imagine he'd want you to leave immediately.'

'You're not serious?'

'I'm not saying Jack would break up with you,' he said hastily. 'I'm sure he has feelings for you. He's certainly never had a long-term relationship before. I've known Jack all his life, and I think if he genuinely cares for you, he will leave Rowan Vale for you. Give up his job on the railway. Give up Honeywell House. He's just that type of person, isn't he?'

From what I knew of Jack, I had to agree. If Jack wanted our relationship to last, he'd leave Rowan Vale for me. I had a feeling I'd only have to say the word.

'He loves this place,' I said angrily. 'It's not fair!'

'And as I said, rules are in place for a reason,' Sir Lawrence repeated, shaking his head regretfully. He tilted his head, as if trying to work out a compromise.

'Perhaps,' he said eventually, 'there is a way. But it would involve you keeping a big secret from Jack for as long as your relationship lasts. Perhaps forever. Who knows?'

I eyed him suspiciously. 'You mean, don't tell him who I am?'

'Exactly. And you stay away from Harling Hall, and from Aubrey. If you see him in the street, you cross over. You do not approach him. You do not try to speak to him. Any communication from a descendant of James would only distress him, you understand?'

'Wow,' I said. 'He really did hate his son, didn't he? Some father.'

'Do we have an agreement?' Sir Lawrence asked, ignoring my comment.

'So, if I agree to keep away from Aubrey and Harling Hall, and don't tell Jack who I am, I can stay here?'

'Yes,' Sir Lawrence said. 'But not just Jack. You mustn't breathe a word to anyone. It would set a precedent, you see, and that simply won't do. Your family, for example...'

'I don't have any family,' I said. 'None that I'm in touch with anyway. My mum died twenty years ago, and Dad passed away four years later. Car accident. Dad didn't have any living relatives. My mum had some, but I don't see anything of them these days. They moved to South Wales after Mum died, and we lost touch. So you see, it's just me. No one to tell.'

'You're the last of the Wyndhams?'

'I am.'

He looked rather sad at that. 'I know I must seem rather cruel, Clara,' he said, 'but as custodian of the Harling Estate, I have a duty. I don't always like what I'm called upon to do, but my feelings don't matter. And – well, even ghosts are entitled to have their wishes respected. You understand?'

'I understand,' I said. 'I know how important this place is, and what it means to be the owner of it. I thought, to be honest, that Dad made most of the stuff up, but I listened anyway because it was so wonderful. Now I realise he was telling me the truth, and it seems even more amazing. I just wish Aubrey would give me a chance.'

'I'm afraid it's out of the question,' Sir Lawrence said. 'If I allow you to remain here, you must swear you'll leave him alone.'

I sighed. 'Okay, Sir Lawrence. I get it. I swear I'll do as you ask.'

He held out his hand and I shook it.

'Welcome to Rowan Vale, Clara,' he said warmly. 'And please, call me Lawrie.'

19

As I finally finished my tale of deception, I raised my gaze to meet Callie's, dreading what I'd see in her face.

She was staring out of the window, absent-mindedly stroking Toby's head, and I wondered if I'd bored her, and she'd drifted off into a world of her own. Then she shook her head.

'Wow.'

It was one word, but it carried a whole weight of disgust. I felt sick.

'I'm really sorry I didn't tell you, but how could I? I don't want to leave Rowan Vale. Jack's lived here his whole life – he loves it, and the boys are settled. I know I shouldn't be here, honestly, I do get it. But it wasn't deliberate. I mean, yes, I knew about the estate's history when Jack invited me here, and maybe I should have said no, but I'd put it off for a whole year, and I really liked him, and besides – I wasn't convinced any of what Dad had told me was true.'

I shut up as she slowly turned to face me.

'What did you think when Lawrie stepped down and sold the estate to me?'

'Wh-what do you mean?'

'I mean, didn't it make you angry that he and Brodie were still living here? Davenports. The gift had been lost to that family and a new family had taken over. If it's forbidden for previous owners to return to Rowan Vale, didn't it bother you that Lawrie was still here? Or Brodie, for that matter?'

'Well, no,' I said slowly. 'I mean, it did cross my mind, but I thought maybe it didn't count because they never actually left, whereas my family did. All the previous families who owned the estate did, from what Dad told me. And I suppose I just thought – well, maybe once you've gone, you're supposed to stay gone, but if you stay...'

I shrugged. I wasn't sure what to think really. I supposed, now that it had been pointed out to me, it didn't really make sense, and it *was* unfair.

Callie sighed. 'Lawrie and Brodie are here because, why the hell not? I never understood that rule. Lawrie says it's because the tenants – alive and dead – would have difficulty adjusting to a new owner if the old one was still around. He says the new owner has to put their own stamp on the place, and that's why the old ones leave.'

'You don't agree?'

'I sort of see his point,' she acknowledged. 'It was really hard for me when I came here, and I think even now, some of the villagers take more notice of Brodie than they do of me, even though he never actually owned the place. Although, I suppose, that could be because he's a man.'

'More than likely.' Some of the older villagers were *very* set in their ways. And, let's face it, there were no older villagers than the ghosts. I didn't envy Callie having to deal with so many of those.

'I always suspected,' Callie continued, 'that the real reason the owners left and never returned was because they simply couldn't bear to see their old home in the care of someone else and be unable to interfere in any way. I should think some of them loved being in control and would have felt inferior somehow once they'd relinquished that power. It must feel like quite a comedown. Imagine what it would be like to walk around knowing this place once belonged to your family, and now you're no one.'

'Hmm,' I said wryly. 'Imagine.'

'Does it bother you?' she asked sharply. 'Has it always bothered you, all this time?'

'No,' I said honestly. 'I'm not interested in reclaiming the Harling Estate, if that's what you're worried about.'

'I'm not,' she said. 'But I am wondering if that's why owning the model village was so important to you. What was it you said? "Making our own stamp on Rowan Vale".'

'It would be nice to have a stake in the place,' I admitted. 'And to have something to leave my sons. Is that so wrong?'

'I suppose not. Having something to pass on to Immi was my main reason for accepting this job in the first place, so I get it.'

'It was more than that, though,' I insisted. 'I want a life, Callie! I want to get back out there and be someone again. Someone other than Mum. But how can I get a job when I have children to look after?'

'Other mums do it,' she said gently. '*I* did it. Not going to pretend that it's easy because it isn't, but it is possible. But I think you know that, deep down. I think you're scared and that's why you wanted to set up your own business, so you didn't have to go outside the village looking for a job. You *want* a life outside but you're afraid to take it, aren't you?'

'Of course I'm not!' But the hot tears pricking my eyes betrayed my fears. Toby evidently sensed my unhappiness, because he left Callie and padded over to me, resting his head on my lap and gazing up at me with a mournful expression.

'There's no shame in being afraid,' she said. 'You've been a stay-at-home mum for twelve years. It's a big deal, going back to employment.'

'Terrifying,' I said, wiping away a tear. 'And that's if I can even get a job in the first place. I mean, look at me, Callie! Who's going to employ me? My skills are completely out of date, and I'm fat, spotty, hormonal...' I shook my head. 'When I came to this place, I was young, attractive, full of confidence. I knew who I was and what I wanted. But now...'

'So many women feel like that, Clara,' she said. 'You're not on your own. And you're still young and attractive.'

As I snorted with laughter she put her arm around me. 'Yes, you are! Don't forget you're eight months' pregnant, so your hormones are all over the place. You may have gained a little weight, and maybe got the odd blemish, but that will all settle once the baby's here. Besides, there's so much more to you than looks. You've brought up a family of three boisterous sons! You must have loads of transferrable skills. And you can bring your training up to date. There are courses. That's if you even want to do the same kind of work as you did before. I mean, the world's your oyster. You can be anything. You just have to believe in yourself.'

As I shook my head in denial, she said kindly, 'I think you can do so much more than sell tickets to tourists who want to wander round a model village during the holiday season.'

I gave a half-laugh. She had a point. It wasn't much of a job, but it was safe.

Right now, safety was my priority.

'What will happen now?' I asked her. 'Will I have to leave?'

'Don't be daft!' Callie nudged me, a smile on her face. 'As if I'd make you leave. I couldn't care less if a Wyndham's back in the village. If it's okay with you it's fine by me.'

'Really?' I could hardly believe it. 'Are you sure? You sounded a bit angry when I told you what had happened.'

'I *am* a bit angry,' she admitted, 'but not with you. Now I understand why you won't visit Harling Hall. Scared of ghosts indeed! Can't believe I fell for that. How come you came to the 1940s ball? You could have bumped into Aubrey then.'

'I asked Lawrie's permission. I really didn't want to let you down, and I knew Jack was desperate to go. And, to be honest, I really wanted to go, too. I wanted to see the Hall, and I wanted to have some fun.'

'And Lawrie just agreed?'

'Reluctantly. He said he'd discuss it with Aubrey and let me know. Then the next day he rang me and said Aubrey had agreed that I could attend if I stayed in the ballroom. He would keep out of my way.'

'Aubrey said that, did he?' Callie murmured. 'Hmm. Something's not right about all this, and I think I know what's happened. I've dealt with it before.'

'What do you mean?' I asked, puzzled.

'I'll explain later. I must go home now and find out if I'm right.'

She got to her feet, inadvertently dropping bits of churro onto the carpet, which made Toby abandon me immediately, the fickle creature.

'What about those?' I asked, nodding at the rest of the snacks that sat untouched on the coffee table. 'Do you want to take them with you?'

'You can reheat them in the air fryer later,' she said. 'Give them to the kids. They'll be home from school soon, won't they?'

I nodded. 'Jack's picking up the two youngest. He finishes a bit earlier on a Thursday, so he said he'd go straight to Kingsford Wold and collect them.'

'There you go then. I'm sure the boys will enjoy them, and I've lost my appetite.' Seeing the look on my face she added hastily, 'Honestly, I'm not mad at you. I need a word with Lawrie.'

'Jack mustn't know!' I begged her. 'He has no idea I'm a Wyndham and if he found out… I mean, after all this time. You can see how it looks, can't you?'

'We'll sort something out,' she said briskly. 'Just one thing before I go. What you said about Aubrey. You couldn't be more wrong. He's the kindest, gentlest person I know, and he would never be so dismissive towards you. I just think you should know that.'

After she left, I sat shaking on the sofa, not sure what was going to happen next. It sounded like she was going to have a showdown with Lawrie, and then all this might come out. It was the last thing I wanted.

Whatever Callie had said, I wasn't convinced about Aubrey. Maybe she didn't know him as well as she thought she did.

One thing was for sure, he wasn't worth breaking my family up for. I wished I'd never said a word.

20

AGNES

Agnes and Lawrie were together in his sitting room, listening contentedly to an album of Christmas carols, sung by the choir from King's College, Cambridge.

As their sweet voices delivered a beautiful rendition of 'The Holly and The Ivy', Agnes found herself wishing, just for a moment, that she could visit the village and see this year's Christmas lights for herself. She had no doubt that Rowan Vale looked stunning, and it had been so long since she'd seen it dressed for the festive season.

How wonderful it would be to walk arm in arm with Mr Wyndham, young Florence skipping beside them, admiring the views, conversing with some of the more refined ghostly villagers, and strolling through the market, eyeing the exciting goods on display. She wondered if roast chestnuts were available. She would like to smell those again.

Wistfully, she gazed at the crackling fire, reminding herself that she had a lot to be thankful for, even if a visit to the village was out of the question.

She glanced over at Lawrie, who was leaning back in his chair, his eyes closed, a smile on his lips.

He looked so contented that Agnes couldn't help but smile, too, at the sight of him. She was grateful he was listening to the carols in silence. Dear Lawrie. He had always loved music, but sadly he had no talent for the pianoforte at all, and frankly, his singing voice was bad enough to curdle milk. Ah well, one couldn't be good at everything.

The door banged against the wall, and Lawrie's eyes flew open, as Callie stormed in, looking unnervingly angry.

'Good heavens,' Agnes said reprovingly, her warm and cosy festive feelings evaporating instantly, 'is there any need to open a door like that? Have you never heard of manners?'

'Where's Aubrey?' Callie demanded.

Agnes's eyes narrowed. 'He's in the schoolroom. He volunteered to help Walter Tasker with the children's lessons. Since there's to be a Dickensian weekend, Mr Tasker felt it would be appropriate to teach them about the works of Charles Dickens, and what life was like for the poor in Victorian England.' She sniffed. 'I can't say I approve, but you know Mr Wyndham. He has a heart of gold.'

'Hasn't he just!' Callie plonked herself down on the sofa and glared at Lawrie in a most insolent fashion.

He eyed her with some amusement.

'Something seems to have upset you,' he said, reaching over to turn off the music box contraption and silencing the poor choir mid-song.

It suddenly felt deathly quiet in the room and, somewhat unnerved, Agnes sat up straight, adjusting her bed jacket.

'Well,' she said, 'now you've ruined our pleasant afternoon listening to carols, perhaps you'll tell us why you're so desperate to see Mr Wyndham that your ability to behave with propriety has been lost to you. Really, Callie! It's the choir from King's College! I take it that even you can appreciate good festive music?'

'Absolutely,' Callie said sarkily. 'Nothing I love more than "A Wombling Merry Christmas".'

Agnes winced, remembering that dreadful song from when William, Lawrie's son, was young. Surely Callie didn't really consider that to be *good festive music*? But Callie had moved on. 'I don't want to speak to Aubrey. I want to speak to you two, and I wanted to make sure that he wasn't going to interrupt us. I don't want him hearing what I've got to say – at least, not yet.'

Agnes and Lawrie exchanged worried glances.

'Meaning what?' Lawrie asked. 'What's all this about?'

'Remember a few months ago, when I found out that Mia was related to Florrie, and that you'd made her keep her mouth shut?'

Agnes didn't like the way this conversation was going. She gave Lawrie a nervous look, but he was gazing steadily at Callie.

'I do indeed. Thankfully, all that business has been sorted now. All's well that ends well.'

'Except,' said Callie, 'you've neglected to tell me one thing, haven't you?'

Lawrie raised an eyebrow. 'I have?'

'Yeah. Like, how you did exactly the same thing to Clara Milsom about Aubrey.'

Agnes gasped and Callie swung round to look at her. 'You're in on it, too, aren't you? Lawrie would never do anything without your say-so, and this smacks of you giving him instructions and him running to do your bidding, just like he did with Mia.'

'I – I have no idea what you're talking about,' Agnes said indignantly.

'Oh, come off it!' Callie threw up her hands in despair. 'I just don't get it. What is it with you two? Why did you do that to Clara? Why would you do that to Aubrey? You're supposed to love him!'

'Of course I—' Thankfully, Agnes remembered herself in time and said, 'I am exceptionally fond of Mr Wyndham, as well you know, and I resent any implication that I would do anything to hurt him.'

'But you did! Can't you see that? Just like you hurt Florrie. You're keeping Aubrey from his family, and that's unfair and cruel. As for you!' She turned back to Lawrie. 'I can't believe the things you said to Clara when she first came to the village. You practically threatened her. Saying she'd be thrown out of the place if she opened her mouth, like some second-rate gangster! What is this? *Peaky Blinders*?'

'Really, Callie, I don't know what Clara has told you—'

'Everything! She told me everything! You took advantage of her, Lawrie. She loved Jack and wanted to stay with him, but she knew if it came right down to it, he'd give up everything to be with her. She couldn't have that on her conscience, so she did as you asked. Because of that, she's had to live with this secret that's weighing heavily on her, and she's lost the opportunity to get to know her ancestor. And he's lost the chance to get to know her! And the Milsom boys! Can you imagine how thrilled Aubrey would be to know them all? I just...'

Her voice trailed off and her eyes widened. 'Oh, my God! That's it, isn't it? That's why!'

'Why what?' Agnes asked faintly.

'Why you won't let Aubrey go into the village!'

'That – that has nothing to do with it. Silas Alexander—'

'Was giving you grief for decades and it never bothered you enough to keep you inside the grounds of the Hall. Someone told me it had been ten or fifteen years since you two last went into Rowan Vale. I'm willing to bet it was fifteen years. As soon as Clara arrived here, in fact. You couldn't risk her breaking her promise, so you kept Aubrey away from her. You've kept him prisoner in this house!'

'I've done no such thing!' Agnes leapt to her feet, but Lawrie gestured to her to sit down.

'The jig's up, I'm afraid, Agnes. We may as well confess.'

Agnes dropped back onto the sofa, feeling quite ill. 'You don't understand. You mustn't tell him.'

'Why shouldn't I?' Callie demanded. 'Right now, it seems I'm the only real friend he's got, and it wouldn't be very kind of me to let you two carry on with this deception. Poor Aubrey deserves so much better.'

'I'll admit,' Agnes said weakly, 'I did ask Lawrie to have a word with the young woman.'

'Aubrey's great-great-great-great-granddaughter,' Callie reminded her. 'Clara. Her name's Clara.'

'Yes, yes. Well, I saw her that day, as I was out walking with Mr Wyndham, and it was apparent that she could see him but had no idea I was with him. I knew what that meant, but I had to be quite certain, so I asked Lawrie to visit her and ascertain what her credentials were.'

'In other words,' said Callie, 'find out how she was related to Aubrey, then bully her into promising never to go near him – or else.'

'Really, Callie,' Lawrie said, 'you make it sound so crass.'

'And you don't think it is?' Callie laughed in disbelief. 'You two are bonkers, you know that? You've learned nothing! After everything we went through with Mia and Florrie, too!'

'It's not as simple as you think,' Lawrie said.

'Yes, it is. Agnes wants to keep Aubrey by her side like some pathetic lapdog, and when Agnes gives you an order, you jump to it.'

'Well, really!' Agnes couldn't believe the nerve of the girl. 'You make me sound like some sort of despot.'

'Hmm. Do I? Well, if the cap fits...'

Callie stared pointedly at Agnes's nightcap, and Agnes automatically adjusted it, as if it had somehow become dislodged.

'I would thank you to remember your manners when speaking to Agnes,' Lawrie admonished her. 'She doesn't deserve to be spoken to in such a fashion.'

'Maybe not, but did Clara deserve to be spoken to the way you spoke to her? Did Aubrey deserve to be separated from his family and kept hostage in the grounds of Harling Hall?' Callie turned back to Agnes, her eyes shining with tears. 'You know how much he loves you. He longs to go into the village. He misses it, Agnes. He misses everything and everyone in it, and he wanted so much to go to the Christmas lights switch-on. Instead, I had to open a window for him so he could lean outside and catch a glimpse of the illuminations from upstairs. Why on earth would you treat him so badly?'

'Oh, come on!' Lawrie said impatiently. 'He's hardly The Man in the Iron Mask, is he? He has this enormous house to roam in, as well as extensive grounds. He has the gardens and the orchard and the acres and acres of parkland to explore. It's not like he's in manacles in the basement.'

At such an image, Agnes could bear it no longer. Had she really been so unkind to her beloved Mr Wyndham?

'No, Lawrie,' she said. 'Callie's right. It was unforgivable. I should never have made you go to see Clara. And I should never have lied to Mr Wyndham and kept him here against his will.'

'Not against his will,' Lawrie said firmly. 'He chose to remain here with you.'

'Yes,' Agnes said wretchedly, 'because he's a good, kind man, who wants only to please me. And I have repaid his kindness with nothing but deception and cruelty. I do not deserve him.'

'Steady on,' Callie said, looking surprised at Agnes's turnaround. 'I never said that. Aubrey adores you. He'd be lost without you. I just don't think it's right that you've lied to him all this time.'

'It's not right,' Agnes agreed. 'Considering how badly he was treated all his life, that he should receive the same poor treatment in his afterlife, and by me, of all people, is not to be borne. In my defence, all I can say is that I thought I was doing the right thing. Any descendant of James is not to be trusted. I do not want to see Mr Wyndham hurt by one of his own yet again.'

'Clara would never—' Callie frowned. 'What do you mean, *yet again*? And *was* Aubrey treated badly all his life?'

'You have no idea,' Agnes said heavily. 'I know. I was there. I saw it all and it broke my heart.'

'Well...' Callie glanced at Lawrie, who nodded in agreement. 'Maybe – I mean, if you like – you could tell me about it. I'd really like to know more about Aubrey, and I want to understand why you've done this. Really, I do.'

Agnes swallowed. 'It's been so long, I hardly like to think about such times. But you're right. Perhaps, after all, it's time you knew. Maybe then you'll see why I wanted only to protect him and keep him safe from that wretched family.'

21

AGNES

Agnes settled back in the sofa and prepared to revisit some distinctly uncomfortable memories. Where to begin? At the beginning, she supposed. And that was the day the estate passed from the Ashcrofts to the Wyndhams.

'Miles Ashcroft – my stepson – was forced to sell the estate when it was revealed that, like his father before him, he had no ability to see the ghosts. This was in 1818.' She hesitated. 'Coincidentally, the year of my own passing.'

As Callie opened her mouth to speak, Agnes pressed on, not wanting to hear any words of sympathy or, worse, personal questions. It was hard enough to talk about Mr Wyndham's past. She certainly wasn't going to discuss her own.

'The only candidate was an unlikely one. Thomas Wyndham was the Ashcrofts' gamekeeper – a duplicitous wretch if ever there was one. Poacher-turned-gamekeeper springs to mind, and I never trusted him as far as I could throw him. Nevertheless, it was clear that there was no choice. No other villager possessed the gift. For some reason, fate had decreed that the Harling Estate was to pass into the hands of the Wyndhams.'

'So what relation was Thomas to Aubrey?' Callie asked.

'Thomas was Aubrey's father,' Lawrie explained. He nodded gently at Agnes. 'Do continue.'

Callie took the hint and shut up. Agnes cast her mind back to those days, when she'd been forced to share her home with the insufferable Wyndhams.

It was enough to make her shudder, even to this day.

'Thomas had married just a few months before he purchased the estate for ten pounds. His wife was a common baggage and couldn't believe her luck when she became lady of this house.' She sniffed. 'I say lady, but of course, she was anything but.'

'Some would say I'm no lady either,' Callie reminded her. 'I don't think I'd deserve to be called a common baggage because I'm not a member of the aristocracy, Agnes.'

'That, my dear girl, had nothing to do with it. I had an open mind, believe me, but that woman... No, I'm sorry. Janie Watson was no lady. She worked as a kitchen maid here at the Hall, and she was known to be coarse, crude and cruel. Becoming the owner of the estate didn't change her. She treated her former friends, the other servants, abominably. Made their lives a misery, if you must know. So, there you have it.'

'Seriously? And she was Aubrey's mother?'

Agnes nodded her head sorrowfully. 'I'm afraid she was. Mr Wyndham – Aubrey – arrived in 1820. I will say, I felt for Janie that day. She suffered greatly in her labours and was unable to have any more children. You would think, wouldn't you, that would make them treat Mr – Aubrey – with more kindness, if anything. After all, he was their only child. But instead, they showed him indifference at best, callousness at worst.'

'Poor Aubrey,' Callie breathed. 'I never knew.'

'No, well.' Agnes nodded furiously. '*I* knew. I watched it all. I sat with him when he was left alone in his crib to cry. It broke my heart that I couldn't make myself heard to him, nor offer him any comfort. His parents were determined to act like gentlefolk and sent him away to boarding school as soon as he was old enough. You can imagine how he suffered there, having parents that had once been a gamekeeper and a kitchen maid.'

'When did Thomas and Janie find out that Aubrey didn't have the gift?' Callie asked, sounding almost afraid to know the answer.

'By the time he was ten years old it had become evident that he wasn't suddenly going to be blessed,' Agnes explained. 'They had barely tolerated him before, but now he became an object of hatred. As far as they were concerned, he'd been their meal ticket. The guarantee that the Wyndham family would always own property and land. Be respected. Deluded fools! They bullied and scorned poor Aubrey dreadfully, and he was beaten regularly.'

'Poor Aubrey,' Callie whispered. 'Gosh, I've already said that haven't I? But I don't know what else to say.'

'His parents decided that their only hope of hanging onto their newly founded dynasty was for Aubrey to marry and give them a grandchild who possessed the ability of Thomas. In 1845 they selected The Honourable Elspeth Cook-Warren as a suitable candidate.'

'She sounds posh,' Callie observed. 'Didn't her parents mind about the Wyndhams' background?'

'Elspeth's parents had died abroad,' Agnes said. 'She was the ward of her uncle, and he apparently had no concerns about her marrying into the Wyndham family. No doubt he was pleased to be rid of the responsibility for her. She, of course, had no choice in the matter.'

'Sounds awful,' Callie said. 'Did she and Aubrey get on?'

Agnes shook her head. 'He tried,' she insisted. 'He was nothing but kindness and politeness to her. What else would you expect of Mr Wyndham? But she was a cold fish, who treated him with contempt. She may have been forced into the marriage, but she gave no thought to the fact that he'd been forced into it, too. She didn't accept the Wyndhams as people of her own class. She viewed them as peasants and was furious to find herself living with such a family.'

'Well,' Callie said slowly, 'you can't really blame her, can you? Having no choice in who you marry. Can't be fun.'

Agnes exchanged glances with Lawrie. He gave her a sympathetic smile.

'No indeed,' Agnes said heavily. 'It cannot be much fun at all. Which was why I tried to understand her and like her. But I could not. Mr Wyndham didn't deserve the treatment she gave him. She showed him no respect, no kindness.'

She shuddered at the memory. 'A year after their marriage, their son James arrived. Elspeth promptly informed Mr Wyndham that she had done her duty and that he must never bother her again.'

'Whoa!' Callie's eyebrows shot up. 'And she got away with that? I thought women in those days did as they were told.'

'Many unfortunate women indeed did as they were told,' Agnes said, her voice little more than a whisper. 'But not everyone had a husband like Mr Wyndham. He would no more force himself on a lady than he would shoot her. Surely you know him well enough by now, Callie?'

'I do,' Callie agreed. 'You're right. I wasn't thinking. Sorry.'

'That's quite all right, as long as we understand each other,' Agnes said.

'Now, James was the apple of Elspeth's eye. All the love she refused to give to Aubrey, she lavished on their son. I hardly like to speak ill of the child, but he was a little beast. Spoilt, wilful, sly. He had no time for Aubrey, of course, because Aubrey was always trying to make him behave himself and be kind and helpful to people. A waste of time. Between Elspeth and Janie there was no chance of that. They ruined him.'

'Wait, so Janie was actually *nice* to James?'

'She was. She liked the fact that he had aristocratic blood on his mother's side. It made her respect him in a way she'd never respected her own child. She pressured Mr Wyndham that he must have another son, but never Elspeth – which was, of course, nonsensical. The two of them would sit together,' she added bitterly, 'spending many a merry hour listing all his imagined failings and discussing how weak and unmanly he was.'

Callie puffed out her cheeks. 'No wonder you didn't like them. They sound bloody awful.'

'Quite.' Agnes didn't approve of Callie using such words, but she agreed with the sentiment. 'Thomas died when James was twelve, and Janie blamed Mr Wyndham, saying his father had been killed by the stress of the situation that he had caused by not being able to see the ghosts. *That he had caused!* Can you imagine?

'Oh, I was so angry! Poor Mr Wyndham tried his best to forge a relationship with James, but the pampered brat wanted nothing to do with him. Indeed, he laughed at him. Any other father would have beaten him black and blue for such insolence, but Mr Wyndham never laid a hand on him. Instead, he withdrew. He spent a lot of time alone, walking the grounds, working in his study. At least, he imagined he was alone, but he rarely was. I tried to keep him company.'

Agnes's mind flew back to those dark days, when she'd sat with him as he worked, or walked beside him as he patrolled the parkland, finding comfort in conversations with the staff.

Sometimes, she'd watched him head out on business, away from the estate to Gloucester or Cirencester. Sometimes even to London. How she'd wished she could go with him. She'd longed to be beside him, wherever he went.

She couldn't admit it to Callie and Lawrie, but she'd fallen in love with him even then. He'd been twenty-six when Elspeth had rejected him, and despite Agnes being in her forties, she'd given her heart to him at that moment. The pain of being so close to him but unable to make herself known had been almost unbearable.

'That last Christmas before he passed...' Agnes murmured, perhaps to herself.

Remembering where she was, she spoke directly to Callie. 'James had become engaged to a young woman of some means called Frances Croft. The Crofts invited the Wyndhams to spend Christmas with them at their country home in Hampshire. James, Elspeth and Janie made it quite clear that Mr Wyndham would not be welcome.

'There'd been a huge row, you see. Aubrey was desperately trying to find someone with the gift – someone who could take over the estate, since it was clear by then that James couldn't. His so-called family accused him of treachery and informed him they wanted nothing to do with him. They took some of the servants with them to Hampshire and left him to spend Christmas without his family.'

She rubbed her eyes as they misted over. 'He didn't even have a present to open! There was no roasted goose that year. He gave the remaining servants the day off and spent the day alone. I remember, he dined on leftovers and went to bed early. He...' She shook her head, unable to continue.

'I'm so sorry, Agnes. It must have been really hard for you to see all that,' Callie said gently.

'You can't imagine.' Agnes pulled herself together. 'But it was nothing, compared to how Mr Wyndham suffered.'

She gazed sadly down at the carpet, unable to remove the image of that sad, lonely Christmas night from her mind.

Lawrie cleared his throat. 'And then, unfortunately, just a few weeks later Aubrey died of a sudden heart attack. He was only fifty. And James, Elspeth and Janie clung on at Harling Hall, refusing to look for a new owner for the estate, despite not being able to see the ghosts. They had already announced to the villagers that they wouldn't be leaving, and that the ghosts would just have to fend for themselves.'

'Are you joking?' Callie gasped. 'Seriously?'

Agnes recovered herself enough to explain. 'The Wyndhams didn't care about the future of the estate. They cared only about their wealth and privilege. They weren't about to give that up so easily. And there was talk that the Crofts were having second thoughts about their daughter's marriage to someone who would soon be homeless.'

'So what happened?' Callie asked. 'The Davenports were next to own the estate, weren't they?' She nodded at Lawrie. 'How did that happen?'

'Sir Ambrose Davenport – plain Ambrose back then – lived in the village,' Lawrie explained. 'He was a smart man, who despite his poor upbringing, had great ambitions. Aubrey saw his potential and ensured he received an education. When Ambrose came of age, Aubrey gave him money – an investment in his talent, he'd called it – and Ambrose sailed to America where he made his fortune. When he returned to England, he was most distressed to hear of Aubrey's death and went straight to Harling Hall to pay his respects.'

'Where he found the Wyndhams not in the slightest bit saddened by their loss, but furiously refusing to move out,' Agnes said angrily. 'Luckily, Ambrose had a weapon that meant they had no choice.'

'Which was?'

'His son, Jeremy. He'd been a tiny child when the family left for America, but he was an adult upon their return, and as soon as he entered the village it was obvious that he possessed the gift. He was the natural successor to the estate and Ambrose made it very clear that the residents of Rowan Vale wouldn't tolerate the Wyndhams clinging on to power any longer. They were very much disliked, and there would probably have been a riot if they hadn't gone when they did.'

'So they finally agreed to give it up, just like that?' Callie asked.

'Oh no,' Lawrie said. 'To *persuade* them, Ambrose gave them a parting gift. Enough money to ensure that they could buy a home of their own and have enough to live on if they maintained a modest lifestyle. A good job, as it happened, because I did a little digging after I'd spoken to Clara, and I discovered that Frances Croft broke off her engagement to James not long after he left Rowan Vale, and married a distant cousin instead. Without Ambrose's generosity the family would have been in dire straits.'

'But that's not all,' Agnes said. She glanced at the door, as if checking no one else was listening. 'After they left, it was discovered that they'd taken quite a few paintings and other objects with them. Objects that belonged, not to them, but to the Harling Estate.'

'So they were thieves, too? Wow, they sound real charmers. How the heck is

Aubrey related to those people?' Callie asked. She frowned. 'How the heck is Clara related to them, come to that?'

'Bad blood will out,' Agnes said. 'Now do you understand my fears? I don't want Mr Wyndham to be ill-treated again. He needs to be protected from that family. They hurt him enough, and I will not allow them to hurt him any more.'

'But – but Clara's not like that!' Callie assured her. 'Really, she's not. She's a good person, and you'd know that if you'd just give her a chance.'

'The young woman who came to Rowan Vale to be with a man she wasn't even betrothed to?' Agnes asked. 'Who moved into his house with him, unchaperoned?' She sniffed disapprovingly.

'Things are different these days,' Callie said impatiently. 'It's not like when you were young, and there were all those ridiculous courting rituals.'

'Hardly ridiculous,' Agnes protested.

'Oh, please! I've seen *Bridgerton*. I know how daft it all was.'

'You can't deny, Callie,' said Lawrie, 'that Clara didn't tell Jack the truth about herself. She met him – perhaps by chance, perhaps not – on a holiday in Scotland, and within a year she'd moved here. And would she have conducted a long-distance relationship with him all that time if he'd lived anywhere but Rowan Vale? You must surely agree that it's suspicious.'

'You told me you liked Clara!' Callie burst out, clearly furious at the way the conversation was heading. 'That day you first took me to see the model village, you said she fitted right in here.'

'And so she does,' he said with a nod, raising an eyebrow. 'Almost as if she was born to it.'

'You honestly think she can't be trusted?' Callie gasped.

'I like Clara,' Lawrie said. 'She's always struck me as a very pleasant woman. After our initial meeting we settled into an amiable enough relationship, and I appreciated that she never seemed to hold a grudge and that she kept her end of the bargain. Nevertheless, I will admit I'm wary of her. If she's capable of such deceit, perhaps she has more of James Wyndham's personality than Aubrey's. I wouldn't want to put Aubrey through any more pain, which is why I agreed when Agnes asked me to find a way to keep her away from him.'

Callie was quiet, thinking things through. Agnes twisted her hands in her lap, wondering what the outcome of this conversation would be. Lawrie gave her a reassuring smile, clearly certain that Callie would understand and that would be the end of the matter.

'This doesn't sit right with me,' Callie said finally. 'You talk about Clara's deceit, but what about yours? And can you honestly tell me, Agnes, that this has nothing whatsoever to do with you being afraid that Aubrey would want to be with his living family, rather than with you and Florrie?'

'Aubrey would never leave them!' Lawrie said, shocked.

'I know that, and you know that,' Callie said. 'But does *she* know that?' She nodded at Agnes, who stared at her, hardly knowing how to respond.

'Of course,' she said at last.

'Really? Because I remember all too well how terrified you were that Florrie would abandon you for Mia, and as much as you love that child – and I know you do – I think you'd be even more devastated if you lost Aubrey. Isn't that the real reason you want to keep him away from Clara, Agnes? Be honest.'

Agnes stared at her in dumb misery. She wanted so much to deny the accusation but found herself unable to. It would, after all, be untrue.

She was indeed wary of Clara, and afraid that she would somehow break Mr Wyndham's heart all over again. But, in all honesty, she was even more afraid that Clara's blood ties to Mr Wyndham would tear their family apart and leave Agnes alone.

What could she offer him that Clara couldn't? Clara was, according to Lawrie, a lively and vivacious young woman. And she had three young boys whom, no doubt, Mr Wyndham would dote on.

Plus, she lived in the heart of the village and would encourage Mr Wyndham to get out and about and enjoy his afterlife to the full – unlike Agnes, who had stifled him and made him miserable for years.

She gazed down at her fingers twisting nervously in her lap, as Cyril Ashcroft's voice flooded her mind.

'Second best, that's what you are! Just someone to warm my bed and run my house. I don't love you and I never will, so get those ridiculous notions out of your head! You'll never match up to her, and if I could walk away from you tomorrow I would.'

'You see?' Callie asked gently. 'I'm right, aren't I? And what kind of friend would I be to Aubrey if I didn't tell him the truth?'

'Please,' Agnes whispered. 'I can't lose him.'

'You won't lose him!'

'Callie's right, Agnes,' Lawrie said quietly. 'If this really is about your fears and insecurities over Aubrey's feelings, you have nothing to worry about. He adores you.'

'You're so lucky, Agnes!' The memory of her younger sister's voice drifted through her mind. 'Cyril adores you!'

No one really knew what was in another person's heart, did they? In her experience, one could take nothing for granted.

'I'll have to talk this over with Brodie,' Callie said, getting to her feet. 'I really need someone who isn't biased to help me work out what I should do next. But look, I promise I won't say anything to Aubrey without warning you first. That's the best I can do, right now.'

Agnes nodded, aware that Callie was trying to be fair. She had a point, after all. What kind of friend would Callie be if she didn't inform Mr Wyndham that he had living, breathing family in the village? He deserved so much more than that.

What a pity that she, the woman who professed to love him, was far too much of a coward to be as honest with him.

22

AUBREY

Having finished telling Florence, John and Robert, plus an enthralled Walter Tasker, about life in Victorian England, Aubrey headed into the suite of rooms he occupied with his family to tell Agnes all about the lesson, only to discover that she wasn't there.

Disappointed, he went back onto the landing, which was when the sound of beautiful voices singing Christmas carols drifted up the stairs towards him. He guessed that Agnes was with Lawrie, enjoying a musical interlude as they sometimes did.

He thought to join them but then changed his mind. He knew how much they valued the time they spent together, and he didn't want to disturb them. Perhaps he would go for a stroll in the garden instead.

He left the Hall through the front door. He'd initially intended to make a circuit of the gardens, but gazing out of the drawing room window while he considered what to do, his attention had been caught by a crowd of people at the end of the drive, who were peering through the gates. Some of them had those pocket telephones that Callie and Brodie seemed so reliant upon and seemed to be using them to take photographs of the house.

It still struck him as incredible that one could carry in one's pocket a small device that served as both a telephone and a camera. Technology was a marvellous thing.

He'd made up his mind to walk up the front drive instead. Perhaps he could get a good look at the devices and see how they worked.

'Tourists,' he said, shaking his head as he arrived at the gates. Even on this drab December day the village was full of them. Then again, it would be. The market was in full swing, and with the fairy lights and the beautiful Christmas trees dotted around the village it was bound to attract visitors.

He glanced back at the house, feeling wistful. He would so love to see Rowan Vale in all its festive glory, but he'd promised Agnes. She would be so hurt if he went against her wishes.

He couldn't help feeling resentful towards the Reverend Alexander. Why did that man have to make so much fuss about their living arrangements? What business was it of his anyway?

As the thought entered his head, Aubrey straightened. Maybe, just maybe, it was time that he gave Silas a piece of his mind. Stood up to him. His mother and Elspeth had repeatedly told him he was pathetic and weak, and perhaps in some ways he was, but dash it all, there was a limit to how many times one could turn the other cheek.

He was sick and tired of having to stay within the grounds of the Hall, and he was sure that, deep down, Agnes was too. How wonderful it would be if he could reason with the crotchety old vicar and get him to see sense! He could tell Agnes her worries were over, and together they could venture into Rowan Vale with their heads held high at long last.

He nibbled at his thumbnail, uncertain what to do. He had given Agnes his word, and he didn't like to even consider breaking it. But surely, if this was for the greater good, it didn't count? If he could improve their afterlives by taking matters into his own hands, it had to be the right thing to do, didn't it?

He thought of Florence, her thin arms wrapped around his own, begging him to come into the village with her, then her matter-of-fact statement that she hadn't bothered to tell him she was taking part in *A Christmas Carol* because she already knew her parents wouldn't see it. That bitter memory made up his mind. He longed to be a proper father to her, in a way he'd never been allowed to be with James.

He wanted – needed – Florence to love and respect him in a way his son never had. That meant showing her that, sometimes, one had to have the courage of one's convictions and stand up for what was right.

Besides, after his rather embarrassing lack of self-control last Friday, when he'd let his passions run away with him, he felt he had to do something to win back Agnes's respect. She hadn't referred to the incident since, for which he was profoundly grateful, but he was sure that he'd shocked her. The way she'd pulled away from him and rushed to her room was evidence that he'd deeply disappointed her, and he felt honour-bound to put things right somehow. Dealing with the Silas problem would surely win her over?

Without allowing himself time to change his mind, Aubrey strode purposefully through the gates, past the crowds, and headed along the street towards the church.

He wasn't sure if he would find Silas in the vicarage or All Souls itself, but either way he was determined to seek him out. Now he'd made his bolt for freedom he couldn't let it be in vain. When he told Agnes what he'd done – because, of course, he would have to upon his return – he needed to be able to assure her that his act of rebellion hadn't been for nothing.

He tried to dismiss the nerves that suddenly attacked him at the thought of Agnes's reaction. He really didn't want to hurt her or trigger another panic attack. When he saw her eyes widen in fear and her whole body start to shake, it made him feel quite ill. He hated the thought of her being distressed in any way. He would have to be extremely careful when he broke the news to her.

He just prayed Silas Alexander would be reasonable, otherwise he would have to tell Agnes that he'd failed, and the thought of seeing disappointment in her eyes was unbearable.

To distract himself from such dismal thoughts, he concentrated on enjoying the freedom of being out in the village again. Above him, fairy lights twinkled against the darkening sky. Little pieces of Christmas to gladden any heart.

He could hear music in the distance – if he wasn't mistaken, they were playing 'Good King Wenceslas'. Smiling to himself, he began to hum along. Maybe, if all went well with Silas, he could pop to the village green for ten minutes or so, just to have a quick look at the market and see how everything was going. He shouldn't really, but in for a penny and all that.

Across the road, he noticed a small child skipping along the pavement, hand in hand with a dark-haired man. Behind them an older child dawdled, absorbed in what appeared to be a similar device to the pocket telephone, but larger. Both boys had bright red hair, and the younger one was chattering ten to the dozen.

The man turned round and yelled, 'Come on, Declan! Put the game down until you get home or I'll tell your mother.'

Aubrey shook his head, smiling. Then he frowned. The man looked familiar. Wasn't that Jack Milsom? He knew him because he'd sometimes come to Harling Hall to drive Lawrie into town if Brodie couldn't. In fact, Aubrey was almost certain that it was Jack who'd brought Callie and Immi to Harling Hall on the day they moved in.

Ah, it *was* Jack! Nice chap. Engine driver by profession. Aubrey hadn't even realised he'd got married, but those must be his sons, so hopefully he had.

The village Christmas tree loomed up before him, and he stared at it in wonder. It looked utterly beautiful, with its twinkling lights and a variety of baubles that seemed quite enchanting to him. He wondered who'd decorated it, and thought it was about time that the Christmas tree was put up at Harling Hall. It was overdue. He'd have to remind Callie about that when he got home.

His steps slowed as he made his way to the lychgate of All Souls, bracing himself for a confrontation with Silas. He just hoped he was in there. It would be too much if he'd sneaked out of the Hall and then couldn't find the vicar!

Casually, he glanced over at Jack and the boys again and stared in astonishment as the youngest hesitantly waved at him.

Aubrey turned around to see if anyone was coming down the path of the church, because surely the child was waving at someone else, but there was no one else there.

Astonished, and feeling a little foolish, Aubrey waved back, and the boy beamed in return. Before Aubrey could gather his thoughts, Jack had led him round the corner, momentarily out of sight.

Aubrey shook his head, dazed. He must be imagining things. There was no reason that this child would be able to see him. Unless... Good heavens, supposing the boy had the gift? All that panic about finding a replacement for Lawrie, and all the time there'd been a youngster in the village who could see ghosts!

Well, it was too late now. Callie was in place and that was that, and a splendid job she was doing. Even so, it seemed a shame, given the child was a local.

'Well, I'll go to the foot of our stairs!'

Aubrey jumped, startled, as a hand rested on his arm.

'Aubrey Wyndham as I live and – well – don't breathe!' There was a chuckle and Aubrey relaxed slightly as he recognised one of the village ghosts. With her dark hair and cotton dress, she had always struck him as a kindly, attractive young woman.

'Mrs Herron,' he said politely. 'How lovely to see you.'

'Polly, love,' she reminded him. 'Mrs Herron was my mother-in-law, thanks very much. Fancy seeing you out and about! We'd given up on ever clapping eyes on you again. Why have you been hiding yourself away?'

'Hardly hiding, Polly,' he said, embarrassed. 'But you know how it is.'

'I do, love. It's that vicar, isn't it? The things he said to you both! Shocking, I call it. But you don't want to take any notice. None of us do, you know. And between you and me, his bark's worse than his bite. Fancy me saying that, eh?' She let out a peal of laughter as Aubrey's eyebrows shot up in surprise. 'I never thought I'd say it either, but let's just say he's done a very good turn for my family recently, and I don't think he's all bad. There's a kernel of humanity in there, and if I were you, I'd let whatever he says about you and Agnes wash over you. Not worth getting upset about, if you ask me.'

'No, well... As a matter of fact, I'm just on my way to see Reverend Alexander. I think this situation has gone on long enough, and it's time to put a stop to it.'

'Ooh, really? Well, good for you. Do you want me to come with you? I could be one of them whatchamacallits. Mediators. What do you say?'

'Thank you very much, Polly, that's terribly kind of you, but I really don't think it will be necessary. This is between Silas and me, and I must deal with it in my own way.'

He noticed the faintest trace of disappointment in her green eyes, but she nodded and patted his shoulder firmly. 'Well, I hope it all goes well then. I'll expect to see you and Agnes out and about in the village very soon. We've all got a lot of catching up to do, and I know there are loads of ghosts dying to see you.' She burst out laughing. 'Well, you know what I mean.'

He smiled at her little joke and nodded, wondering what more today was going to throw at him.

'I'll see you later, love. Good luck,' Polly said, then added, 'and if it doesn't go well and I don't see you again for who knows how long, well, a merry Christmas to you and yours.'

'Thank you, Polly. A merry Christmas to you, too.'

As she hurried off, Aubrey gazed after her. It was the first time someone outside Harling Hall had wished him a merry Christmas in years, and it had given him a warm feeling inside. With 'Good King Wenceslas' replaced by 'Hark! The Herald Angels Sing', the buzz of conversation drifting over from the market, and the sweet expression on that little boy's face, he felt a sudden determination that he wasn't going to have this taken away from him again.

He wanted this afterlife. Not just for himself, but for Agnes and Florence, too. He wanted them to enjoy themselves as a family, mixing with the other villagers, and joining in with celebrations such as Christmas and the 1940s weekend that he'd longed to go to, but had missed.

'Damn Silas Alexander,' he said. 'I won't put up with this a moment longer. I simply won't.'

He walked through the lychgate and up the path towards the church. He wasn't going to return to Harling Hall until he'd got the result he wanted.

23

AUBREY

Inside, the church was decorated for the festive season, with an advent wreath complete with four purple candles on the outside and a white one in its centre, a Christmas tree with purple, white and gold baubles, and of course, the nativity scene.

There was no one around, and Aubrey thought that Silas was perhaps at the vicarage or had gone for a walk. He slipped into a pew and bowed his head in prayer. He had missed the church and felt the need to apologise for his absence.

For many years after his death, Aubrey had prayed that he would be released from this earthly plane and allowed to move on to wherever it was most people seemed to go.

But after he'd fallen in love with Agnes, he'd stopped praying for that, because he wouldn't want to be separated from her ever again. And now they had Florence, he couldn't possibly abandon his little family. So instead, he prayed for understanding, for forgiveness if he'd done something terrible that had left him stranded as a ghost, and that – should he ever be taken to the Great Beyond – he would be accompanied by the woman he considered to be his wife, and the child he considered to be his daughter.

He shuffled forward, his hands folded under his chin, his eyes closed. His thoughts strayed to the day he'd died and how disarming it had been to find himself still present in Harling Hall.

That terrible day, he'd looked down at himself, lying so still and deathly white on the carpet in the upstairs drawing room, and had thought how typical it was that he should become a ghost when there was no one alive in Rowan Vale to communicate with. Unless, he'd thought hopefully, James or his mother could see him.

For the last few years, he'd tried to find someone to take over the estate, but there seemed to be no one with the gift. And now it was too late. What, he'd wondered, would become of Harling Hall and the rest of the village now?

For some time – he wasn't sure how long – he'd sat beside his body, wondering what to do next.

His mother had been the one to find him, and clearly, she'd had no idea his spirit was lingering in the Hall. She'd been in her seventies by then and looked every day of her age and more. But her tongue was as sharp as ever, and if he'd hoped for a word of sorrow or grief from her, he was to be disappointed.

She'd nudged his corpse with her foot then tutted. 'Typical of you to die in here,' she'd said in her broad West Country accent. 'You could have snuffed it downstairs. It would have made it so much easier.'

Then she'd called for James, who'd shown little emotion over his father's passing.

'Well,' he'd said grumpily, 'this is dashed awkward. We needed a bit more time.'

'We haven't got time,' his grandmother replied. 'But don't worry. They'll not get us out. I'd like to see them try.'

So clearly James couldn't see him either, and as Aubrey realised how little grief his mother and son felt at his demise, he'd decided it was perhaps a good thing they couldn't. No doubt they'd have continued to ignore or belittle him even after death, if they'd been able.

He'd cast one last pitying look at his body, then left the room, unable to bear another moment of their indifference.

He'd wandered downstairs into the library, and it was there he'd found Agnes.

Lord, she'd frightened him! Even though he knew that Rowan Vale was home to many ghosts, and even though his father had told him about Agnes, it had still been a shock to see her in the flesh, so to speak.

Bless her, she'd looked more frightened than him, though. She'd stared at him in bewilderment, and it was then that he'd realised her eyes were wet with tears, and she seemed quite distraught about something.

'I thought – I thought you'd have passed on,' she'd said in amazement. 'I heard them shouting that you had died.'

'I rather think I have,' he'd replied with a shrug. 'It's all rather perplexing.'

Agnes had risen slowly to her feet and walked towards him. Tentatively, she'd touched his arm, and he'd seen her gulp when their forms connected. He supposed she'd been expecting her hand to pass straight through him, but they were as real and solid as each other, as far as he could tell.

'You *are* a ghost?' he enquired, wanting to be absolutely certain.

'Agnes Ashcroft,' she said, staring up at him in the most peculiar way. 'And you are Aubrey Wyndham.'

'Yes, I know I am.' Did ghosts usually lose their memory or something? 'So, is this it then? Am I to remain here for – well, forever, I suppose?'

She blinked away her tears. 'I have no way of knowing, but believe me, you have no reason to be afraid. There are many of us on the Harling Estate, and it's not so bad once you get used to it. I'll introduce you to everyone, and you'll soon make new friends. And, after all, it will be nice to have company in the house after all this time.'

'You've been here a while then?' He'd surveyed her attire with some embarrassment. She was, it appeared, dressed for bed.

'Over half a century,' she confirmed.

'And you're the only one in the Hall, aren't you?'

'I am. Well, I was. Now I have you.'

A sudden smile lit up her face and he'd realised she was thoroughly delighted to see him. He supposed that it was only natural considering how long she'd been the only ghost in this place, but even so, it was nice to feel wanted for a change.

'I'm very pleased to meet you, Mrs Ashcroft,' he'd said, holding out his hand as he remembered his manners.

'Oh, Mr Wyndham,' she'd murmured, her eyes shining as she took it in hers. 'And it is so very good to meet *you* at last. So *very* good.'

Aubrey opened his eyes and sat back in the pew, remembering those early days together, and how, gradually, their friendship had blossomed before turning to love. He wasn't entirely sure when his feelings towards Agnes had changed, but he did know that it had been many, many months before he'd dared express them.

He'd expected a rejection and had been overwhelmed when he discovered she felt the same way about him. Of course, they'd known they could never live as husband and wife; they may be dead, but standards still had to be maintained. Even so it hadn't been too long before they started to refer to each other in that fashion.

They were lucky, because Jeremy Davenport had fully accepted them as a couple, and had even suggested they move into the east wing, where he would prepare a suite of rooms for their own use.

After the cruelty he'd experienced from his father, Aubrey considered himself a lucky man to have found such kindness and compassion from the new owner of the estate and had been loyal to the Davenports ever since.

And as for Agnes...

He closed his eyes again and murmured, 'Thank you.'

His gratitude knew no bounds. Whoever had decided that he and Agnes should spend eternity together, he would never stop thanking them for it.

'Good grief! It's you!'

Aubrey leapt to his feet, recognising that rough bark immediately. The Reverend Silas Alexander!

'Ah, Reverend, there you are,' he said, raising his chin as if daring the vicar to send him away.

Silas, who had died in 1927, was a scowling, bespectacled man with a shock of snow-white hair, a large nose and thin lips.

He had been rather intimidating when he was the incumbent at All Souls, and Aubrey didn't find him any less intimidating now. But Aubrey was on a mission, and nothing was going to stop him.

'What the devil are you doing here?' Silas demanded. 'Haven't seen you in years. Been hiding away in your little love nest, haven't you? Disgraceful behaviour.'

'I came here to see you,' Aubrey said sharply. 'And for your information, Harling Hall isn't our love nest. Nor is it a den of iniquity, however much you delight in telling people it is.'

'Hmm! If you say so. What have you come to see me for anyway? If you want me to pray for your soul it's all a bit pointless, isn't it?'

To Aubrey's surprise, Silas dropped into the pew behind him and heaved a heavy sigh.

'Christmas,' he said, gazing round him. 'The birth of our Lord, eh? What do you make of that then?'

Aubrey frowned. 'What do you mean, what do I make of it? What do you expect me to say to that? Is it a trick question?'

Silas stared at him, then to Aubrey's amazement he gave a snort of laughter. 'Trick question? Good heavens, man. It's simple enough. Mind you, maybe it's *all* a trick. What do you think? We were all hoodwinked perhaps. Me most of all.'

He shook his head, staring gloomily at the nativity scene while Aubrey tried to fathom what on earth was in his mind.

'Are you all right, Reverend? You're behaving very oddly, if you don't mind me saying so.'

Silas turned to face him. 'I always liked you, you know. Good chap. Decent. But a bit wet, if I'm being completely honest. Why did you hide away in that old house, eh? Why didn't you come out and hold your head high before now? Be a bloody man? Tell me to stick it?'

Aubrey's mouth fell open. 'I beg your pardon?'

'So you should! Let me down badly, didn't you? Where's the fun in a sparring partner if you won't fight back?'

'Are you telling me that all the abuse you've hurled at Agnes and me was a bit of fun?'

Silas leaned back and stared at him with an intensity that was quite unnerving.

'Not much else to bloody do, is there? It's only winding people up that keeps me going. And to be honest, I'm angry. Furious, if you really want to know.'

'With me?'

'Pah! Not with you, you idiot. With this!' He waved a hand around the church. 'With Him! With all of it!'

Aubrey felt quite dazed. 'Are you sure you're all right?'

'Seventy-five I was when I died,' Silas told him, suddenly looking quite fierce. 'Seventy-five years on this earth! And I spent over seventy of those years in prayer. Religious parents,' he explained. 'Bible forced down my throat along with the nursery food. Sunday School. Church services. Theology studies. When I became vicar of All Souls, I was so proud, Wyndham. So proud.'

'Well...' Aubrey tried to fathom what was going on. He'd never seen Silas like this before. 'You had every right to be proud.' He gazed up at the stained-glass window depicting the Adoration of the Magi. 'It's a beautiful church.'

'But what did it all mean, eh?' Silas asked. 'What was it all for? I thought –

afterwards – I'd spend eternity in heaven. A reward for my services, as it were. Instead, here I am, stuck in this village. The indignity of it! And with a woman vicar in that bloody pulpit every Sunday, too. An abomination! Pah!'

He got to his feet, glaring down at Aubrey as if it was all his fault. 'So you tell me, eh? You tell me what the point of it was. What was the meaning of my life? My work? I might as well have been a coalman or a bus conductor.'

'Or lived in a den of iniquity,' Aubrey said wryly.

For a moment he thought Silas was going to explode, then to his relief, the old man sat down again and ran a hand through his nest of white hair.

'How do you do it, Wyndham?'

'Do what?'

'How do you stay so calm? You're always so cheerful and balanced. I've never seen you get angry. What's the secret?'

'I suppose,' said Aubrey thoughtfully, 'because I'm happy. Of course, I sometimes question why I'm here. Sometimes I think, *did I do something wrong*? But generally, I'm content with my lot. Because, you see, I have a family now, which is more than I ever had when I was alive. I have my daughter, Florence. And I have Agnes, whom I love with all my heart. And that,' he added firmly, 'is what I'm here to see you about.'

'Eh? What? Agnes, you mean?'

'Yes. Now, look here, I won't have this any longer. All this abuse and name-calling. It just isn't on. Have you any idea how much you've upset Agnes? She's a lady, and this sort of thing is simply too much for her. Why, it's because of you she's hiding away in Harling Hall and doesn't want me to come into the village. You've made us virtual prisoners in our own home and it's simply not cricket. A lady's reputation is everything. I can shrug it off, but she can't, and I won't have it. So, what are you going to do about it, eh?'

Silas frowned. 'What are you talking about?'

'You know what I'm talking about,' Aubrey said patiently. 'The insults you hurled at us when we came into the village. The way you stood at the gates of the Hall, warning other ghosts to stay away from us. We've done nothing to deserve it.'

'Yes, yes.'

'Never mind, "yes, yes". You won't fob me off this time. There has been no impropriety between Agnes and me. Yes, we have referred to each other as husband and wife because that's how we feel about one another. And, of course, there's Florence to consider now. We wouldn't want to shock her. But as for marital relations...' He cleared his throat. 'We have separate rooms, and there has never been any suggestion of—'

'Oh, do shut up, Wyndham,' Silas said with a sigh. 'I know perfectly well that you don't live as man and wife, even if you think of each other as such.'

'What?' Aubrey blinked, astonished. 'You know?'

'Of course I know. Didn't your *wife* tell me so herself? She made it very clear what the situation was at Harling Hall, before telling me exactly what she thought of me and how utterly contemptible my behaviour had been.'

'*Agnes* did?' Aubrey could barely take it in. 'When was this?'

'Oh...' Silas shrugged. 'I can't really remember. Years ago, now.' He smirked suddenly. 'It was all rather enjoyable. She's quite a firecracker, that one, when she gets going. I can see why you're attracted to her. She really gave me what for.'

'*Agnes* did?' Aubrey gasped again.

'My dear fellow, is that all you can say? Yes, Agnes did. Stormed into the vicarage and yelled at me for at least ten minutes. Most fun I've had in decades.'

'I – I didn't know. She never said.'

'Hmm. Maybe she didn't want to embarrass you. Bit humiliating, after all, having to do your *husband's* dirty work. You didn't have the guts, so she did it for you.'

'I simply thought it best to ignore you,' Aubrey said indignantly. 'And I *have* asked you to cease your vile insinuations on several occasions.'

'Yes, all very polite and gentlemanly, I'm sure. Where was the fun in that? But Agnes, now, she knows how to put a chap in his place. You're a lucky man.'

Aubrey was so stunned by this turn of events that he couldn't speak. Luckily, he didn't have to as Silas barely paused before continuing.

'And then, just as I thought we were going to start having some proper high jinks – you know, rows in the street, that sort of thing – what did you both do? Threw in the towel and hid yourselves away in the Hall. Most disappointing. I've really missed you both. That's why I stood outside the gates when they had that ridiculous meeting for the ghosts. I thought if I yelled loudly enough, you'd both come out to tell me off. There you go. Let down again. Such is life – or afterlife.'

Aubrey had no idea what to do with all this information.

The fact that Silas was now claiming he knew the truth about the Wyndhams' relationship, and that it clearly didn't bother him in the least but had been a way of stirring up some excitement was astounding enough... but to think that Agnes had been to see him and put him straight!

It didn't make sense. If she'd given Silas a piece of her mind, why had she then retreated into the Hall, keeping Aubrey with her?

'So,' he said, puzzled, 'you don't have any objection to Agnes and I living together?'

'What is there to object to?' Silas asked sadly. 'Of course, I was quite outraged when I first found out about the situation. But things changed. Over the course of my afterlife, these rules and regulations hardly seem to matter any more. If God doesn't care enough about me to call me to His side, why should I care about obeying Him? That's if He even exists.'

'Reverend!'

'Don't sound so shocked, Wyndham. It must surely have crossed your mind, too? I find myself growing less and less convinced of that fact with every passing year that I remain here. When it comes right down to it, what does any of it matter? Not,' he added sternly, 'that I approve of women vicars. That's simply a step too far.'

He got up and wandered over to the Christmas tree, examining it in silence for a few moments. Aubrey watched him, not entirely sure what to make of this entire conversation.

'And when Agnes told me your living arrangements – well, there was nothing else to say, really. It was all a terrible letdown.'

Silas nodded sadly at the tree then turned back to Aubrey. 'So you see, there's no need to hide away in the Hall on my account. I really don't care one way or the other what you do.'

'And you'll stop hurling insults at us, or telling the other ghosts that we're committing some dreadful sin?'

'Oh, come now. Allow me *some* pleasure.'

'Reverend Alexander!'

'Oh, all right! But really, you ask a lot of me. I suppose I'll have to find someone else to insult now. Trouble is, everyone seems to find me amusing. Or they ignore me. I can't get a good argument out of any of them these days, and it's all so dreadfully tedious, don't you think? Eternity is a long, long time. What on earth shall we do with ourselves, Wyndham?'

Aubrey joined him by the tree. 'How about making friends?' he suggested kindly. 'Being with Agnes and Florence, chatting to Walter Tasker when he visits the Hall, the conversations I used to have with the other ghosts – all those things helped the time pass. As you say, eternity is a long, long time. We can't spend it alone. I should think anyone who tries to would go quite mad.'

'Perhaps,' Silas said thoughtfully, 'I *have* gone a little mad. I'll mull over what you've suggested, though I have to say there are slim pickings in this place when it comes to intelligence or scintillating conversation.'

'I've heard that Quintus Severus has moved into the village,' Aubrey said. 'You might find *him* interesting. I'm certainly hoping to seek him out and have a conversation with him. Now that I've chosen to come into Rowan Vale again, that is.'

'Quite, quite. Of course, he's a heathen so...' Silas shrugged. 'Then again, perhaps I am, too. Sad state of affairs, Wyndham. Sad state of affairs.'

Aubrey patted him on the shoulder and turned to leave. A few steps down the aisle, he paused and looked over his shoulder.

'You know,' he said, 'if you ask me, the very fact that we are here now is proof of God, don't you think?'

Silas raised an eyebrow. 'How on earth do you make that out?'

'Well, if there was no God, there'd be no afterlife, would there?' Aubrey said. 'And this may not be heaven, but it's certainly not hell.'

'Then what is it?'

Aubrey shrugged. 'A waiting room of some sort perhaps? Somewhere we stay until we learn our final lessons before we can move on?' He gazed up at the stone carvings and the beautiful stained-glass windows. Everything in this church was, after all, a symbol of man's faith in something greater than himself. 'I really don't know. But surely the fact that we're here to question these things means there's something bigger than you or me? And for my own part, I choose to believe that something is God.

'I may be wrong, of course, but it makes me happier to hold on to that belief than to let it go. I believe God is in each and every one of us, so maybe, Reverend, if you connect with other people, you'll find Him again. You've pushed Him away for long enough. Open your heart to the villagers, and you'll let Him in once more.'

'But I feel forsaken,' Silas said, a bleakness in his eyes. 'We are in no man's land. If there is a God, is He really likely to find us here?'

'He'll find us wherever we are,' Aubrey assured him. 'He's our God, too. Merry Christmas, Silas.'

He nodded a farewell and headed down the aisle. He'd reached the door before Silas responded.

'Yes, yes. Merry Christmas,' he called, sounding distracted. Then, a welcome hint of mischief in his voice, 'And a merry Christmas to that firecracker of yours.'

Aubrey shook his head. 'Really, do show some respect. That's my wife you're talking about.'

As he pushed open the church door, Silas called to him one last jibe.

'Not in the eyes of God, she isn't! Don't you forget that, Wyndham! No shenanigans. Do you hear me? No shenanigans!'

Smiling to himself, Aubrey left the church – and the wayward vicar – behind.

24

The market was heaving that Saturday, despite the cloudy skies which held the threat of rain, and the strong gusts of wind that caused the fairy lights strung around and between the market huts to swing wildly at times.

Jack and I had arrived with three boys, but within a few moments we were left with just Declan and Freddie. Ashton refused to be accompanied by his parents and said he was meeting his mates, so could we just give him some money to spend instead?

'I suppose we're going to get a lot of this from now on,' Jack said with a sigh, as we watched our eldest son running into the crowd, twenty pounds richer. 'Now he's turned twelve he's not going to want to hang around with his mum and dad, is he? Before you know it, Declan will be just the same. We should really make the most of it while he doesn't mind our company.'

'You should see him at school drop-off,' I told him. 'He already escapes from me the minute we arrive in case someone should spot him with his mother. Mind you, I can't blame him. State of me!'

Jack put his arm around me. 'You look beautiful,' he said. 'You're blooming.'

'Blooming awful,' I replied.

He laughed. 'You're not going to believe me, no matter what I say, so I won't bother arguing. I know I'm right and that's all there is to it. Right now, I just want you and the boys to enjoy the market and get into the Christmas spirit.'

The Christmas spirit had been sadly lacking at home, it had to be said. We still hadn't got the decorations down from the loft, and normally we'd have bought a tree by now. The boys were getting antsy about the whole thing, demanding to know why Christmas had been delayed this year.

The market was our way of both apologising and appeasing them, I suppose. We planned to take them round it, stuff them full of treats, then get some fish and chips on the way home. Maybe that would buy us some time, and we'd be able to sort out the Christmas decorations tomorrow.

'There's a stall selling Christmas trees over there,' Jack whispered. 'If they're cheap enough, I'll get one before we leave.'

'Can *you* pay for it?' I asked, hoping he wasn't expecting me to dip into my purse. I was supposed to be getting the fish and chips and that was going to cost me a small fortune.

But Jack had just put down a deposit on a pram, and he'd already promised to pay for the treats at the market, as well as giving Ashton that twenty quid…

I sighed, wondering when our fortunes would change and if we'd ever be able to buy what we wanted, when we wanted, as some people seemed to.

He bit his lip, then nodded. 'Of course. Er, you're okay for money? If you need anything—'

'I'm fine,' I said quickly. 'It's just the fish and chips. You know.'

That and the credit card bill that I'd received yesterday. It was higher than I'd expected it to be, and the payments for the Christmas presents hadn't even kicked in yet. I wondered if we could look at a consolidating loan. Or maybe we could get a nought per cent balance transfer credit card and move the debt over to that?

I'd almost shown the statement to Jack, but I didn't want to burden him. He had enough going on, putting up with me, and besides, it was my problem. He earned the money, while I did nothing but spend it. I needed to get my act together and start earning too, but how was I going to do that with a new baby about to arrive in a matter of weeks?

The thought of the financial mess that faced me in January made my head ache, and I'd abandoned the frantic calculations I'd made on the kitchen jotter to see how I was going to make even minimum payments and made up my mind to forget about it all and do as Jack wanted. Just enjoy the market and get into the Christmas spirit. Or try, at least.

Freddie's face was bright with excitement as he gripped my hand and stared in delight at what must seem to him to be a magical winter wonderland.

The village green had been transformed, with dozens of wooden huts dotted around, each selling enticing festive goods. The smells that were coming from some of them were so divine they made my mouth water, and with the Christmas songs and carols playing over the speakers it was easy to dismiss my troubles and focus on my two youngest sons, who were clearly enchanted. Declan even seemed to have forgotten about his games console for once.

There were some truly fabulous goods on display. One stall sold hand-crafted glass baubles in all manner of shapes, sizes and colours, and I was really tempted to buy a couple for our tree until I saw the price. Bloody hell! The whole tree should cost less than those!

There were some beautiful wreaths on sale, too, and I wished I had the spare cash to buy one for our front door. I could see Amelia and Tully eyeing one up, and I was sorely tempted to do the same, but right now I just wanted to treat the boys. Today was supposed to be about them.

'What are *they*?' Freddie enquired, pointing to a stall selling snow globes – some of them huge.

Jack lifted him up to show him, and the woman behind the counter grinned and shook one for him, making his eyes widen as the flakes of snow drifted down over the little cottages and people inside the globe.

'Can I have one?' he begged immediately.

I saw Jack glance at the price and give the woman a sheepish look as he lowered Freddie to the ground. 'Maybe on our way back,' he fudged. 'Don't want to drop it and break it in the market, do we?'

The woman gave him a wry smile, as if she'd heard that one many times before, but luckily her attention was drawn to another customer – hopefully one who intended to buy something.

There was a strong Christmassy smell as we passed a stall selling scented candles. I got a distinct whiff of cinnamon and cloves and closed my eyes, breathing it in and feeling a sudden uplift in my mood.

'Christmas cards!' Declan cried suddenly. '*Please* can you get me some? Everyone else brought theirs to school for the postbox ages ago.'

'*I* want some Christmas cards,' Freddie pleaded.

The cards weren't a bad price, surprisingly. In fact, they were cheaper than the ones in the card shops I'd visited in Kingsford Wold, so I bought a couple of packs each for the boys and a couple of packs to send to our friends and neighbours. I'd get the special ones from the card shop during the week.

Declan looked highly relieved and insisted on carrying the bag. I felt awful, and realised I'd been promising to buy him some for ages now. I'd never been so disorganised and felt bitterly ashamed.

'Ooh, mulled wine,' Jack said as we approached a drinks stall. 'I could just fancy a glass of that. Or a paper cup of it,' he added, grinning.

'Lucky you,' I said. 'No alcohol for me.' *Better late than never, anyway*. 'But,' I added, 'don't let that stop you. Go ahead.'

'No, I won't bother.' He tucked his arm in mine and hurried on past the stall.

'Honestly,' I told him. 'I don't mind.'

'I do! Did you see how much they were charging? We could get a whole bottle of it from the supermarket for the price of one of those servings.'

'Oh, Jack.' I sighed, feeling fed up all over again. 'It's Christmas. We shouldn't be worrying about the price of a glass of mulled wine at Christmas.'

'A cup,' he reminded me. 'Anyway, I'm *not* worrying. I'm just too tight to pay it.'

He pressed his forehead against mine, smiling, and I smiled back, knowing he was just trying to make me feel better and loving him for it.

'Anyway,' he said, 'never mind mulled wine. I think we should all have a hot chocolate, don't you?'

'Ooh, yes please!' Declan said happily.

'*I* want a hot chocolate,' Freddie announced.

'You want everything,' Jack told him. 'You're a waste disposal unit on legs.' He ruffled Freddie's hair. 'As if I'd leave you out, anyway.'

To be honest, when we found a stall selling hot chocolate, it wasn't much cheaper than the mulled wine, especially as Jack insisted that we all have one, including the full works: whipped cream, chocolate sprinkles and tiny marshmallows.

To my relief, they did kid-sized cups with lids – a lot safer and easier for the boys to carry round. Jack held on to Freddie's until it had cooled off sufficiently, which didn't please our youngest at all, so we distracted him by buying him a Father Christmas cookie to munch on in the meantime.

I wondered what the experts would say about our so-called parenting skills.

We stayed at the market for a couple of hours, but by then my back was starting to ache, and I was feeling pretty tired.

'Right,' Jack said, seeing I was struggling, 'time for home. Let's go back to that stall and see how much the Christmas trees are, and if they're not too extortionate I'll buy one. Then I'll drop it at home before I go and get the fish and chips.'

'We were all going to go to the chippy,' I reminded him.

'You're worn out, love. I can see it in your face. You stay at home and put your feet up, and I'll take the boys with me.'

'Really?' I hugged him gratefully. 'You're a star.'

'Not really,' he said with a shrug. 'I'm just trying to get on Santa's nice list.'

'*I* want to be on Santa's nice list,' Freddie said.

'Of course you do.' Jack shook his head, amusement in his eyes. 'I think I'm going to change your name to Veruca Salt.'

'From *Charlie and the Chocolate Factory*!' Declan let out a cackle of laughter.

'I don't want to be called Veruca Salt!' Freddie cried in dismay. 'I'm Freddie.'

'Hallelujah,' I said. 'We've finally found something he *doesn't* want.'

'Having fun?'

We looked round, and I gave an embarrassed greeting to Brodie and Callie, who were with Immi. It was the first time I'd seen Brodie since my little tantrum.

'We were just about to leave, actually,' Jack said. He sounded strangely awkward. 'We've been here a while now and we're all shopped out.'

'Jack's just going to buy a Christmas tree,' I added.

'We were just looking at those,' Brodie said. 'We thought we might order a few for the Hall. We've got the big one for the entrance hall coming in a couple of days, but it would be nice to put a smaller tree up in some of the other rooms.'

'Did you buy anything interesting?' Callie asked, glancing at our carrier bags. 'Did you get some of those handmade chocolates? Every time I pass that stall, I think I'll treat myself. Maybe I will today.'

'No,' I said. 'I didn't see those.'

I *had* seen them, but they were way out of my price range. Sadly, I just couldn't justify it.

'We got Christmas cards for school,' Declan said, swinging his carrier bag at her. 'And hot chocolate.'

'And Father Christmas cookies,' Freddie added. 'And a nutcracker.'

'A nutcracker? Whoa, that sounds amazing,' Brodie said.

'It's a shoulder really,' Freddie told him, having given up trying to pronounce soldier. 'We're going to put him on the mantelpiece, aren't we,

Mummy? We're getting the tree up tomorrow,' he added, his eyes shining. 'And all the decorations. And our stockings are going to be hanged up on the fireplace.'

'That sounds smashing,' Brodie agreed. 'Not long to go now, so it's best to be prepared.'

'Would it be okay if we popped round later?' Callie asked. 'We've something we'd like to talk to you about.'

Jack and I looked at each other. Last time they'd come round to talk to us it hadn't ended well. Still, that was hardly their fault, and they *were* our friends.

'Sure,' Jack said. 'Look, we're heading home now and we're getting some fish and chips for dinner. Do you all want to join us? My treat.'

I gaped at him. Was he off his head? We'd been saying no to ourselves and the boys this entire visit to save money, and he was offering to buy them fish and chips?

'No, no! You have your dinner in peace,' Brodie said, to my relief. 'We're going to have a quick look around the market, make sure everyone's happy and it's all going as it should, then we're taking Immi and Florrie to The Quicken Tree for tea.'

'Florrie's here?' I swallowed, wondering if anything had been said at Harling Hall about my secret. Not that Florrie could have spilled the beans to Jack, but even so...

'Yes, and she's really excited to be going to the pub, aren't you, Florrie?' Callie said fondly.

As Declan and Freddie began to bombard this invisible girl with questions, receiving answers via Immi, Callie pulled me aside and whispered, 'I won't say anything to Jack, don't worry.'

'Does Brodie know?' I asked urgently.

'Yes, but he knows not to say anything. Look, we really need to talk to you so—'

'After dinner is fine,' I said. 'If you can make it after nine the boys will all be in bed and we'll get some peace.'

'Brilliant,' she said. 'Not that I don't want to see the boys, naturally, but this is important.'

I nodded, feeling a bit sick. Clearly, they weren't going to mention Aubrey in front of Jack, so what was this about?

I guessed I'd find out soon enough.

25

I was on the verge of falling asleep when Callie and Brodie knocked on the door. I'd eaten some yummy fish and chips, washed down with a big mug of tea, then I'd stacked the dishwasher, tidied up, and made sure the boys had their baths and brushed their teeth, while Jack took Toby for his regular evening walk.

Upon his return we were immediately called upon to referee a mighty row between our errant offspring when Ashton – who had arrived home just in time for dinner – produced a bag of fudge, purchased at the market, which he refused to share with Declan and Freddie.

'I bought it with my own money,' he protested, as they clamoured round him. 'Don't tell me Mum and Dad didn't buy you stuff while you were at the market cos I don't believe you.'

'Only a hot chocolate and a Father Christmas cookie,' Declan whined.

'And Christmas cards,' I said, feeling terrible all over again. We'd shuffled them past so many stalls selling delicious treats. Were we terrible parents?

'You all said you wanted fish and chips for dinner,' Jack reminded them. 'Do you know how expensive they are? You can't have everything.'

'I suppose you need all your money to buy baby clothes now,' Declan said sulkily.

'Oh, shut up moaning,' Ashton told him smugly, as he dipped into the bag of fudge. 'Hope you enjoyed your *Father Christmas cookie*.'

His smirk was wiped off his face as Jack reached over and took the bag from his hands.

'You needn't think you're eating all that tonight,' he said. 'Think of your teeth which, by the way, you'll now have to brush again. I'm sure you've had enough to eat at the market before you even came home for dinner.'

'Please tell me you didn't spend all that money on sweets and snacks,' I pleaded.

'It's my money. I can spend it on what I like,' Ashton said.

'Lucky you.' Jack rubbed the back of his neck wearily. 'If only your mother and I had the same luxury.'

Ashton informed us that we were the worst parents in the world and never treated him fairly, while Declan moaned that he hadn't even wanted a Father Christmas cookie and would have much preferred a bag of fudge if we'd only given him the option, and Freddie wailed, '*I* want fudge,' on a loop until I wanted to scream.

'Right,' Jack said. 'Bedtime.'

'But it's not school tomorrow!' Declan gasped.

'You can't mean me,' Ashton said. 'I'm twelve!'

'And you're behaving like a spoilt six-year-old,' Jack told him crossly. 'No offence, Freddie.'

'You can read in bed for an hour, Ash,' I offered.

'*Read?*' Ashton's lip curled in scorn.

'Can I have my Switch?' Declan asked.

Jack nodded. 'Yes, until nine. I'll come up then and take it off you, so make the most of it. Now bed.'

His voice brooked no further arguments, and he'd ushered them all upstairs, settled Freddie into bed, then made me a mug of cocoa.

'This is the worst thing I could have really,' I said, even as I accepted it gratefully. 'Honestly, I'm ready for bed as it is.'

'Do you want me to call Callie and Brodie? Tell them to make it another night?'

'No. We may as well get it over with. Unless *you* want to cancel?'

Jack hesitated. 'No. Let's hear what they have to say.'

Luckily, Callie and Brodie arrived at ten to nine, just as I was on the verge of nodding off, and apologised for being a bit early.

'No worries,' Jack said politely. 'Come in. Would you like something to drink?'

'We've brought this,' Brodie said, handing him a bottle of wine. 'It's non-alcoholic,' he added, smiling at me.

'And I've brought you these,' Callie said, passing a carrier bag to me. I opened it, surprised and touched to find a box of the handmade chocolates she'd been talking about earlier.

'Oh wow, that's so kind of you. Thanks. What have I done to deserve them?'

'It just seemed a shame you'd missed them, that's all,' she said with a shrug. 'It's no big deal.'

No big deal to her maybe, but I knew how expensive they were.

'We saw the tree outside,' Brodie said, giving Jack his coat. 'Looks good.'

'Yes, we were pleased with it. It wasn't too pricey either.' Jack took Callie's coat from her. 'Did you buy one for the Hall?'

'Four,' she said, rolling her eyes. 'One for the main sitting room, one for the living room in mine and Immi's suite, one for Lawrie's sitting room, and one for the drawing room in the Wyndhams' suite. They were delighted. Immi's going to decorate it for them tomorrow following their instructions – after Brodie's put the lights on it.'

I felt uncomfortable immediately at the mention of the Wyndhams, convinced that guilt showed on my face, but Brodie and Callie gave nothing away and Jack remained oblivious.

He hung up their coats in the hallway then hurried upstairs to take Declan's Switch away before he forgot, while I poured the non-alcoholic wine into four glasses and our guests made a big fuss of Toby, who seemed delighted to see them again.

'Right, that's the boys all sorted,' Jack said, returning to the living room. 'Freddie's already fast asleep,' he assured me, 'and despite their protests, the other two look as if they won't be awake much longer.'

'Immi fell asleep half an hour ago,' Callie told us, stroking a blissful Toby's neck. 'Fresh air and excitement, I expect. She loved the market, and was thrilled to visit the pub. So was Florrie.'

'It's odd that they're such good friends,' Jack mused. 'But it's nice, too.'

'Nice now,' Callie said with a sigh. 'I do worry what will happen in a couple of years' time, though.'

'What do you mean?' Jack asked.

'Well, Immi will be a teenager, and she'll hopefully make friends at school. Will she still want to hang around with a perpetual ten-year-old? I can't see it, can you? And what will Florrie do then? It's a bit worrying. I have a feeling Florrie's going to be really hurt. I'm just hoping she doesn't go back to her old ways when it happens.'

'I hope so, too,' Brodie said. 'For John's and Robert's sakes as much as anyone else's.'

'John and Robert?' Jack frowned. 'Are they the ragamuffin children from the eighteenth century?'

'That's right,' Callie said. 'Florrie used to boss them around terribly until they all started having lessons with Walter Tasker. Having a routine, making friends with Immi, and finding she's related to Mia – all those things have really changed her. I'm hoping she's come on far enough that she won't go back to her naughty ways. Time will tell, I guess.'

She took a sip of the wine. 'Hmm. That's actually quite nice. Much better than I expected.'

'You could have brought real wine for yourself,' I told her. 'I wouldn't have minded.'

'Certainly not!' She grinned. 'I'd never do that to my pal.'

I smiled back. Callie really was a friend in a million. How she'd seen past all the hormonal rages and sniping and tears of the last few months, I'd never know.

'So, what is it you wanted to talk to us about?' Jack asked.

'Well...' Brodie glanced at Callie, who nodded. 'It's about the model village. We wanted to put something to you.'

I saw Jack tense. 'Go on.'

'We've been talking it over with Lawrie and Mia – and the Wyndhams,' he added, not looking at me, 'because this would affect them, too, and we had to be sure it was okay with them before we said anything.'

'And they're all fine with it,' Callie said quickly.

'I'm intrigued.' Jack swirled the wine in his glass and watched them through narrowed eyes. 'What are you thinking?'

'Well,' Brodie said, 'we know how disappointed you both were not to find a solution to opening the model village here, and we still think it's a good idea. We're pretty sure it would be a great tourist attraction, but probably not one that would pull in huge crowds all year round. Even so, it would potentially make quite a bit of money during the holiday season, so we were thinking about opening it from Easter until the end of September only.'

'Okay,' Jack said slowly. 'Makes sense. But it doesn't solve the problems we came up against, does it?'

'Not if we keep the village at Honeywell House,' Brodie said. 'But how would you feel about moving it across to the grounds of Harling Hall?'

I glanced at Jack. I knew how much the model village meant to him. He'd grown up helping to maintain it and associated it with his much-loved grandad who had taught him how to care for it. Moving it away from the paddock at Honeywell House to someone else's home might be a step too far.

'What do you think, Clara?' Jack asked.

'Me? Well...' I considered the matter. 'It would solve a lot of our problems. We wouldn't have to worry about access and privacy. Are you sure no one would mind it being situated in the grounds of the Hall?'

'No,' Callie said. 'There's acres of space and it wouldn't be difficult to create a pathway to wherever we situate it. We've been considering opening the gardens to the public during the main season anyway, so this would be another attraction to draw them in.'

'But wouldn't you then have the same problem?' Jack asked. 'Lack of privacy. Especially with having Immi to consider.'

'No, because the family lawn at the back of the house is walled off and the gate would remain locked during opening times. It's a huge space – plenty of room for Immi and Florrie and John and Robert to play, not to mention Brian.'

Callie smiled at the thought of the kitten. 'If I'd thought there was any threat to Immi's privacy there's no way I'd go ahead, but there isn't. The family lawn runs the full length of the house, and you know how big that is!'

'Are you sure there were no objections?' I asked, giving her a meaningful look. 'From *anyone*?'

'None,' she said firmly. 'Agnes was a bit dubious at first, but she came round to my way of thinking eventually.'

It sounded like a good solution to me, except for one thing. 'Would I still be able to work at the ticket office?'

Because, presuming the ticket office would be situated in the grounds, would Lawrie allow me near the Hall every day? Would *Aubrey* allow it?

'Even if it's only Easter to the end of September it would be something,' I added.

'Right through the school holidays?' Jack said, frowning. 'How would that work?'

I glanced at him impatiently. 'We could work something out, couldn't we?'

'I don't see what,' he said. 'I have to work, too, and we'll have a young baby to look after.'

'Yes, *we* will,' I said pointedly, feeling my frustration and anger bubbling up again. 'Maybe I could find a childminder or a nursery somewhere. There's nothing in Rowan Vale, but maybe in Kingsford Wold...'

'You'd spend more on childcare than you earned.' Jack shook his head. 'What would be the point?'

To make me feel like a normal human being again. To give me some sort of life outside the family home.

Why couldn't Jack see that? But there was no way I wanted to get into another row in front of Callie and Brodie, so I bit my lip and stared stonily at the carpet.

'Well, er... We can discuss that later,' Callie said awkwardly. 'We've got months yet before we need worry about that and maybe you'll have a clearer idea of what you can manage by then.'

'So what do you think?' Brodie asked Jack. 'I know it's a big deal to you, and I know the model village has always been associated with Honeywell House but—'

'Not so much with the house,' Jack said quietly. 'But with my family, yes.'

'You think your mum would object?' Brodie asked, aware that it had been her grandfather who'd created the model village in the first place.

'No. She never took much interest in it,' Jack said. 'That's why, when Grandad died, he left it to me. I can do what I like with it, which is why I have another proposal for you.'

I lifted my head, baffled. What proposal?

'Go on,' Brodie said.

Jack took a steadying breath. 'How would you feel about buying it from me? Then you could put it wherever you like, open it to the public or not. I'd want a fair price, but I wouldn't make a ridiculous demand, and you'd make the money back over time with entrance fees, I'm sure.'

Brodie and Callie stared at him in surprise. They weren't as surprised as I was, though.

'Sell the model village?' I gasped. 'When did you decide this?'

'Been thinking about it a while,' he said with a shrug.

'And you didn't think to consult me?'

'I didn't think I had to,' he said evenly.

'Well, that's bloody charming,' I snapped. '*Your* family, *your* model village, *your* decision. I get it. Thanks for keeping me in the loop.'

'Like you've been keeping *me* in the loop?' he demanded.

I felt the blood drain from my face and cast a desperate look at Callie and Brodie. Surely they hadn't told him my secret? Callie gave a slight shrug, as if to reassure me that, whatever Jack was talking about, she hadn't a clue.

'What do you mean?' I asked faintly.

'Did you really think I wouldn't find out, Clara? Look, I get why you didn't tell me, but we're supposed to be a couple. A team. You can't carry the burden on your own, love. Don't you think you have enough to worry about?'

I was totally confused. He sounded concerned about me. If he knew my family history, it didn't look as if he was bothered.

'I saw it,' he said heavily.

'Saw what?' For a moment, I could only think of my drawing of Aubrey. But Jack had never seen Aubrey, and I'd already given him an explanation for the sketch anyway. How would he know who he really was, let alone of our connection?

My heart sank as he said, 'The calculations you were doing on the bit of paper you'd chucked in the bin, along with the invoice for the kids' Christmas presents. I saw the figures you'd written down for the credit card statement, too. We're in real trouble, aren't we?'

He threw up his hands in an appeal to Brodie and Callie. 'Yeah, I know, I probably shouldn't be saying this in front of you two, but the fact is we're struggling financially. It's hard enough to make all our repayments now, but once the kids' presents get added to the credit card balance, and we have to pay the outstanding amount on the pram and buy a cot and everything else we're going to need...'

He massaged his temples, clearly stressed. 'Look, we're in over our heads – we need an injection of cash. If we could pay off the credit card and the Christmas spending, buy everything we need for the baby and put a bit away for emergencies and the kids' futures... You understand?'

'Yes, of course.' Brodie sounded sympathetic. 'Of course we understand.'

'Of course we do.' Callie gave me a look that held a hint of shame. 'I'm so sorry. We should have thought.'

'We'll be fine,' Jack said firmly, tilting his chin. 'We're not charity cases and we don't need sympathy. But a fair price for the model village would see us out of this mess, and if you're willing to give us that, I'd be happy to sell it to you.'

'Really, Jack?' I murmured. 'Are you sure about this?'

'I've been thinking about it all week,' he admitted. 'And when I found your workings out this morning, my mind was made up. When I saw you two at the market, I was going to suggest a meeting, but you beat me to it. And the fact is, if you're not interested, I'll probably put it up for sale anyway.'

'Jack!' I exclaimed, shocked.

Callie and Brodie looked at each other with expressions I couldn't quite read.

'Well,' Callie said, 'I think that's clear enough.'

'I'm not trying to be difficult,' Jack assured them.

'No, no of course you're not. We get it, honestly,' she said. 'Look, we need to think about this. We can't make a hasty decision.'

'I realise that,' he said.

Callie smiled. 'I'll have to discuss it with my accountant,' she said, nodding at Brodie. 'But I promise we'll get back to you as soon as we can.'

'We realise you need an answer pretty quickly,' Brodie assured him. 'We'll get on to it straight away.'

'So you're not saying no?' Jack asked hopefully. 'I'll be honest – I'd far rather sell it to you two, knowing it will stay with people I can trust, but...'

'Surely no one outside the village would be interested?' I asked, perplexed. 'It's a model of Rowan Vale. Where else is it going to go?'

Jack rolled his eyes, and I realised I wasn't helping. Brodie, however, wasn't so sure I was right.

'There are plenty of people who want a slice of the Cotswolds and loads of opportunities in the tourist industry. I can think of a few places nearby that would happily add a model village of such good quality to their attractions. Doesn't matter that it's of Rowan Vale. It's close enough to be a draw for visitors. But we don't want that to happen any more than you do, Jack. Like I said, we'll be as quick as we can.'

'Thanks, Brodie. Callie. I appreciate that.'

They all got to their feet and Jack shook their hands, while I remained on the sofa, stunned by what I'd just heard.

'Right,' Callie said, 'we'll go home and start crunching some numbers. Well,' she added, 'Brodie will. I'll probably scoff chocolates and admire him in action, so to speak.' She giggled, and Jack visibly relaxed, clearly realising he hadn't caused a rift between us and our friends.

She bent down and hugged me. 'Don't get up,' she said. 'We can see ourselves out. Enjoy the rest of the evening. Make the most of the peace and quiet while you can.'

Jack nodded. 'I'll get your coats,' he said. I heard them mumbling in the hallway and sat there, feeling numb. How could Jack have been thinking about this for days without even mentioning it to me?

This affected me, too. It affected the kids as well, because the model village was their heritage – the only thing we had to pass on to them. A slice of the estate.

If I was honest with myself, I had to admit that it hurt. My family no longer owned the Harling Estate, but when I married Jack, it had sort of owned a miniature version of it, and now even that was to be taken away. It just didn't seem fair.

Though, lately, not much did.

26

AUBREY

'Imogen has made a wonderful job of the tree, don't you think, Mr Wyndham?'

Aubrey nodded. 'A very fine job indeed,' he said, glancing at the Christmas tree in the corner of their drawing room, which Immi had spent all afternoon decorating for them.

Brodie had put the fairy lights in place first, then left her to it, and Immi had carefully placed the baubles where Agnes and Florrie told her to.

'It's really brightened up the room,' Agnes said, nodding approvingly. 'I'm starting to feel very festive now, aren't you?'

Aubrey made some non-committal reply and turned back to the television. Immi had kindly put *The Crown* on for them to watch before she left, but it had to be said that he'd barely taken in a word of the last couple of episodes, despite finding Claire Foy utterly charming.

He was distracted, much as he'd been ever since he'd got back from the village early on Thursday evening after his little chat with Silas.

Rushing back to Harling Hall, his intention had been to find Agnes and clear up the mystery of why she hadn't told him about her conversation with the vicar and ask her why – knowing Silas's true feelings – she hadn't changed her mind about them leaving Harling Hall.

Upon seeing her, though, he'd decided against confronting her. She'd seemed upset about something, and although he'd pressed her to tell him what had happened, she would only say that it was nothing more than the realisation that they couldn't partake of so many of the festive celebrations, and that he should think no more of it as she was merely being a foolish woman.

Aubrey hadn't been convinced, and there was a part of him still fretting that his ungentlemanly behaviour towards her had affected her even more deeply than he'd imagined.

Fearing that he'd already damaged their relationship in some way, he hardly liked to jeopardise it even further, with the result that he'd spent the entire weekend puzzling over the situation with increasing confusion and despondency.

That she'd kept such a secret from him was bad enough, but it was her motivation for doing so that worried him. Yet he feared, more than anything, that their warm and affectionate relationship would become cold and distant if he pressed the matter.

If his 'marriage' to Agnes became a replica of the one between him and Elspeth, he didn't think he could bear it.

He tensed as Agnes came to sit beside him on the sofa.

'You're not yourself today, Mr Wyndham,' she said nervously. 'In fact, you haven't been yourself for some days now. Is – is there any reason for your melancholy?'

He didn't want to lie to her, but equally, how could he possibly tell her the truth? If he revealed where he'd been early on Thursday evening, it could bring their entire house of cards tumbling down. He couldn't risk it.

'Nothing for you to worry about, my dear,' he said eventually, not looking at her.

She hesitated, then said, 'So there *is* something?'

Aubrey heaved an inward sigh. Must she persist? He made himself face her and forced a smile.

'Are you not interested in *The Crown*? Perhaps I could find Callie or Lawrie and ask them to search for something more to your taste this evening.'

Agnes swallowed and he noticed her fingers twisting the ribbons of her bed jacket. Had he brought her to this? He knew she was highly sensitive, and the thought that his morose behaviour had upset her to such a degree was a distressing one.

Difficult or not, he must tell her the truth. They had to clear the air. Maybe there was a perfectly logical explanation and once explored they could put the whole thing behind them and work on restoring the previous goodwill between them.

'Agnes, I must talk to you.'

'Mr Wyndham, I must talk to you!'

As they each realised what the other had said, they both laughed nervously.

'You first, my dear,' he said politely.

She shook her head. 'Not here. Would you care to take a turn around the garden?'

He looked at her in surprise. *In the dark?*

'Florence,' she murmured. 'She is asleep in the next room, but I wouldn't want to wake her.'

'Why would we wake her?' he asked, confused.

'Please, Mr Wyndham. Outside.'

Nodding his assent, he followed her out of their suite and downstairs, through the hallway and kitchen and out into the family garden. There was little moonlight, and in the darkness, it was hard for him to see her.

He reached for her hand, and they made their way to the picnic table where Immi and Callie often had their lunch on summer days, with Florence sitting beside them joining in their chatter.

As Agnes settled herself on the bench, Aubrey said, 'Are you sure about this? I can barely see your face and it's hardly conducive to a conversation. Shouldn't we go inside?'

Agnes shook her head. 'I would prefer to stay out here,' she said in a low voice. 'I would prefer that you didn't see my face clearly, nor I yours.'

Aubrey felt a twist of fear. Why would Agnes not want them to see each other's faces?

It came to him in a sickening rush that perhaps she was about to tell him that she no longer wished to be considered his wife, and that he should move out of their family suite.

He had kissed her! He had kissed her on the mouth and held her and... Oh, lord. He had frightened her away. How could he have been so stupid? He didn't deserve her affections. He was nothing but a cad and a bounder.

'Mr Wyndham,' she said brokenly, 'I have done you a grave disservice, and I cannot tell you how sorry I am.'

That was not what he'd expected to hear, and he frowned, not understanding what she could possibly have done to be sorry for.

'Agnes, I am quite sure—'

'Please,' she said. 'Let me finish.'

He stared at her. She was gazing down at the ground and seemed rather hunched and smaller somehow. Whatever she was about to say, it was obviously huge. Afterlife-changing, in fact.

He would have to ask Callie if he could move into another room. There were lots of empty ones, after all. But maybe that would still be too close? Perhaps he should do the decent thing and offer to find alternative accommodation. There were plenty of other buildings in Rowan Vale. There must be a vacancy for a ghost somewhere.

If the worst came to the worst, there was always The Monastery. He shuddered, imagining having to live in the desolate old building near the boundaries of the estate, where the ghosts who wanted nothing to do with the villagers dwelt. Could he really bear to live among them? Would they even allow him to?

And what of Florence? She would come from a broken home. He understood that was quite common these days, but he didn't want that for *his* daughter!

'Mr Wyndham,' Agnes said urgently. 'Are you listening?'

He'd been lost in his thoughts, staring into the darkness towards the home he might soon have to leave, his fevered imagination running away with him. He turned back to her, full of contrition.

'I'm so sorry. But Agnes, whatever this is, we can fix it, can't we? Surely, if we're just honest with each other and admit our mistakes, we can forgive and forget? After all this time—'

'Mr Wyndham,' she said, her voice shaky, 'I have done something that you may not find so easy to forgive. I have kept a secret from you. I have lied to you. I have behaved in a deplorable manner, and I will fully understand if you want nothing more to do with me. But I must tell you the truth now, because Callie has made me see that I have done you a terrible injustice, and you have never deserved to be treated in such a fashion. I am truly, truly sorry.'

Aubrey, full of compassion for her, reached out and took hold of her hand.

'Whatever it is, I accept your apology,' he said kindly. 'You needn't be afraid to tell me. I think I know what you've done anyway, and I'll confess I'm a little bewildered as to why you did it, but I am not angry with you, my dear. Far from it.'

She lifted her face to his. He couldn't quite make out her expression, but he saw her rear back a little.

'You know?'

'I have a confession of my own to make,' he said. He braced himself. Time to tell the truth and shame the devil. 'I went to see Silas Alexander the other day.'

Agnes pulled her hand from his. 'You did what?'

'I wanted to put things right for us, you see,' he explained nervously. 'Missing out on the Christmas market and the switching on of the festive illuminations was the final straw. Why should we hide away here in Harling Hall? So I went to see him to tell him once and for all that we had done nothing to be ashamed of, and that he needed to stop this vendetta against us.'

'And – and what did he say?' she managed, in strangled tones.

'Well,' Aubrey said slowly, 'I expect you can guess what he said. He told me that you had already explained the situation to him some years ago, and that he was fully aware that there was no impropriety between us.'

He was glad she couldn't see the flicker of shame he was certain was in his eyes. It had to be said, if she hadn't spurned his disgraceful advances the situation might well have changed. It was lucky that Agnes was a woman of such high principle, because he had been decidedly weak.

'I see,' she murmured.

'I'll admit, I'm baffled as to why you didn't tell me. And more than that, why you still insist that we should remain within the grounds of the Hall. All this time I assumed it was because of Silas, but it hardly seems as if you are afraid of him after all, and I'm at a loss to understand what your motivation is for keeping us here all this time.'

For a long moment, she was silent. Then she said, 'You didn't assume, Mr Wyndham. You were told. You were told by me repeatedly, and each time I blamed Silas for the situation, I was lying. There is another reason I wanted you to stay away from the village, and that's what I must confess to you now.'

Aubrey rubbed his chin, utterly confused. If it wasn't Silas, why were they virtual prisoners in their own home?

'Go on,' he urged.

Agnes got to her feet and turned away from him. Her voice, shaky but resolute, drifted through the darkness towards him.

'I kept you here because you have family in Rowan Vale. A great-great-great-great-granddaughter, to be exact. And I didn't want you to meet her, so I lied and said it was because of Silas's vicious slurs that we must remain behind the gates. So now you know the truth.'

Aubrey gaped at her. She still didn't turn around and he didn't know what to make of anything she'd just told him.

'A – a descendant of mine is in Rowan Vale?' he asked incredulously. 'But, who? When? How?'

'She is descended from James,' Agnes said. 'Her name is Clara and she's been living in this village for around fifteen years. She came here because she met a man on holiday and fell in love with him, and he was a resident here.'

She gave a little cry of despair and dropped back onto the bench. 'I'm so sorry!'

'I can't take any of this in,' Aubrey admitted. 'A Wyndham in Rowan Vale! But the rules...'

'Lawrie knows,' she told him. 'He allowed her to remain in the village, providing she never told her husband or anyone else about the family connection, and—'

She shook her head and Aubrey frowned.

'And what? And *what*, Agnes?'

'And that she never approached *you*,' she whispered.

Aubrey's thoughts were racing so far ahead of him he couldn't keep up. Then suddenly, a memory pierced through the jumble of images, and he said sharply, 'This woman. Is she married to Jack Milsom?'

Agnes started. 'Why, yes. She is. How on earth did you know?'

'He's my family,' he murmured. 'The little boy with the red hair. I *knew* he could see me!'

'What did you say?' she demanded, sounding almost like her old self again.

Aubrey barely heard her. He had seen his own great-grandchild. Forget all the generations that divided them. He would think of the child as his great-grandson and this Clara as his granddaughter. He had seen the boy, and the boy had seen him, and all the time they were related, and he hadn't known.

All that time. Fifteen years Clara had been in Rowan Vale. His flesh and blood. And Agnes had known. Lawrie had known. Why?

'I don't understand,' he said, feeling utterly wretched. 'Why would you and Lawrie keep us apart?'

'She's a descendant of James,' Agnes repeated. 'You know how badly he treated you. Who's to say she won't be just as awful? James scorned you and mocked you, and after you passed away, he stole from the Hall and was utterly shameless. You know that, Mr Wyndham. I didn't want you to suffer like that again. I was protecting you.'

'And Clara definitely knows I am at Harling Hall?'

'Yes – yes, she knows. She saw you and me one day just after she arrived and followed us. That's when she realised who you were. I saw her, but you didn't notice her watching, and of course, she couldn't see me. I told Lawrie because I knew what it must mean, and he visited her at Honeywell House and explained the situation to her.'

'Explained what situation, exactly?'

'Well, that a member of a family that has formerly owned the estate should not return. She already knew that yet she chose to ignore the rule and come here anyway. Doesn't that tell you all you need to know?'

'You said she came here because she fell in love with Jack?'

'Well – yes. But it's a bit convenient, isn't it? Anyway, Lawrie and she made a deal that she could stay on his terms.'

'And she just accepted that? She didn't argue?'

'No,' Agnes said. 'She accepted it. She wanted to stay.'

'Right.' Aubrey couldn't deny he was hurt. Clara had clearly had no desire to see him. Maybe his entire family had despised him through the generations. 'I see.'

Agnes gave a sob. 'Oh no, Mr Wyndham! Don't be downhearted. It's not what you think.'

'Well,' he said with a bitter laugh, 'clearly, it's exactly what I think. She has no more interest in me than James had. I was a fool to think otherwise. You know, for a moment there... Ah well.'

'No!' Agnes reached for his hand and clasped it tightly in hers. 'You mustn't think such things. I-I must explain. Clara was told...'

She put her hand to her mouth, shaking her head frantically.

'What?' Aubrey asked roughly. 'What was she told? Agnes! What was she told?'

'Oh, Mr Wyndham. I'm so sorry.' She released him from her grasp, no doubt due to the harsh tone of his voice. He felt a fleeting shame for that until she continued, 'She was told that you had no interest in seeing her and wanted her to stay well away from you and from the Hall.'

Aubrey put his head in his hands. Bad enough that he'd had family in the village all this time, but that Agnes and Lawrie had conspired to keep Clara from him and had lied not only to Aubrey, but to his granddaughter, too, was almost too much to bear. What must she think of him?

'You never did think much of my family, did you?' he said at last.

'I did not,' she admitted. 'But can you blame me? They were dreadful people. Liars, thieves, opportunists. They clung to the estate long after they should have left and would have remained if Ambrose Davenport hadn't bought them off. Even then, they stole from the Hall and took things that never belonged to them – no doubt to sell for a tidy profit.'

'And that's why you wanted to keep Clara and me apart?'

'Indeed. She came here despite knowing the rules. She admitted as much to Lawrie. What is that, if not deceitful? Wilful. Selfish. A sure sign that she had inherited the ways of James and your parents, if ever there was one. Bad blood will out, will it not, Mr Wyndham?'

Aubrey got to his feet and ran a hand through his hair, feeling sick with grief.

'All these years you have kept me here under false pretences,' he said, the pain searing through him as he realised the full depths of her deception. 'You have made decisions on my behalf. You have lied to me. You have lied to Clara. You have alienated us from each other. You have colluded with Lawrie to deceive me and my granddaughter. You have deprived me of getting to know her, and my great-grandchildren. You have made me worry and grieve for you, believing as I did that you were wounded by Silas Alexander's ramblings.'

He shook his head, bewildered at how blind he had been. 'In short, you have behaved despicably, and I have no words to express how disappointed I am in you.'

Agnes gave an anguished sob, but Aubrey made no attempt to comfort her. He paced up and down, trying to make sense of this new reality he found himself in: a reality where the woman he'd loved and trusted more than anyone he'd ever known had betrayed him so completely.

'Does Callie know about this?' he asked. 'You said she had made you see that you'd done me a grave injustice.'

'She does,' Agnes said, guiltily. 'Clara told her the truth and Callie sought me out. Oh, Mr Wyndham, she said some dreadful things to me and to Lawrie.'

'But she still didn't tell *me*?' Had even Callie betrayed him? He'd expect it of Lawrie, but *Callie*?

'She said she would discuss it with Brodie, and then she told me this morning that she couldn't in all conscience live with this, and that if *I* didn't tell you the truth *she* would, so—'

'So you were forced to come clean,' he said, feeling some relief that at least *someone* had been on his side. 'And if she hadn't given you that ultimatum?'

Agnes stared at him dumbly.

'Well,' he said heavily, 'I should not be surprised. Nothing is as I imagined it to be, and I cannot say I would expect you to behave any differently.'

'I did it for you,' Agnes wailed, grabbing his arm. 'You were always too good for that family! I couldn't let them get their claws into you again and hurt you.'

Aubrey shook off her hand. 'You forget yourself, Mrs Ashcroft. It wasn't your decision to make.'

Agnes sank back against the picnic table, and Aubrey was suddenly very glad he couldn't see her expression clearly. He didn't want to feel pity for her. He didn't want to feel obliged to tell her it was all right and he understood and everything she'd done could be forgiven.

It was bad enough that Lawrie had deceived him, but he knew Lawrie had always been on Agnes's side, no matter what. Look how they'd colluded to keep Mia and Florence apart. One would have thought they'd have learned from that mistake.

But no, they'd taken it upon themselves to play God yet again, and he wondered if he could ever forgive them for it.

He could hear Elspeth's voice in his head, telling him how stupid and gullible he was, and how pathetic and unmanly. He heard his mother mocking him, saying what a disappointment he'd turned out to be. His father's scornful declaration that he was no Wyndham, and that if only he'd never been born, they might have had the chance of a real son, who had the gift and would have saved the Harling Estate for them.

Now Lawrie and his own dear Agnes had humiliated him, and he felt the pain of that betrayal deeper than anything even his own parents and wife had inflicted upon him.

Without another word he headed back to the house, leaving Agnes alone in the garden.

He simply had nothing more to say to her.

27

As promised, Jack and I spent Sunday afternoon decorating the Christmas tree and hanging holly and mistletoe around the house, as well as attaching bunches of balloons to the ceiling because Freddie begged us to.

The boys contributed by hanging baubles on the tree, removing each other's baubles, arguing over which bauble should go on which branch, and sneaking chocolate coins into their mouths when they thought we weren't looking.

Toby, meanwhile, joined in by barking noisily and joyfully at the general melee before jumping on a balloon, which promptly exploded and frightened me so much it was a wonder I didn't go into labour.

The tacky and tasteless singing Snowman and the battery-draining dancing Santa, which we'd bought for Ash when he'd been even younger than Freddie was now, were on the mantelpiece, either side of the more dignified Nutcracker, and five stockings hung over the fireplace waiting for the big guy to stuff them on Christmas Eve.

'Just think,' Jack said, 'next Christmas there'll be six of them!'

'Probably just four,' I said wryly. 'I think Santa will be so broke trying to fill stockings for all the children in this house that he'll decide Mum and Dad can do without from now on.'

By some miracle there was still chocolate left in the advent calendars, but they were looking a bit ragged now, with most of their doors torn off in the frenzied excitement of getting to the treat behind them each morning.

On Monday, the two youngest boys finally took their Christmas cards into class for their respective postboxes. It was the last week of term but I felt quite pleased with myself because not only were the cards done, but I'd wrapped presents for their teachers, ready for them to take in on the last day of term, and I'd even remembered it was the school nativity play on Thursday and had drawn a big ring around the date on the calendar.

On Tuesday night Jack brought his costume home for the Dickensian weekend and tried it on for me after the kids had gone to bed.

'What do you think?' he asked, giving me a twirl.

'Very, er, nineteenth-century train driver,' I said helpfully.

'Very *sexy* nineteenth-century train driver?' he asked, waggling his eyebrows suggestively.

'Sexy isn't an adjective I'd use with nineteenth-century train driver,' I admitted.

'Charming.' He sat beside me on the sofa and put his arm around my shoulders. 'Shame you couldn't wear that dress you'd hired, love. I'll bet you'd have looked gorgeous in it.'

'I'd have looked like a sack of potatoes,' I assured him. 'To be honest, I'm very relieved not to be wearing it. Freddie's going to look adorable, though.'

We'd hired Freddie a cute little costume that would make him look like a small Oliver Twist. We could have got him one that would have made him look more like Little Lord Fauntleroy, but we had a feeling it wouldn't suit him half as much.

'Though really,' Jack mused, 'I can imagine him more as the Artful Dodger than Oliver, can't you?'

'It's a shame the other two wouldn't wear a costume,' I said wistfully. 'I'd love to have drawn them looking like little Victorian boys.'

'Drawn them?' Jack pulled away and gave me a hopeful look. 'You're drawing again?'

I shook my head. 'No, only *thinking* about it. I haven't actually tried it. I'm not sure I'd even know how to any more.'

'Why don't you try now?' he suggested. 'You could draw me in my sexy Victorian costume. I'll even pose for you.'

I laughed awkwardly. 'Sorry, but no. I'm just not ready yet.'

'Okay.' He didn't push me but cuddled up to me again. 'Hey, when you do decide to give it a try, you could draw Ash and Declan wearing Victorian clothes anyway. Who's to stop you?'

I grinned. 'Good idea. Though they'd be mortified if they found out.'

'Good. If they don't keep their rooms tidy, we can threaten to show the pictures to their classmates and tell them they modelled for them.'

'Blackmail!' I giggled at the thought of it.

'You can't deny it's a good idea.'

'No, I can't really.'

'Maybe we can buy you some new drawing and painting materials,' he said, 'now we're coming into money at last.'

I bit my lip, still not happy that he'd offered the model village to Callie and Brodie. We'd had quite the argument after they'd left, as I insisted it should remain in the family.

'It's our boys' heritage,' I'd pointed out. 'And the only thing we'll ever have to leave them.'

'Not if we get a good enough price for it,' Jack said reasonably. 'We can invest some cash for their futures. They'll thank us for it when they're old enough.'

'But it won't be a slice of Rowan Vale,' I'd argued. 'Don't you want them to have that, at least?'

Jack had shrugged. 'Not particularly. So long as the model village stays here and is maintained the way Grandad would have wanted, I don't mind that we won't own it any longer. My main concern is getting us out of debt. I need to take care of my family. The future can take care of itself.'

On Monday evening, Callie and Brodie had accepted his offer and terms had been agreed. I'd felt a sense of desolation that my last connection with the estate had been severed, even though I knew, deep down, that the model village had never really been mine anyway, any more than the estate had.

Even so, there was a part of me that wished our sons could have had that at least. Just a little piece of what their ancestors had once owned.

There was no point worrying about it now, though. Jack had agreed and the estate solicitors were drawing up a contract even now. I supposed at least it meant we could get everything we needed for the baby and pay off our credit card debts. Brodie had very kindly transferred some of the money into Jack's account in advance, as a favour, so we could buy a carrycot and a few supplies for the baby. I couldn't deny that was a huge weight off my mind, and Jack looked years younger overnight.

'I'm not spending any money on art materials just yet,' I said now. 'Let's not run before we can walk, eh? If anything, I need some things to pack for the hospital. I'd die of shame if I had to wear the pyjamas I've got now.'

'Fair enough.'

I yawned and rubbed my tummy, rewarded instantly with a sharp kick. 'Whoa!'

Jack's eyes widened. 'Baby?'

I nodded. 'I don't think he approves of our plan to trick his siblings.'

'He'd better get used to it. Are we making a start on wrapping the kids' presents tonight or do you want to leave it until tomorrow?'

'I know I should say tonight, but I honestly haven't got the energy.'

He squeezed my shoulders. 'Would you like a mug of cocoa, or will it send you to sleep?'

'At this point, I don't care if it does. I'm ready for an early night anyway. Cocoa would be lovely, thanks.'

'I'm on the case.' He jumped up and headed into the kitchen, and Toby scrambled up from his position in front of the fire to follow him.

'I think Toby needs to be let out,' I called, hearing Jack's muffled, 'Okay,' in response.

I leaned back and closed my eyes, wondering if I had the energy to stay awake even to drink the cocoa.

I yawned again, picking up my phone as I thought I heard a beep.

A message from Callie.

I tapped the screen and began to read, then my heart thumped.

> CALLIE
>
> Just to let yuo know Orbrey's been to see me and he nowes cos Agnuss apperentley came clene I was rite it wos'nt what Lory told you at all he did'nt nowe you wear heer and hes reely upset abuot the hole thing xx

I stared at the message for ages, reading it repeatedly, and not just because of Callie's spelling and punctuation. Aubrey hadn't known I was here? So, when Lawrie told me that Aubrey wanted nothing to do with me, he'd been lying? The whole time?

My fingers trembling, I managed to tap out a reply.

CLARA

Why? Why did Lawrie lie? xx

There was quite a gap before the reply came pinging back, but that wasn't surprising as I knew she was dyslexic and struggled to put down her thoughts in writing, which was why she usually rang me, rather than sent a text.

CALLIE

Long stroy I think heel explane. He reely wonts to see yuo Calra hees askt if it wood be okay for him to visit yuo I've side Ill check with yuo is it? xx

Was it? Everything I'd heard about my ancestor had been negative, but Callie seemed to really like him, and she'd insisted something wasn't right about the whole situation. Turns out, she'd been spot on. Maybe she was right about him, too?

Another beep.

CALLIE

No pressher heel totaly understand iff you do'nt wont to meet him xx

Would he? That didn't sound like the Aubrey I'd heard about. But after all these years, I owed it to him and to myself to find out what he was really like, didn't I? I couldn't deny, now that there was the real possibility I'd talk to him at last, I felt a thrill of excitement. It's not often you get the chance to meet your Victorian ancestor, is it?

And if the worst came to the worst and he was a total git I could always send him packing again. Couldn't I?

CLARA

Yes. Would love to meet him. Tomorrow afternoon okay? Say 1 p.m.? xx

There was an agonising wait of what felt like hours but was in fact no more than a minute. Then:

> **CALLIE**
> that wood be perfect hees looking forwood to it xx

I put the phone down and absently rubbed my stomach, as the enormity of what I'd just done hit me. Oh, my God! I was going to meet Aubrey Wyndham. What if he really was horrible? What if the stories about him were true and I'd invited a monster into my home?

The phone pinged again.

> **CALLIE**
> sorry Orbrey was with me so cuold'nt say anything before. Calra, give him a chance wont yuo this has reely noct him for six and hees such a sweethaert he reely is xx

I swallowed. It was as if she'd read my mind.

> **CLARA**
> Of course I will. Fingers crossed we like each other xx

Another ping.

> **CALLIE**
> Yule love aech other! Yuor both fabbuluss xx

Bless her. She was such a lovely friend. If Callie thought Aubrey was a sweetheart, then surely, I had nothing to worry about?

'What are you smiling at?'

I jumped as I realised Jack had come back into the room, carrying mugs of cocoa. My heart sank as it occurred to me that things had taken a decidedly risky turn.

If Aubrey was going to be a part of my life, Jack would have to know. I couldn't, in all conscience, keep lying to him. Nor did I want to lie to Aubrey or ask him to lie for me. What sort of start would that be to our relationship? If we were to have one.

With all the lies Aubrey and I had been told, I knew it was time to wipe the slate clean. Jack had to know the truth.

'You all right, love?' he asked, concerned. 'You were smiling a minute ago. Now you look as pale as a ghost.'

'Well,' I said, putting my cocoa on the coffee table and turning to him, my pulse racing, 'it's funny you should say that, Jack, cos there's something I've got to tell you.'

* * *

Jack sat very quiet and still as I told him the truth about my heritage and what had happened between myself and Lawrie all those years ago.

When I finally told him about the text messages I'd received from Callie, he shook his head slightly but didn't speak.

'So that's it. Now you know it all,' I said, my heart pounding as I finished explaining the situation to him.

He didn't reply, and I watched nervously as he stared bleakly into the fire.

'Jack, please say something,' I begged when the silence became unbearable.

'You're a Wyndham,' he said at last.

'Well, yes. Sort of.'

'No *sort of* about it as far as I can see. You said it yourself. You're a direct descendant of this Aubrey Wyndham who lives at the Hall.'

'Okay. Yes then. I *am* a Wyndham.'

'And you've always known that?'

I swallowed. 'I grew up hearing about Rowan Vale and how our family used to own this whole estate. It was sort of a bedtime story that my dad used to tell me when I was little.'

'But you never came here until you met me?'

'No, Jack, of course not! I knew better than to break the rules even if I didn't understand them.'

'But you came anyway,' he said flatly.

'In the end,' I said. 'I put it off for a whole year, remember?'

'Yeah, I remember.' He gave a short laugh and rubbed the back of his head. 'But even so. Bit of a coincidence meeting me in Scotland, right? That I came from Rowan Vale, of all places.'

I frowned. 'What's that supposed to mean? You surely don't think I conspired to meet you there? That's the most ridiculous theory ever. I was shocked when I heard where you were from. I had no idea.'

'I know, I know.' He shook his head. 'Just... I suppose I always wondered why, that's all. Why someone like you would hook up with someone like me.

Richard said it didn't make sense. Said I was punching. He thought you were after somewhere to live, with you losing your job and everything.'

'*Richard* said that?' I gasped. 'Richard who was the best man at our wedding? Bloody charming!' It was a good job the two-faced rat had moved to London over a decade ago or I'd have hunted him down and kicked his sorry arse.

'He changed his mind,' Jack said hastily. 'When you went back to Lancashire and found all those temping jobs, he had to admit he'd been wrong. Even so, you knew you were a Wyndham and you should never have risked coming here.'

'I know, and I tried to stay away,' I said. 'But our relationship got serious so what was I supposed to do? And anyway, it worked out fine, didn't it? I mean, the sky didn't fall in when I set foot on the estate, did it?'

'But it could have done! You didn't know that. None of us did. Anything could have happened, but you did it anyway, putting us all potentially at risk.'

'Are you seriously telling me that you'd have stopped me from coming here if you'd known I was a Wyndham?' I asked, laughing nervously. He couldn't possibly mean it. No one was that superstitious and Jack was as down-to-earth as they came.

'Yeah. Maybe. I don't know. The point is, I *didn't* know, did I? And *you* didn't know what would happen!'

'What *could* happen? You sound paranoid now.'

'This isn't any ordinary village, Clara. You, of all people, know that! With your family history, and the fact that your Victorian ancestor is coming here to meet you tomorrow, I'd have thought you'd have realised that the Harling Estate isn't like anywhere else. We have no idea why it's the way it is, and no clue what might happen if we mess with the rules. They must have been put there for a reason.'

'Yes! To stop the previous owners interfering with what the new owners do,' I cried. 'It's as simple as that. Even Callie thinks so.'

'Callie's been here five minutes so what does she know?' He gave me an anguished look. 'And while we're on that subject – how come she knew about all this, and I didn't? This is the second time you've told her something you've kept from me. First the baby and now the fact that you're a Wyndham. Is there anything else she knows that I'm not aware of?'

'Of course not! I wanted to tell you, Jack, really I did, but I was scared.'

'Of what? That night in the hotel. You lied to me. I told you I was from Rowan Vale and you never for a moment let on who you were. You pretended you'd vaguely heard of the place. Oh my God!'

He reared away from me, staring at me in disgust. 'It took me ages to pluck up the courage to tell you about the ghosts! I practised and practised, and agonised over how to break it to you in a way that wouldn't scare you off or make you think I was insane. I was so bloody terrified that you'd leave me.'

'I'm sorry,' I said miserably, my face burning as I remembered that awful afternoon.

'And at first you acted as if you were going to! You made out as if you thought I was playing a stupid game with you, then you asked me if I was on medication! You made me beg you to believe me!'

'I know,' I whispered. 'I'm so sorry, Jack. I had to play dumb, and I hated every minute of it, but I didn't know what else to do.'

'You could have told me the truth. At *any* point over the last sixteen years, you could have told me the truth. From that moment when I first said I came from Rowan Vale to the day you arrived here, to catching sight of Aubrey, to accepting my proposal, to having the kids—' He shook his head. 'Bloody hell! The kids! They're Wyndhams, too.'

'No. They're Milsoms. Jack, this doesn't have to be a bad thing, does it?' I begged. 'I know I should have told you before, but really – what does it matter? You know now. I couldn't tell you because Lawrie said—'

'Yeah, I'll be having words with *him*, too,' Jack said bitterly.

'But he said I had to keep it quiet from everyone or he wouldn't let me stay. I had no choice.'

'You did have a choice, Clara. You could have told me, and we'd have faced Lawrie together.'

'And what if he'd insisted I had to leave?'

'Then I'd have left with you!' Jack yelled. 'What the bloody hell did you think would happen? I loved you. Adored you. I'd have given up this place like that.' He snapped his fingers.

'But why should you?' I said tearfully. 'You love it here, and you love your job. I couldn't ask you to give all that up for me.'

'You didn't mind me giving up my job when you wanted me to run the model village with you, did you?'

'That's not fair...' Although, thinking about it, he had a point.

Jack sighed. 'You just don't get it, do you? We're a team, Clara. I thought we always were. We clicked from that first night in the hotel in Scotland, or so I thought. But you lied to me from the first and you've been lying to me ever since.'

'Once I'd started, I didn't know how to tell you the truth. And then when I finally came here and Lawrie blackmailed me... I just couldn't see a way out.'

'Is that why you wanted to hang on to the model village? In your own weird way did it make you feel as if you still had a piece of the Harling Estate? No wonder you kept banging on about wanting to keep it for the boys. No wonder you gave me so much grief the other night after Callie and Brodie left.'

'Because you offered to sell it without talking it over with me first!' I protested.

'And God forbid I should do anything without your say-so, eh, Clara? Only you're allowed to keep secrets and make unilateral decisions, right? Even massive ones like keeping me away from the scan.' He ran a hand through his hair, and I was horrified to see the gleam of tears in his eyes. 'Was even that a lie? Did you know you were pregnant the whole time?'

'Of course I didn't!'

'I'm not so sure. How can I believe anything you say now?'

'Why would I keep it a secret?' I asked incredulously.

'Who knows? Who knows why you do anything? Do *you*? Maybe I should ask Callie. She seems to know all your darkest secrets. I suppose even Brodie knew. Have they been laughing at me behind my back all this time?'

'Jack, you've got this all wrong,' I said, tears rolling down my face as I saw the unmistakeable pain in his eyes and heard the heartbreak in his voice. 'No one's laughing at you. Callie and Brodie think the world of you. Callie begged me to tell you about the baby, and Brodie knew nothing about it, I swear.'

'You swear? What's your word worth to me now, Clara?'

He got to his feet, shrugging me away as I reached for his arm.

'Where are you going?' I sobbed.

'To take Toby for a walk,' he said. 'I need to think. While I'm gone, please go to bed. I'll sleep down here tonight and be out of the way by five-thirty. No need for you to get up. In fact, I'd really appreciate it if you stayed out of my way completely.'

'Jack, please—'

'I can't, Clara.' He turned to face me, and I gave a smothered gasp as I saw his face, wet with tears. Jack never cried. He'd got a bit emotional on our wedding day, and his eyes had shone with tears of pride and joy when the boys were born, but I'd never seen any tears escape to roll down his cheeks before.

I'd never seen that anguished look in his eyes or heard the desperate sadness in his voice.

'I just can't. I thought we told each other everything. I thought we shared it all. All this time you were a Wyndham. You shouldn't have been in this village at all. You didn't tell me who you were when I told you I came from here. You didn't explain why you kept saying no every time I invited you to stay with me. You kept quiet when Lawrie blackmailed you instead of coming clean and letting us face it together. You didn't even tell me when you realised you were pregnant again. Your first thought was to keep it a secret from me and confide in Callie. What does that say about us? What does it say about the state of our relationship? How can I ever believe in you – in us – again?'

He patted his leg and Toby, who'd been watching us both with a puzzled expression on his face got up immediately and loped over to his side.

'Your lucky night, boy,' Jack said bleakly. 'Extra walk. Let's fetch that lead, shall we?'

I didn't say anything to stop him because I knew he wouldn't change his mind, and I had nothing to bargain with. No defence for what I'd done.

Whatever happened next, it was on me, and if Jack chose to leave...

I covered my hand with my mouth as I let out a terrified sob. I loved him so much! What would I ever do without him?

28

I was in two minds whether to call Callie and ask her to cancel my meeting with Aubrey. The last thing I felt like right now was a family reunion – particularly one that had caused so much trouble before it even took place.

I'd done as Jack had asked the previous evening and made myself scarce before he got home, but I'd barely slept a wink all night. I'd heard him moving about downstairs early this morning and had longed to make him his breakfast as I usually did, but I didn't dare face him in case I saw a look of contempt in his eyes.

Maybe, I thought hopefully, he just needs some time. Maybe.

I'd got the boys ready for school and dropped the two youngest off before heading straight home to tidy the house, hoover up the dog hairs, and try to make myself presentable – not easy given my swollen eyelids and the dark shadows under my eyes.

'What am I even doing?' I murmured as I gazed into the mirror, mascara wand in hand. 'I'm tarting myself up to impress a ghost! Bloody hell. I can't even remember the last time I tried to impress Jack.'

And it was true. It had been months since I'd last worn make-up or made any real attempt to look nice. We hadn't been to the pub quiz at The Quicken Tree for weeks, but even when we had gone, I'd done nothing more than run a comb through my hair.

I'd not only let myself go, but I'd also let the romance in our relationship die. Life had become all about getting through the day: looking after the kids, cooking, cleaning, washing clothes, shopping, ironing, the school run, working out budgets, worrying about the bills...

If Jack decided he wanted out of this marriage, who could blame him?

I made myself a sandwich for lunch but barely touched it. I was worried sick about Jack, and nervous as hell about meeting Aubrey.

If he gave me any trouble, I decided, I'd send him packing. I'd get Amelia to perform an exorcism if I had to. I had enough to deal with without a bullying ancestor who'd died nearly a hundred and fifty years ago.

I was just refilling Toby's water bowl when I heard an embarrassed, 'Ahem' behind me.

I dropped the bowl in the sink and spun round in shock, which didn't lessen when I saw I'd been joined by a distinguished-looking man in Victorian clothing. I'd never seen him close up before and was surprised how young he looked. He couldn't have been much older than Jack really.

'I'm terribly sorry,' he said. 'I did knock but you didn't hear me. Well, I say knock. I stood on the step and called, 'Knock knock,' because there's not much else I can do, you see. But I did call out quite loudly. Anyway, you were in the kitchen, clearly, so wouldn't have heard me.'

My first thought was how polite and gentle his voice was. My second thought was even more surprising: Aubrey was nervous. Maybe even more nervous than I was.

'Is it inconvenient?' he asked, shuffling from one foot to the other. 'If it is, I can come back another time.'

I found my voice at last. 'Sorry. I mean, no, it's not inconvenient. I was just getting some fresh water for Toby.'

'Toby?'

'Our dog.' I realised he was still in the garden and opened the door to let him in. He came loping in as usual, but to my surprise he stopped suddenly and growled quite menacingly.

'Don't worry,' Aubrey said. 'Animals usually react that way the first time they meet ghosts. Once they're used to them, they settle down quite well. It's just understanding what we are, I suppose.'

Toby padded over to Aubrey and walked around him, sniffing the air as if trying to catch a scent that would give him some sort of explanation for who or what this person was.

'Good boy,' Aubrey said kindly. He looked over at me, smiling. 'Handsome chap, isn't he? What sort of dog is he?'

'A-a Bernese mountain dog,' I said weakly, filling Toby's water bowl and putting it down on the floor for him. He ignored it completely, still focused on Aubrey.

'Really? We always had Labradors and spaniels. For the shooting really.' Aubrey straightened suddenly, looking horrified. 'I'm so sorry. I haven't even introduced myself! I'm Aubrey Wyndham, your... Well, you know who I am, I expect.'

'My great-great-great-great-grandfather,' I said.

'That's an awfully long title,' he mused. 'Perhaps plain old grandfather would be better.' His eyes widened in horror. 'Not,' he added hastily, 'that I'm expecting you to call me Grandfather! Good heavens, no. I wouldn't dream of making such an assumption. I do realise I'm nothing to you whatsoever, and—'

'I'm Clara,' I said, deciding he'd suffered enough. 'Clara Milsom. And I guess, in that case, I'm your granddaughter.'

Aubrey stared dumbly at me for what felt like forever.

Toby gave one final, fruitless sniff and seemed to decide that this strange man was no threat to our safety. He lolloped over to the water bowl and began to show me up by drinking loudly and messily, water slopping over the sides of the bowl and all over the floor as usual.

I cleared my throat and gave Aubrey an apologetic smile. 'I'd love to offer you a drink but obviously...'

He blinked, pulling himself together. 'Think nothing of it. But please, don't feel you have to deprive yourself. I don't mind. I'm used to people eating and drinking around me.'

'Doesn't it bother you?' I asked, pouring myself a glass of fresh orange juice with shaking hands.

'Sometimes,' he admitted, 'but one gets used to it. There really isn't much choice, is there?'

'I guess not. Would you like to come through to the living room? We'll leave that messy creature to his own devices for a while.'

Aubrey followed me into the living room and waited until I'd sat down in an armchair before sitting down in the other.

We gazed awkwardly at each other.

'I, er, I understand that you saw me in the village when you first came here,' he said at last. 'I just wanted to say...' He shook his head, looking ashamed. 'Clara, I'm terribly sorry for what happened. I promise you; I had no idea you were here. What Lawrie and Agnes did to you – to us – was unforgivable.'

'Agnes? Is she your – I mean, that's the Regency lady from the Hall, right? Lawrie said she'd seen me watching you and had told him I must be related to you. I don't get it. I sort of understand why Lawrie was wary of a Wyndham returning to the village, but what did Agnes have to do with it? Why wouldn't she want me to see you?'

He looked uncomfortable. 'Agnes... She had her reasons, I suppose. The main thing now is that we know about each other, and I would really like, if you feel the same of course, to start afresh. Believe me, if I *had* known I would never have told you to stay away from me. Why, to meet a descendant of mine is a dream come true. I never thought to see the day.'

'Even knowing there was a chance that I'd bring catastrophe to the estate?' I asked. 'That's what I've always been told, ever since I was a little girl. "Wyndhams cannot return to Rowan Vale". It was practically the family mantra.'

'Yes, I know,' he said, shrugging his shoulders slightly. 'Yet here we are, none the worse for wear. I really don't think it's a curse, or anything like that, you know. I believe it was just to ensure that the changeover happened smoothly, with no interference from the previous owners of the estate. Well, you've been here fifteen years, after all, and nothing's happened, has it? I should imagine we're safe now.'

He smiled, and I thought how different he was to what I'd expected. Callie had told me he was a sweetheart, but I hadn't really believed it, even though I'd wanted to.

In our family, we'd always been told that Aubrey had been a stern, unemotional man, with no interest in his family. He didn't strike me that way at all. Unless he'd changed. I supposed he'd had plenty of time to do that.

'So, tell me,' he said, 'if you wouldn't mind, that is, who your parents were. Are you a descendant of mine through your father's or your mother's line?'

'My father's,' I said. 'Hang on.' I hurried over to the sideboard and pulled out the family tree I'd quickly mapped out that morning, showing only my dad's side. He'd been obsessed with his ancestry – joining various genealogy sites to keep track of it all – and had drummed the Wyndham line into my memory.

I put the piece of paper on the coffee table for Aubrey to see. 'That's my dad, there. He was born in 1959. Then the line runs upwards from his mother to her father, to his mother, and then to her father, who was James, your son, born 1846.'

Aubrey stared at the line, his eyes wide. 'How marvellous. Thank you for this. All these people, descended from me. It's incredible.' He swallowed. 'And James? What sort of life did he have? Did he marry Frances Croft?'

'Who?' I wrinkled my nose, trying to remember the name.

'She was his fiancée when I – passed. One of the Hampshire Crofts.'

'No, her name doesn't ring a bell. My great-great-great-grandmother was called Ellen. She came from Ireland.'

'*Ireland*?' Aubrey's eyebrows shot up in surprise. 'James married an Irish girl? Good lord.'

'We think that's where the red hair comes from.' I grinned. 'He was a lot older than her, though. According to the census returns my dad had, she was eighteen years younger than him.'

'The census returns?'

'Yeah, my dad was really keen on genealogy. He made a family tree online. Got the birth, marriage, and death certificates, printed off the census returns, parish records, all that sort of thing.'

I still had most of them, locked away in an old suitcase in the loft. I'd told Jack it contained old art magazines that I wanted to hang on to. Another lie.

'Ellen was twenty-one when she married James. He was thirty-nine.'

'Thirty-nine? He waited a long time to marry then,' Aubrey mused. 'I wonder why.'

'Probably just hadn't met the right girl,' I said.

I barely knew Aubrey, but a few minutes in his company had already convinced me that it would be cruel to tell him the truth about his son. James had been in prison for theft and embezzlement and had married Ellen six months after his release.

She'd been a neighbour of his mother's. Elspeth, it seemed, had fallen on hard times since leaving the estate, as, according to the 1881 census, she'd lived in a terraced house in Manchester and took in lodgers to make ends meet.

I wasn't sure James and Ellen had ever been a love match either, as their daughter had arrived just four months after the wedding, so it might have been forced upon them. Looking at this gentleman sitting in my living room, I had a feeling he wasn't ready to hear such things.

The story had always been that James was a bit of a rat, but the blame for that had been put squarely on the fact that he'd been so badly treated by his father. Somehow, I had a feeling that the truth had been buried along the way. I decided to be gentle with this man.

'They were very happy,' I told him. 'And I remember their great-granddaughter, my grandma a bit. She seemed lovely. Sadly, she passed away when I was four.'

'And your parents?'

I bit my lip, aware that this was turning into a tale of woe.

'Both gone,' I said briefly. 'It's just me now.'

'I'm so sorry,' he said kindly.

'Thank you.' I took a sip of orange juice. 'Anyway, I have Jack.' *For now.* 'And I have three children.' I patted my stomach. 'And one on the way.'

His face brightened. 'You're expecting a baby? How wonderful! You know, I saw two of your boys in the street on Thursday. Red hair, like yours. One of them waved at me. It was quite apparent that he could see me.'

'One of the boys saw you?' I gasped.

'Yes. Little chap, about five or six years old. The other one was distracted. He had some sort of device in his hands. Perhaps a pocket telephone.'

'They don't have mobile phones,' I said. 'It must have been his Switch. Little bugger must have sneaked it into school. I'll be having words with him.'

'Oh dear. I didn't mean to cause any trouble,' he said anxiously.

There was something so innocent about him that I couldn't help wanting to reassure him. 'You haven't. Don't worry. It's not really that big a deal.'

'I don't suppose...' Aubrey hesitated. 'These documents your father collected. I don't suppose there was anything about me? I mean, did – did you know about me?' He gave a nervous laugh. 'Or had I been forgotten about entirely?'

I couldn't hurt him. Those gentle navy-blue eyes of his made me want to protect him somehow.

'Only your birth, marriage, and death certificates,' I said, 'and the brief mentions in the census returns. But Dad said he'd heard you were a gentleman, and someone to be proud of.'

His eyes shone as he beamed at me. 'Really? Ah, well, that's – that's excellent. I mean, I don't know about 'someone to be proud of', but anyway... Wonderful. And my wife, Elspeth? What became of her?'

After James went to prison, she moved to a pretty dodgy address, took in the sort of lodgers she'd once have turned up her nose at, and died of tuberculosis aged sixty-one.

'Lived to a ripe old age and died peacefully in her sleep,' I said.

'I'm very glad about that,' he said softly. 'It's a great relief to me. I've worried you see. Over the years.'

I had no idea where the stories about Aubrey had started, but I was no longer in any doubt that Callie was right about him. He *was* a sweetheart, and I already liked him a lot.

'When is your little one due, if you don't mind me asking?' he said.

'January.'

'You must be so excited.'

'Well, it was a bit of a shock to be honest. We've only just found out ourselves, and there's a lot to do before he arrives. But we've got to get Christmas over with first. With three boys that's a major production in itself.'

'Ah yes.' He laughed. 'I can imagine.' He glanced around, admiring the Christmas tree and eyeing the balloons that were pinned up on the ceiling in rather suggestive bunches of three, thanks to Jack's juvenile sense of humour. 'Very festive.'

'Hmm.'

We sat in silence for a few moments while I racked my brains trying to figure out something else to say. I really wanted to ask him more about Agnes, and why she'd interfered in our business, but I had a feeling he didn't want to discuss it, and I wasn't going to nag him.

'I understand you're selling the model village,' he said suddenly, 'and it's being moved to the grounds of the Hall.'

'That's right,' I said. 'We wanted to open it up to the public, but unfortunately, we just don't have the space to accommodate paying visitors here, so Jack decided it would be better to hand it over to Callie. I expect you've seen it, haven't you?'

'Oh yes. When it was completed, there was a grand opening for the villagers, and we all popped along to have a look. There's a little model of me at the Hall, you know. Doesn't look much like me, but then none of the ghosts look truly accurate. How can they? The craftsmen only had Sir Edward's description of us to go by, and maybe the odd photograph or portrait of some of us. Sadly, my portrait was only rediscovered fairly recently, so...'

'I've seen a portrait of you when you were very young,' I said.

He stared at me in amazement. 'You have?'

'A miniature portrait of you and your wife. You looked to be in your twenties.'

He thought for a moment then nodded. 'That,' he said heavily, 'would have been our engagement portrait.'

He didn't sound as if the engagement held any happy memories, so I didn't push it.

'Sadly, we don't have it any longer,' I admitted. 'When Dad died, we had to pack up his belongings quickly, and I think the portrait got put into the wrong bag. I think it must have gone to the charity shop. I'm so sorry.'

He shook his head. 'It really doesn't matter. Don't give it another thought.'

'Would you like another tour of the model village?' I suggested.

'May I? That would be most agreeable.'

'Of course.' I was glad to have something to do, and led him back through the kitchen, where Toby eyed him with interest but made no attempt to growl at him, then through the back door into the garden.

I opened the paddock gate and together we walked into the miniature world of the Harling Estate, complete with a scale replica of Rowan Vale, the woodland, the parkland, and even The Wyrd Stones.

'This is incredible,' Aubrey said. 'I'd quite forgotten how well-built this is. Ah, and look! There's that Roman chap, Quintus Severus! They'll have to reposition him, you know. He no longer spends all his time at the stones. For some reason, he's moved into the village. I was hoping to catch a glimpse of him on my way here today, but no such luck.' He gave a hoot of laughter. 'And look! There's old Walter Tasker, bowing as usual.'

'Wasn't he Shakespeare's teacher? Or is that just something people say?'

'Oh no! It's quite true. Of course, that has given Walter a few ideas above his station, but his heart's in the right place. So to speak.' He smiled and peered down at another figure. 'And that's Peter the baker. Oh, and there's Isaac Grace. He was the landlord at The Quicken Tree Inn, you know. Oh, it is good to see them all here. I've not spoken to them in years. Although, clearly, some are missing.'

'Callie's talking about putting models of the more recent ghosts in place,' I told him. 'Did she mention it?'

'Not to me,' he said. 'You mean, there might be a model of Florence?' He turned to face me. 'Florence is my daughter. Well...'

'I know,' I said quickly. 'I know all about Florence.'

Didn't I just! I'd had Callie ranting on about her enough times when she'd first moved here, though lately it seemed the little wartime evacuee had settled down and was much easier to live with these days.

I knew Aubrey and Agnes adored her and treated her just like their own child. It was quite sweet really.

'There you are,' I said, pointing to the two figures standing outside the Hall. 'You and Agnes.'

'Yes.' He stared down at them, seeming lost in thought. 'Indeed.'

It was so cold that I shivered, and he noticed immediately.

'Good heavens, you shouldn't be out here in this weather, especially in your condition! Let's get inside immediately. I'm so sorry, I didn't think. I don't feel it, you see. The cold. Or the sunshine. Or – or anything in the physical realm.'

We headed inside, and I huddled by the fire, glad to feel the warmth on my skin again.

'Perhaps, now that we've become acquainted,' Aubrey said cautiously, 'you would like to visit me at the Hall? It would be good to get to know you a little better. Only if you'd like to, of course.'

'I think I'd like to very much,' I told him, with barely a moment's consideration. 'But how will Agnes feel about that? She didn't want me near you, did she?'

'No.' For the first time Aubrey's face took on a grim expression. 'No, she didn't. But that shouldn't stop us from becoming better acquainted. After all, Harling Hall was once your family home, too. And I would love it if you could bring the boys. And Jack, too, of course.'

'I'll – I'll talk it over with them and let you know,' I said, not wanting to admit that, right now, the chances of discussing anything to do with my heritage with Jack were zero.

'I've seen Jack a few times,' he told me. 'He's been to the Hall on occasion. He used to drive Lawrie around, didn't he? I believe he drives the steam engine.'

'He does,' I said. 'He loves it.'

'So you're happy, Clara? You seem to have built a very pleasant life here with a good husband and your children.'

'Yes, of course,' I said, not wanting to burst his bubble. 'Very happy.'

'I'm so glad.'

'And you? I know it must be hard for you, being a ghost and everything. But you've got your lovely home, and people to talk to, and Florence, and Agnes of course. You're happy?'

Aubrey gave me a wide smile. 'Me? Of course. Very happy. Everything's wonderful.'

'Well,' I said, valiantly attempting to sound cheerful, 'aren't we the lucky ones?'

'We are,' he agreed. 'Very lucky indeed.'

29

AUBREY

Aubrey had mixed feelings as he walked slowly back to Harling Hall. He had thoroughly enjoyed meeting his 'granddaughter' Clara and had been overwhelmed by the kindness and generosity she'd shown him, especially after she'd been given to believe he wanted nothing to do with her.

Hearing that his wife and son had been happy, and that Aubrey himself was thought of as 'someone to be proud of', filled him with joy, as he'd been convinced he would be remembered with scorn, if at all.

But he had a niggling feeling that all wasn't well with Clara. Oh, she'd been lovely to him – far nicer than he'd dared to imagine – but beneath the smiles he was certain there was a deep unhappiness there. She'd put on a good show for him. He recognised it because he'd put on quite a show for her. Frankly, neither of their declarations of happiness had been convincing.

He mentally shook his head, wondering what to do about the situation with Agnes. He couldn't deny that he missed her terribly, even though it had only been a couple of days since their discussion in the garden. He'd done his utmost to avoid her in the Hall, and when he'd been unfortunate enough to meet her in the hallway or on the landing, he'd merely averted his gaze and passed by.

He simply couldn't believe she'd deliberately kept him away from Clara and the boys all these years. That she'd lied to him, blamed Silas, kept them prisoner at Harling Hall, spoiled events for Florence like the 1940s weekend and the

Christmas lights switch-on by making sure she never had her parents with her, and had conspired with Lawrie behind his back, judging her own opinion to be far more important than his own.

She'd had no right! She'd pointed out that James had been a rogue. Well, he'd never denied it and yes, it did fill him with shame. But the man had come good in the end, hadn't he? Besides, just because James had been somewhat ungentlemanly at times, that didn't mean Clara was cut from the same cloth.

Agnes had condemned Clara for coming to Rowan Vale, even though she'd been aware of the rules. But was what Clara had done anywhere near as bad as what Agnes – with Lawrie's aid – had done? Aubrey didn't think so, and it hurt him deeply to think the woman he loved had been so duplicitous.

'It's like she didn't care about my feelings at all,' he murmured despondently to himself as he strode through the gates and up the drive to the Hall. 'As if they never mattered to her or weren't as important as her own.'

He wasn't sure what he was going to do with himself this evening. He didn't want to go up to their suite because he didn't want to be with Agnes. On the other hand, he didn't want to abandon Florence. Maybe he'd see if their daughter would like to take a stroll around the grounds.

He straightened, jutting his chin out in defiance.

Or maybe, he thought suddenly, he would ask her if she would like to accompany him to the market. He would love to see it in the evening light, with all the illuminations glowing against the dark sky.

He'd seen it as he'd left Clara's, glancing longingly across the river at the green, where crowds of people were seemingly having a wonderful time, and snatches of 'The First Nowell' drifted over to him on the sharp December wind.

He imagined walking between those sweet little huts, smelling the delicious food that Florence had told him about, her little hand in his.

Of course, it would upset Agnes dreadfully, but should he even consider that, given what she'd done?

His posture slumped as he realised that, whether it should be a consideration or not, he knew it would be. He simply couldn't bring himself to hurt her like that. Wretched woman had a grip on his heart that he couldn't shrug off so easily.

Well, he'd have to work on that.

His eyes widened as Callie hurried towards him the moment he walked through the front door. She looked quite anxious.

'How did it go with Clara?' she whispered.

He nodded. 'Very well, I thought. She's a lovely young woman, Callie. I feel terribly proud of her.'

She smiled. 'I knew you two would get on,' she whispered.

'Are we hiding from someone?' he whispered back, for what reason he couldn't imagine.

'Jack's just arrived,' she told him, pulling a face that told him this wasn't good news. 'He's come to tear a strip off Lawrie for what he did to Clara all those years ago.'

'Has he, by Jove?' Aubrey said grimly. 'Well, I'd like to be in on this conversation. Excuse me, Callie.'

'But, Aubrey—'

For once, though, Aubrey paid her no heed. He marched through the closed door of Lawrie's sitting room and glared at his former friend.

Lawrie was sitting in his favourite armchair by the fire, listening quietly as Jack – who was perched on the sofa – told him exactly what he thought of him for playing such a dirty trick on his wife.

'You had no right to do it! And to keep it from me all this time! How could you do that?'

'Exactly,' Aubrey said, nodding his head furiously as he sat beside an oblivious Jack. 'Terrible way to behave. Appalling.'

'Oh, don't you start,' Lawrie said wearily.

'Pardon?' Jack snapped.

'We have a visitor, Jack,' Lawrie explained. 'Aubrey's here now.'

'Aubrey?' Jack glanced around him. 'He is? Well, I should like to know what he thinks of this business.'

'Very much the same as you, I should think,' Lawrie admitted. 'Look, I don't know what else I can say. I've already apologised to you—'

'You haven't apologised to *me*!' Aubrey said indignantly.

'No, Aubrey, I haven't, but I do so now unreservedly. I *am* sorry, Aubrey. I'm sorry, Jack. I did what I thought was right at the time and I got it wrong. Hopefully now it's all out in the open we can put it behind us.'

'Put it behind us?' Jack asked incredulously. 'Have you any idea how much damage has been caused?'

'Quite so,' Aubrey agreed. 'Your actions have caused utter devastation.'

'Because of you and that interfering old woman—'

'Pardon?' Aubrey said, shocked. He gave an unseeing Jack a fierce glare. 'Are you referring to Agnes?'

'—my marriage is hanging by a thread!'

'What?' Both Lawrie and Aubrey chorused the word, then looked at each other.

'You can't mean that,' Lawrie said.

'Of course I mean it. How do you think I feel, eh? Turns out the woman I loved and trusted more than anyone in the world has lied to me ever since the day we met. What sort of future does that give us? Right now, I can't see a way forward for us.'

'What a disgraceful thing to say!' Aubrey gasped.

'A trifle overdramatic, perhaps?' Lawrie asked mildly. 'You two have been married for how long now? Fourteen years, isn't it? I'm quite sure you have a perfectly wonderful future ahead of you. After all, nothing's actually changed. You just know a few more facts than you did before.'

Jack glared at him. 'A few more facts? You mean like the fact that she's a Wyndham, that she came here when she should never have risked it, and that she didn't breathe a word about it until she was forced to because Callie found out and decided Aubrey had a right to know. Or do you mean the fact that she can't be trusted? Because that's pretty clear.'

'Poppycock!' snapped Aubrey.

'What a ridiculous thing to say,' Lawrie said. 'You're married. You have three sons together. You've built a life at Honeywell House. She's loved you and supported you in your career. Are you saying all that means nothing because she kept one tiny detail from you?'

Aubrey nodded. 'Quite so.'

'And *you're* no better,' Lawrie told him. 'The way you've treated poor Agnes is shocking. I thought better of you than that, Aubrey.'

Aubrey gaped at him. 'I beg your pardon?'

'It's not my pardon you should be begging. It's Agnes's. Talking to her the way you did, just because she made a mistake.'

'A mistake?' Aubrey gasped. 'She lied to me and deceived me for fifteen years! She—'

'Yes, yes.' Lawrie waved his hand impatiently, dismissing Aubrey's protests. 'We know what she did. We *all* know what she did. Terrible Clara. Terrible Agnes. Poor, wounded Jack. Poor, wounded Aubrey. Pah!'

Both men stared at him with shocked expressions.

'Don't look like that!' Lawrie chuckled. 'You look like twins. You have identical expressions on your faces.'

Aubrey cast a sneaky look at Jack, but Jack was now looking suspiciously around him, as if wondering exactly where this ghost was lurking.

'The only thing that's been hurt is your pride,' Lawrie continued. 'You've both been deceived and you feel foolish. Neither of you seem to have given any consideration to how terrible your wives must feel.'

Aubrey opened his mouth to speak but found he had no words. Jack's mouth tightened but he said nothing.

'Clara didn't tell you about our conversation because I warned her that if she didn't keep her connection to the Wyndhams a secret, I would be forced to ask her to leave. I thought it was for the best. After all, we all know the rule in this village, don't we?'

'Yes,' Jack said, having recovered his voice. 'We do. And the point is, so did she! And yet she still came to Rowan Vale, knowing what she might be risking. Knowing that it could bring catastrophe to the estate.'

'But it didn't, did it?' Lawrie said with a shrug. 'All those dire warnings came to nothing. And how can I blame Clara for ignoring that rule to suit herself when I did the same thing? I should have left here when I sold the estate to Callie, but I couldn't bring myself to go. I stayed. I allowed my grandson to stay. How is what I did acceptable to you, yet what your own wife did is not?'

'He's got a point there,' Aubrey grumbled. 'And you should think about your children. You can't possibly be considering ending your marriage when you have three boys and another child due in January.'

'Clara's expecting?' Lawrie asked, delighted. 'How lovely. A new baby in Rowan Vale.'

'How did you know?' Jack sighed and rubbed the back of his head. 'Let me guess. A little ghost told you.'

'Her *grandfather* told him actually,' Aubrey said sternly. 'She and I had quite the family reunion today, and we got on splendidly. She's a fine girl. Too good for the likes of you, you callous brute.'

'Aubrey and Clara have met,' Lawrie told Jack. 'They got on very well, it seems.'

'Bully for them,' Jack said grumpily.

'Clara disobeyed the rule she'd kept all her life until that point, because she wanted to be with you,' Lawrie told him. 'Yes, no doubt her desire to see Rowan Vale was a strong one, but would she have risked it if not for you? I find it hard to believe, considering she'd resisted temptation until that point.

'Besides, it was so long ago now. The fact is, she *stayed* here because of you. She stayed even when I'd made it very clear that Aubrey wanted nothing to do with her, and she wouldn't be welcome at the Hall, and that she was to say nothing of her heritage to anyone. Despite all that, she remained here, *because of you*. Because she loves you.'

'Loves me!' Jack snorted. 'Yeah, right.'

'Oh, Jack! Forget your wounded pride and think about it. It must have been quite uncomfortable for her, knowing I didn't want her here. She could easily have left and put it all behind her. If you think she stayed for any reason other than that she loved you, you're a fool.'

'Absolutely,' Aubrey said, nodding vehemently. 'The girl has given you three fine sons, for goodness' sake. There may be another one soon, or a little daughter. You don't know you're born!'

Wasn't that the truth! Some people were never satisfied, he thought ruefully. His own marriage to Elspeth had been seriously lacking in physical affection. She'd done her duty but once James had arrived, she'd put a stop to all that. He'd hoped they could build a loving, tender relationship, with true affection and physical passion, but she'd refused to try. It was quite clear that Jack and Clara's marriage was a very different thing to his own.

'You're right, Aubrey,' Lawrie said. 'Would Clara have married you, Jack, had three children, given up her job, her life, to stay here and play house with you if she didn't love you?'

Jack hung his head. 'But she kept a secret from me all this time, when I thought we were a partnership. I thought we told each other everything. It hurts,' he mumbled.

'I'm sure it does, but you're a big boy. Clara's got enough to deal with, and if you don't mind me saying so, you've treated her poorly. She clearly loves you, or she wouldn't have had a family with you. Didn't you once tell me that she gets up at the crack of dawn with you every single morning to make you breakfast before you go to work?'

Jack sighed. 'Yeah, she does. And sometimes I open my packed lunch box and there's a little note in there telling me how much she loves me.'

'Oh, for heaven's sake!' Aubrey threw up his arms and appealed to Lawrie. 'How much more proof does he need? The man's a moron!'

'All right, Aubrey. Easy for you to criticise. What about your own part in all this, eh?'

'What part?' Aubrey demanded. 'I've done nothing wrong.'

'Perhaps you wouldn't say that if you'd seen the state of Agnes this morning. The poor woman is distraught.'

'She is?' Aubrey's voice was suddenly very small.

'Heartbroken. Terrified. She thinks you're going to leave her and move in with Clara.'

Jack looked horrified. 'He's not, is he?'

'Of course I'm not!' Aubrey said. 'Why on earth would she think such a thing?'

'Well, why do you think?' Lawrie said, shaking his head reassuringly at Jack. 'For goodness' sake, man! You know how she kept Mia away from Florence because she was terrified Florence wouldn't need her any more. How do you think she felt when she discovered you had a living and breathing family member of your own here in the village? She knows how desperately sad you've always been that you had no relationship with your son. She was afraid Clara would step into his shoes.'

'That makes no sense,' Aubrey said. 'Clara is my granddaughter... of sorts... and I'm very happy to meet her, and yes, I'd love for her and the children to be a part of my afterlife, but Agnes is my – well, wife. She and Florence are everything to me!' He stared guiltily at Lawrie. 'Everything.'

Why hadn't he realised? Of course this wasn't about James being a thief and Agnes worrying about bad blood! This was about what it was always about: Agnes's insecurities and her fear of being abandoned for someone else. He knew that much about her. He'd always known. Why had he chosen to forget that?

And he'd called her Mrs Ashcroft!

The shame burned through him. To treat poor Agnes in such a way when she'd done nothing but love him all these years and had given him a home and family that he'd never dreamed he'd have. He'd just criticised Jack for his behaviour towards Clara, but he'd been just as cruel to Agnes.

'She shouldn't have kept this from you,' Lawrie was saying. 'And I totally understand why you're so angry. But you couldn't feel any worse about this than she does, believe me. If you abandon her, Aubrey, I really dread to think how she'll take it.'

'Abandon her?' Aubrey could hardly believe what he was hearing. 'I would *never* do that. How could she even think it? How could *you*?'

'I've been an idiot,' Jack said miserably. 'Clara's my world. Her and the boys. You're right. I felt stupid and used. I didn't stop to look at it from her point of view. I just felt gutted that she'd kept stuff from me, and it made me feel insecure about us – especially with all the stress we've been under lately. How am I ever going to put this right?'

'I'm sure she'll forgive you, though if I were you, I'd grovel to Olympic standard,' Lawrie advised.

'Oh, God! I've been an absolute numpty,' Jack groaned. He got to his feet. 'I've got to go home and tell her how sorry I am. Mind you,' he added, 'this doesn't let you off the hook, Lawrie. I still think what you did to Clara was disgusting, and I'm still annoyed that you kept quiet all this time. And I think you should apologise to her in person, too.'

'Clearly,' Lawrie said ruefully, 'Clara is more forgiving than her husband. But you're right, I *will* apologise to her. Despite what I did to her, she has always been terribly friendly to me. More so than I deserve, no doubt.'

'No doubt,' Jack agreed grimly. 'Right, I'm going home. I've got a lot of fences to mend.'

Lawrie nodded. 'And where are you going?' he asked Aubrey, who had also got to his feet. 'Upstairs to your suite to make it up with Agnes, I hope.'

'No,' Aubrey said. 'As a matter of fact, I'm not. I have other business first.'

'You're going out?'

Lawrie frowned, but Aubrey wasn't about to reveal anything else. Jack opened the door, and Aubrey and he stood for a moment in the hallway, absorbing everything that had just happened.

'I feel like a kid who's just been to see the headmaster,' Jack said with a sigh.

Aubrey shuddered, remembering many such scenarios with horror. Lord, he'd hated boarding school!

'Well, I guess I'd better go home and hope I can put this right,' Jack said. He glanced around unseeingly. 'I *do* love her, you know. I *will* fix this.'

'I'm sure you will,' Aubrey soothed. 'I know you're not a bad man and – oh!'

Jack was already heading briskly towards the front door.

Aubrey sighed and looked up the stairs, wondering what Agnes was doing now. He quickly followed Jack outside and strode purposefully down the drive, determined to do what he must to rescue this situation and save his relationship with the woman he loved.

As he reached the gates, just behind Jack, he stopped and glanced up at the drawing room window on the first floor. As he'd suspected, Agnes was staring down at him, but she was too far away for him to see her expression clearly. Almost immediately, she moved quickly out of sight.

Aubrey squared his shoulders and headed through the gates.

30

It was late. I glanced at the clock on the kitchen wall, all too aware that Jack should have been home well over an hour ago.

As I dished out the boys' dinner, my stomach churned with nerves. What if he wasn't coming home? What if he'd decided that he couldn't get over my deception and he was better off without me? How would I break it to the boys?

Above me, footsteps pounded across the bedroom floor and there were shouts and shrieks of laughter. At least they weren't arguing. Evidently the Christmas spirit was rubbing off on them. With only a few days left of term and Christmas looming ever closer they were bound to be excited. I just wished I could share in their joy because the last thing I wanted was to cast a shadow over it all.

I wondered if I should bother dishing out Jack's dinner. I'd made his favourite steak and chips, aware that it looked like I was grovelling. Normally I wouldn't have spent so much money buying steak, but since we were about to have a bit of money spare and since it was nearly Christmas... Who was I kidding? Yes, I *was* grovelling. And I'd grovel for as long as it took if he'd only try to understand why I'd done what I'd done and could find it in his heart to forgive me.

The front door opened, and my heart thudded. It had to be Jack, and I was gripped with a sudden fear. I'd longed for him to come home, but now that he had I was scared stiff that I was about to hear something I didn't want to.

He walked into the kitchen, and I kept my back to him and reached for another plate, wondering if I'd done the right thing buying him a piece of steak, or if I'd only annoy him for wasting money. Usually, Jack wouldn't dream of lecturing me about my spending. He left all that up to me. Now, though, I wasn't sure what the rules were.

Out of the corner of my eye I saw Toby jump up and trot over to see him. He was greeted with a subdued, 'Hello. Someone's pleased to see me, anyway.'

I rolled my eyes, wondering if he was trying to goad me. Was this how he planned to play it? Coax an argument out of me so that he could justify leaving? Well, I wouldn't play his game.

I heaped chips on his plate, added salad and the steak and, bracing myself, I turned to face him.

'Just in time for dinner.'

He was watching me, a sheepish look on his face.

'I'm so sorry, love,' he mumbled.

I didn't know what to say because it was such an unexpected development I hadn't imagined it in my wildest dreams. I stood there like an idiot, clutching the plate and staring at him.

'What I said to you – I should never have spoken to you like that. What a muppet! You must hate my guts, and I wouldn't blame you, honestly, I wouldn't, and – is that steak?'

'Yes, it is,' I said, my voice coming out all croaky, to my embarrassment. 'I nipped to the butchers over the river after – after Aubrey left.'

'I heard he'd been to see you,' Jack said. 'Did it go well?'

'Never mind that,' I said. 'I can tell you later. Does this mean you've forgiven me?'

He walked over to me and took the plate from my grasp. After placing it back on the worktop, he wrapped his arms around my waist with some difficulty and kissed me softly on the lips.

'Can *you* forgive *me*?' he murmured. 'I was out of order, and I know it. My stupid pride, I guess.'

'But I did keep a big secret from you,' I admitted.

'You didn't have much choice, did you?' he asked. 'I've been to see Lawrie and tore him off a strip about it all.'

'You never did! Jack, he's an old man!'

'Oh, don't worry about Lawrie. He can more than look after himself.

Anyway, he apologised, and he said he's going to apologise to you in person. I should think so, too. But as it happens, he also had plenty to say to me, once he found out how I'd reacted.'

'You told him?'

'Sort of.' He grinned suddenly. 'It seems he got it in the neck from Aubrey as well. Mind, he gave as good as he got there. I think Aubrey had some sort of falling out with that Agnes woman over all this business, and he's really upset her. Lawrie thinks he's behaved badly and should apologise. In fact, he told us both to grow up and make it up with our wives, and he had a point, didn't he?'

'Are you really saying you can forgive me?' I asked, cupping his face in my hands.

'There's nothing to forgive,' he said with a sigh. 'I was just scared. Things have been so rocky between us lately, what with this periwotsit, and then the baby, and all our money troubles. I've been worried for ages, thinking maybe you were going off me. This isn't the life I wanted to give you, and I'm so sorry for that. When I realised you'd been keeping secrets about your heritage all this time, on top of not telling me about the baby and confiding in Callie instead, I suppose my insecurities just got the better of me. I thought maybe our partnership wasn't as strong as I'd always believed, and it scared the hell out of me. I don't know what I'd do if I lost you, Clara.'

'That will never happen,' I told him tearfully. 'I wouldn't want to be with anyone else. And I promise you, Jack, I won't keep any more secrets from you. You must believe me.'

'I do believe you,' he said gently. 'Of course I do. We've somehow, against all the odds, stayed in love all these years, even with three boys causing havoc and all the money worries and even a surprise pregnancy. We're not going to risk what we have, are we? This marriage means too much to both of us, right?'

'I really do love you, Jack,' I told him tearfully.

He pulled me to him and held me tightly. 'I love you too. So much it hurts.'

We clung together for what felt like forever, until I heard a rumbling sound and pulled away, laughing.

'You're hungry!'

'Starving,' he admitted ruefully. 'I didn't make any pack-up this morning, so I skipped lunch.'

'Well,' I said, reaching for his plate, 'you'd better sit down and eat this steak and chips before it gets cold. It cost enough so I don't want you wasting it.'

'Steak!' We looked over to the door, where the boys had gathered and were eyeing Jack's plate hungrily.

'Not for you, I'm afraid,' I said. 'I've made you cheeseburgers to go with your chips as a treat, but you've got to promise to eat the salad that goes with them.'

'If I must,' Ash said with a sigh.

'*I* want steak,' Freddie told me crossly.

'Of course you do,' Jack said, ruffling his hair. 'Now look, I want you all to finish every scrap of your dinner because after that we've got a job to do.'

'What job?' they asked, rushing to the table immediately as I hurried to finish adding salad to their plates, wondering what Jack wanted them to do.

I placed the plates on the table then grabbed my own dinner and sat down with them. Jack looked round at us all expectantly.

'We have something very important to decide,' he explained. 'There are only a few weeks until our new baby arrives, and we haven't even thought about a name for him or her. So, this evening, I want you all to come up with some suggestions – serious suggestions,' he added quickly as Freddie opened his mouth to speak. 'Whoever chooses the boy's name and the girl's name we like best will win a prize.'

'What prize?' asked Declan, digging his fork into his chips.

'You'll have to wait and see,' he said. 'So, come on. Get eating, and not a peep out of you!'

The boys immediately began to eat, and across the table Jack winked at me. I smiled back. He probably hadn't got a clue what the prize was himself, but we'd cross that bridge when we came to it.

In the meantime, we'd have a peaceful meal, then a fun evening choosing baby names. As if on cue, I felt a lurching inside me as the baby shifted position, almost as if it knew something momentous in its life was going to happen tonight and was preparing itself.

I hadn't planned this baby, and to be honest, I hadn't wanted it at first either. But looking round the table at my little family, I knew I had so much to be thankful for, and a new baby was just another blessing.

Whatever Jack decided to give the winner of this impromptu contest, we'd already won the jackpot. We had each other. It was going to be all right.

31

AGNES

It had been a long evening for Agnes. She'd barely been able to drag herself away from the drawing room window, staring out over the drive and praying for a glimpse of Mr Wyndham.

He'd been gone for what felt like hours, and she wasn't sure she could bear his absence much longer. Where could he be?

She knew he couldn't have visited the market because it closed at six o'clock and, according to the chimes of the grandfather clock in the hall it was past seven now.

He must have gone back to see Clara, she supposed. She understood from Lawrie that he'd been to Honeywell House earlier that day and that the two of them had got on famously.

Agnes had begged Lawrie for more information, but he'd been surprisingly cagey about the whole thing, telling her that, as far as he was aware, the meeting had gone well, and he was sure Aubrey would give her more details when he returned.

'He's hardly likely to tell me anything, is he?' she'd wailed. 'Mr Wyndham cannot even bring himself to look at me. I've ruined everything, Lawrie! Everything! What am I to do without him?'

Lawrie had assured her that he was quite certain she'd done no such thing, and that Aubrey had no intention of leaving her and she must keep a sense of proportion about these things.

'He knows his duty to you and to Florence,' he'd said as he shuffled into his sitting room after dinner. 'He won't abandon you, Agnes. He's said as much. Now, do stop worrying and enjoy the rest of your evening. He'll be home before you know it. Would you like to listen to some carols with me?'

But Agnes didn't want to listen to carols, and even the sight of the Christmas trees and the decorations that now adorned the Hall couldn't make her feel any better.

She didn't want Mr Wyndham to stay with her because he knew his duty. What sort of an afterlife would that be for either of them? They had both, after all, had experience of such marriages whilst alive. She couldn't wish it for either of them now.

She'd hoped – even believed – that he had affection for her. Genuine affection. Oh, she knew she wasn't a particularly attractive woman. Cyril Ashcroft had made that abundantly clear to her on more than one occasion. And, of course, there was the tiresome matter of her attire. If she'd known she was about to expire and turn into a ghost, she would have made sure she was wearing something far more becoming than this wretched nightgown, bed jacket, stockings and cap.

Even so, sometimes, when Mr Wyndham looked at her, she'd dared to imagine that he had certain... *feelings* for her.

Indeed, in her most honest moments, she'd hoped that she'd imagined a gleam in his eye that could surely only mean one thing? But, of course, she'd probably imagined it. Why would a handsome man like Mr Wyndham look at her in such a manner? She wished she knew about men's *urges*, but sadly, despite being married to Cyril for eighteen years, she knew very little except roughness and – thankfully – brevity that had left her feeling nothing but used and wretched.

She had certainly never felt any desire for her legal husband and found her imaginings and desires for Mr Wyndham both unexpected and shameful.

When he'd kissed her on the mouth that day... Oh goodness! Agnes could almost imagine herself blushing like a commoner at the thought of it. As his hand had wandered to her breastbone she'd been so overcome with lust that she'd had to fake a headache and rush from the room. What would Mr Wyndham have thought if she'd given in to her base impulses? A gentleman like him would no doubt have been shocked to the core, and she might have put him off her for good.

But then, she thought sadly, as she gazed over the front lawns of Harling Hall, she'd done that anyway. Whatever affection Mr Wyndham had felt for her was surely over now? How could he ever forgive her for what she'd done? And quite rightly, so. She would never forgive herself, after all.

'Mother?'

Florence had entered the room without her even noticing, and Agnes forced herself to smile as she moved away from the window and sat on the sofa, doing her very best to look as if everything was perfectly normal and not at all as if her entire world had just come crashing down.

'Florence, dear. Where have you been?'

'Just in the kitchen with Immi. Mia's baking cookies,' Florence said. She sat beside Agnes and peered up at her. 'Are you all right? You look really sad.'

'Sad! Good gracious, child, what have I got to be sad about?' Agnes said, patting her daughter's hand reassuringly. 'It's only nine days until Christmas, and do you know something? I swear to you that, today, when I was strolling in the grounds, I could smell snow in the air.'

Florence's eyes widened in excitement. 'Really? Proper snow? Are you sure?'

'I'm certain of it. My sense of smell is uncannily accurate,' Agnes assured her. 'I expect we shall have snowfall tonight, or by tomorrow morning at the latest.'

'Oh, wow! Wait till I tell Immi!'

'Did you want me for something, dearest?' Agnes asked. 'You must have left the kitchen for some important reason, with the smell of cookies in the air.'

Florence hesitated, her little face falling. 'Well... To be honest, Mother, I 'eard Brodie and Lawrie talking in the 'allway, and they said Poppa had gone out and 'e'd been gone ages and that 'e'd better get 'ome soon or you'll go off your 'ead.'

Agnes pursed her lips. 'Did they indeed?'

'Is everyfink all right wiv you and Poppa?' Florence asked. 'It's bin a bit funny in 'ere lately, and Poppa's not 'is usual self.'

'Everything's perfectly fine,' Agnes said, determined that, whatever catastrophe she'd brought upon herself, her daughter wouldn't suffer for it.

'So, it ain't me then?'

Agnes peered down at the child, her forehead creased with bewilderment. 'What on earth do you mean?'

'I know sometimes I'm a bit of an 'andful,' Florence said wistfully, 'but I 'ave bin trying real 'ard to be good. Master Tasker's only told me off a few times this week, and I've only played a couple of tricks on John and Robert lately, honest. Poppa ain't mad wiv me, is 'e?'

Tears blurred Agnes's vision. She put her arms around her daughter and held her tightly. 'My darling child, of course he isn't! Why, you know that your father loves you so very much, he could never be cross with you. You mustn't worry. He will be home very soon, I'm sure, and then you will see for yourself that he is perfectly all right, and you have no need to worry.'

'You're sure?'

'I'm absolutely certain,' Agnes promised. At least she could tell the truth about that. Mr Wyndham adored Florence, and he would be horrified that his actions recently had caused her such distress.

One thing was clear: if Mr Wyndham could indeed only offer her a relationship based on duty, she would accept it. It was better to have him in her afterlife under such terms than not have him in it at all, and Florence needed her mother *and* her poppa. She would not suffer because of Agnes's deceitful behaviour.

'Well...' Florence gave her a quick hug then grinned at her. 'In that case, am I okay to go back downstairs? Them cookies smell like 'eaven.'

Agnes patted her on the head. 'Of course, child.'

'Actually, Florence, I would like you to do something for me while you're downstairs.'

Both Florence and Agnes leapt as the sound of a male voice cut through the air.

'Mr Wyndham!'

'Poppa, you're back!'

Florence leapt off the sofa and ran over to him, throwing herself against him as if he'd been gone for months.

'Now, now,' he said, wrapping his arms around her and holding her tightly, 'what's all this about? I've only been gone a couple of hours.'

'I missed you,' Florence mumbled. 'And so did Mother. She's bin ever so sad.'

Aubrey cleared his throat. 'Yes, well, I'm here now. Florence, dear, I would like it very much if you would go downstairs and ask everyone to join us up here.'

Agnes's hands flew to her ribbons, and she twisted them tightly around her fingers as Florence asked, clearly surprised, 'Up 'ere? What – *all* of 'em?'

'Indeed,' he said. 'Lawrie, Callie, Brodie, Mia, Immi.' He smiled. 'You may even bring Brian the cat. I have something to say, and I would like them all to hear it.'

Florence nodded. 'Okay, Poppa!'

She ran through the door without a backward glance, leaving Agnes alone with Mr Wyndham, feeling as if she might faint at any moment, even though it was hardly likely.

'Mr Wyndham,' she said weakly, 'I wonder if I might speak with you?'

'Agnes, *I* wish to speak with *you*,' he said. He sat down beside her, and, to her astonishment, he took her hand in his. 'I have behaved shamefully towards you, and I wish to apologise with all my heart.'

'You – you wish to apologise to me?' she whispered. 'But it is I who should apologise to you! And I do, Mr Wyndham, unreservedly. I behaved so badly. To deceive you in such a manner – I don't believe I shall ever forgive myself for it, and if you—'

'Hush now, Agnes,' he said gently. 'What you did was wrong, but I know for certain that you never meant it unkindly. I understand, my dear. I really do. I'll admit I lost that clarity of thought for a while, which is why I behaved so disgracefully, but I know now that you acted as you did because you were afraid of losing me. And the reason you were so afraid of that was because you love me. You love me deeply, and I rather think I forgot about that.'

Agnes swallowed. They had never spoken of love before. Not to each other. It seemed so intimate, somehow. Of course, they had found other ways to express that emotion. They had talked of deep respect for each other, and affection, and even referred to each other as husband and wife, but to say the actual word...

'I understand,' he repeated kindly. 'When Clara arrived, you were afraid I would leave you to be with my flesh and blood family, so you contrived to keep the two of us separate, just as you did to Mia and Florence for much the same reason. I should have realised that. All your talk of James and bad blood was true enough, I expect, but it wasn't what drove you to lie to me, was it?'

Deeply ashamed, Agnes shook her head. 'I can't bear it,' she murmured tearfully. 'The thought of you leaving me. I can't even... I am so sorry, Mr Wyndham.'

'Agnes, my dear, you don't have to apologise. I know what you went through with Cyril Ashcroft. That I referred to you as Mrs Ashcroft the other night fills me with deep shame. That man damaged you and hurt you so much that you believe yourself to be unworthy of anyone's love and feel you must cling to those you hold dearest, for fear they will abandon you.'

He gently stroked her hair, a look of affection in his eyes that made her feel as if she was melting under his gaze.

'I will never abandon you,' he told her. 'Not out of duty, or pity, or whatever it is you imagine keeps me with you. Don't you understand, my dear? My dearest, beautiful Agnes. I love you. I love you with all my heart. You mean everything to me, and I could no more be without you than you could be without me. We are meant to be together, my love. Through all eternity. And I truly believe that is the reason why we did not move on after we each passed away. We were allowed to stay here so we could find each other and be together forever. I used to think I was here as some sort of punishment, but now I realise it is the exact opposite. I have been given a second chance. You are my reward, Agnes.'

Agnes couldn't speak. She gazed at the man she loved and wondered what on earth she'd ever done to deserve such happiness. How she longed to kiss those lips and stroke his hair, how she ached to tell him how much she worshipped and adored him.

But she didn't dare. It could lead to something neither of them could stop, and that would be wrong. Perhaps, if they gave in to their urges, God might punish them by separating them again. It could never be. But hearing his words – maybe that was enough. If that was all she was ever allowed, she could be happy. Contented. Couldn't she?

'Oh, Mr Wyndham,' she murmured at last. She gulped down her emotions as best she could and squeezed his hand, not knowing how else to respond.

The door opened and they pulled apart, looking round to see Brodie, Callie, Mia, Immi and Florence, along with a rather breathless Lawrie.

'These wretched stairs are getting too much for me,' he said. 'I hope you have a good reason for summoning us up here, Aubrey.'

'Especially,' said Brodie wryly, 'as Mia and I can't see or hear you.'

'I just didn't want the two of you to feel left out,' Mr Wyndham said, smiling. He got to his feet. 'Do come in and sit down.'

Callie quickly repeated what he'd said, and the five of them, along with Florence, sat down.

'Don't worry,' Callie told a bemused Brodie and Mia. 'I'll tell you what he says after he's finished saying it.'

'This evening,' Mr Wyndham continued, 'I went to All Souls to see Silas Alexander. The two of us had quite a long chat – our second in a matter of days, as it happens.'

'The old goat?' Florence asked, wrinkling her nose. 'Whatcha wanna go see 'im for?'

'Florence, darling,' her father said, 'would you mind very much not interrupting me while I tell you what it is I have to say?'

'Sorry, Poppa,' she said meekly, snuggling into Agnes's side when her mother put her arm around her.

'This situation between Agnes and myself cannot go on as it is,' he said firmly. 'It's not fair to either of us.'

Agnes experienced a sudden surge of fear. Even with everything Mr Wyndham had just told her, she was so conditioned to expect the worst that her first thought was that he was about to announce his departure from the Hall.

'I love Agnes deeply,' he said firmly, turning to smile at her. 'And she loves me. We wish to be together for the rest of our afterlives, but the situation at present is far from satisfactory. That is why I have spoken to the Reverend, and after some debate—' His lips twitched in amusement. 'I feel now is the right time to ask a very important question.'

To Agnes's astonishment, he dropped onto one knee and reached for her hand.

'My dearest love, you know you are everything in the world to me. Will you please do me the honour of becoming my wife?'

There was a gasp from Callie, Immi and Lawrie.

Agnes stared at the man she loved in bewilderment. 'But – but Mr Wyndham. How can we?'

'Till death us do part,' Aubrey explained. 'Those are the marriage vows we made to Cyril and Elspeth. The promises we made ended upon our deaths, my darling. I have consulted with Silas on the matter. He can find no reason that compels us to hold fast to those vows any longer. He is perfectly happy to marry us in All Souls. He will even construct some new vows that are more suited for our circumstances. In other words, we will be officially married, my beloved. If you will have me.'

Agnes opened and closed her mouth, too stunned to reply.

'He's asked her to marry him!' Callie cried.

'No way!' Mia laughed and clapped her hands. 'Fantastic news.'

'Has she said yes?' Brodie asked.

There was a long silence.

'Agnes?' Mr Wyndham asked, sounding suddenly uncertain. 'Will you have me?'

'Oh, you beautiful, beautiful man!' Agnes launched herself into his arms and hugged him tightly. 'Of course I will have you, Aubrey! Yes, yes, and a thousand times yes!'

She was dimly aware of a huge cheer going up from the other people in the room, and of Callie quickly informing Mia and Brodie that the proposal had been accepted, although they both assured her that they'd realised that from the cheering.

Everything quickly became a blur as her betrothed's lips found hers and she experienced the very first loving, passionate kiss of her life.

'Well,' Callie said, 'talk about sealing it with a kiss!'

'Good heavens,' Lawrie said. 'How, er, charming. So happy for you both.'

'Blimey,' Immi giggled. 'I think they're stuck together!'

''Ang on a minute,' said Florence. 'Are you telling me they ain't already married? Well, ain't that a bloomin' turn up for the books?'

32

It looked as if the Dickensian weekend would get off to a perfect start, with clear skies and a dusting of snow on the ground. It had started falling early on Wednesday morning, and the boys had got very excited about it. Even Ashton had decided it wouldn't be beneath him to make a snowman after school.

Sadly for them, the snow didn't stay around long enough, but on Friday afternoon, just as I collected the youngest two from school on their last day of term, we'd had more of the stuff, and although it stopped falling at some point during the night, it remained cold enough to prevent a thaw.

Jack was worried about me going out in it. 'What if you slip? You could really hurt yourself or the little one. Maybe you'd be better off staying indoors.'

'Don't be daft,' I said, laughing as I adjusted his cap. 'I'm not going to miss this Dickensian weekend for anything. Besides, I have a date with a hot engine driver.'

Although Jack wasn't usually on duty over the weekend, as the senior driver he'd been asked to take our celebrity guest, plus the reporter and photographer from *The Cotswolds Courier* on a journey between Much Melton and Harling's Halt at eleven o'clock that Saturday morning. He would be driving his favourite engine – yes, he actually had a favourite – *The Lady Davenport*. He'd also agreed to take part in a promo shoot at the station, though he admitted he felt stupid about it.

He looked incredibly handsome in his Victorian train driver's costume, and

I'd already told him as much in the hallway, as I kissed him for the third time that morning.

'You want to get a good look at Cain Carmichael, you mean,' he said knowingly. 'Not that I blame you. Not often we get a bona fide rock star in the village, is it?'

'Pah! He's way too old to interest me,' I said. 'Anyway, why would I look at some boring rock star when I have my very own rock star right here at home?'

'It's a very strange thing,' he said thoughtfully, 'but considering you've been telling me for ages that your hormones have retired, they've certainly had a new lease of life lately.'

'I know! It's a bit embarrassing,' I admitted. 'I can't get enough of you.'

'Well, I'm not complaining.' He grinned and wrapped his arms around me. 'This is the most fun we've had in months.'

'Hmm. Thirty-seven weeks to be exact,' I said wryly.

He laughed and hugged me. 'I really want to stay but I've got to be at Much Melton. Are you really set on coming to the station, love? I won't mind if you don't want to. I'm worried about you walking in the snow.'

'I wouldn't miss it for the world,' I told him, meaning it.

'Just be careful.' He called down the hallway to the kitchen, where the boys were eating their breakfasts at the table. 'I'll see you all later. Look after your mum for me, okay?'

'Yeah, okay,' Ash replied.

'See you later, Dad,' Declan called.

'*I* want to come with you!'

Jack rolled his eyes at Freddie's plea and kissed me lightly on the lips. 'Better go or I'll be late, and we wouldn't want that, would we? See you all around half eleven?'

'We'll be there.'

As soon as he'd left for work, I hurried into the kitchen and began chivvying the boys to finish their breakfasts and help me tidy up the place. Unsurprisingly, there were lots of groans, some jibes about child labour, and the inevitable threat to report me to social services.

'For making you clear up your own mess? I'm hardly sending you up a chimney, am I?' I said, rolling my eyes.

Ash laughed. 'No, for making poor Freddie wear that costume!'

I scowled at him. 'Don't wind him up.'

'I'm not winding him up! He looks stupid in it.'

'He does not!'

'I don't want to wear a costume!' Freddie wailed.

'Now look what you've done.' With some difficulty, I crouched down beside my youngest son, whose lower lip was wobbling dangerously. 'You're going to be just like your dad, aren't you? Only the most important people are wearing costumes today.'

'Only the daftest,' Declan mumbled.

I stood up, aware that I was doing my back no favours.

'And your dad's going to be so proud when he sees you,' I added firmly, my eyes flashing a warning at my two eldest. 'He'll be looking out for you at the station. You might even get your photo taken by the local newspaper. How amazing would that be?'

He eyed me thoughtfully. 'My picture in the paper?'

I nodded. 'Just like your dad.'

His face broke into a smile. 'Okay.'

'I can't wait to see this,' Ashton said. 'It's going to be hilarious.'

Whatever he and Declan thought, to me Freddie looked adorable as Oliver Twist, though from the way he protested as I helped him dress an hour later, you'd have thought I was making him wear his costume as some sort of punishment.

He'd quite forgotten about the newspaper business thank to his brothers howling with laughter and repeatedly asking him if he wanted more. My poor little boy had no idea what they were talking about.

'The part was tailor-made for him,' Jack had said, as we were deciding what costume to hire for him. 'The little boy who asks for more food? If anyone's going to play that character, it's Freddie.'

And who could deny it?

'If you two say one more word I won't let you come to the station with me,' I warned the older boys. 'I'm disgusted with you both. How can you be so mean to him?'

At least they had the grace to look ashamed.

'Sorry, Freddie,' Declan said grudgingly.

'You look great, Freddie,' Ash told him, nudging him gently. 'That reporter's going to love you.'

We took a slow, careful walk to All Souls, where we waited with a few other villagers who'd decided to visit the station. My back was aching badly, so it was a relief that the little Leyland bus came trundling along within ten minutes, and soon we were heading out of the village and along Cotswolds lanes towards Harling's Halt.

I gazed out of the window and thought how stunning the landscape looked. The newly ploughed fields seemed dark and velvety, the ridges between the furrows dusted with white, powdery snow, while others were softened with shoots of winter green poking through their wintry blanket.

The bare branches of the trees were silhouetted against the brilliant blue of a clear winter sky, and I wondered, not for the first time, how this season could be so overlooked.

Everyone raved about the lushness of a Cotswold spring, the golden glory of summer, and the stunning amber and russet of autumn, but in my opinion, there was a stark beauty about the countryside on winter days like this one that was quite unmatched.

It occurred to me that I'd love to paint the landscape like this, and the sudden stirring of longing surprised me. Maybe I should think about buying some new art materials after all.

I winced slightly as my stomach tightened. Braxton Hicks! I'd had a few of those contractions this morning, which I knew was quite common at this stage of pregnancy. I just hoped they eased off as I didn't want to be uncomfortable, today of all days.

We trundled into the car park at Harling's Halt, just as the first flakes of snow began to fall.

'Mummy, look!' Freddie shrieked, pressing his nose against the window. 'It's snowing again!'

Good job I'd made him wear his coat, although it was a shame to hide his cute costume. I wondered about all the visitors to Rowan Vale, and if they'd all be forced to cover up under heavy coats and scarves.

We made our way through the car park towards the station. Already I could hear music drifting over the speakers. The usual First World War songs had been replaced by brass band versions of traditional Christmas carols.

The sound was drowned suddenly by a long, shrill whistle from *The Lady Davenport*, and Declan and Ashton exchanged delighted grins. 'Dad!'

We could hear the engine puffing into the station, and I gripped Freddie's hand even tighter, knowing how impulsive he could be and how excited he'd be to see his father driving the train.

As we arrived on the platform, I could see the usual soldiers and their "sweethearts" standing in groups and posing for the tourists. The women had long, warm coats over their dresses, their cheeks pink from the cold. I knew they'd be glad when their shift was done, and they could nip into The Victory Tearooms for a nice hot cup of tea while their replacements took over for a while.

Even in there, though, they were expected to stay in character. If they wanted to take a real break, they were able to escape to the staff room in the main station building, where they could relax away from the curious and fascinated gaze of visitors.

The engine slowly ground to a halt, and great puffs of steam shot from the funnel.

'Chuff-chuff,' said Freddie, laughing. 'It's just like *Thomas the Tank Engine.*'

Doors opened and a crowd of people stepped onto the platform. Most of them were dressed in modern winter clothing, but a surprising number wore Victorian costumes. I felt a pang for my beautiful dress that I'd never got to wear. Maybe, if Callie thought the event was a success, she'd do something similar next year, and I'd get to wear something a bit more glamorous than leggings, ankle boots, a huge jumper and a big, winter coat.

To my surprise, Callie, Immi and Brodie got off the train – all wearing Dickensian costumes – along with Max and Shona who were not. Immi looked very pretty, dressed, so Callie had told me, as poor Little Nell.

'Immi!' Declan shouted, making Ashton scowl.

They all looked round and there was a lot of waving and smiling as they spotted us. Before we had a chance to say anything, though, the crowds began to cheer as Cain Carmichael himself stepped onto the platform, along with a gorgeous man, a rather beautiful and elegant woman, a boy of around Freddie's age, and a little girl aged about four.

Cain had clearly dressed for the occasion and bore a startling resemblance to most people's idea of Ebenezer Scrooge, whether by design or unfortunate coincidence I wasn't sure.

Shona and Max managed to find their way to us as Callie and Brodie introduced the celebrity party to the station staff.

'Isn't it exciting?' Shona said. 'I managed to wangle a seat through Callie because I wanted to travel with Pippa. Blimey, though, that Cain Carmichael looks ancient. Mind you, he was a big star in the seventies, so he must be getting on a bit. That's his son, daughter-in-law, and grandchildren with him.' She leaned over and whispered, 'American accent, unlike Cain. The son I mean. Should have got him to open the event, if you ask me. Miles more photogenic. Isn't he gorgeous?'

'I am standing right here,' Max reminded her with a twinkle in his eye.

'Aw, and I'm very glad you are, *liebling*.' Shona gave me a wink. 'Look at Pippa over there, next to that cameraman. She's reporting on the event. She's already interviewed Cain at Much Melton. I'm so proud of her.'

'What's a cameraman doing here?'

'Pippa's not the only one reporting,' Max explained. 'Would you believe we have a television crew with us?'

'Oh wow, really?' Ashton looked thrilled.

'A television crew? Callie pulled it off then.'

'Well, it's only local television,' Shona said. '*Your Cotswolds*. To be honest, I think they're only here for Cain Carmichael. He's big news since he got his knighthood in the King's birthday honours in the summer.'

'A knighthood? For singing that terrible music?' Max asked, puzzled.

'Services to music and charity. To be fair, he does loads of charity work. He's set up some organic farms specially for underprivileged city kids to stay and get a taste of life in the countryside. Can't fault him for it really. He seems devoted to the cause.'

'I don't suppose Callie's going to get a chance to talk to us,' I said. 'Ooh, look! There's Jack!'

We all turned to see Jack and Tom heading down the platform towards the press party. I watched, almost bursting with pride, as my husband was introduced to Cain and his family and shook hands with them all before they began posing for photographs.

'Callie's got to give the Carmichaels and the media a tour of the station, and introduce them to the staff in the Tearooms, so they'll be a while yet,' Shona said. 'Shall we get the bus into the village? I'm dying to see the market with a whole bunch of people in costume wandering around.'

'We have the perfect weather for the occasion,' Max said, smiling up at the snowflakes that were falling even faster now. 'It could not be more *A Christmas Carol*, could it?'

'I thought Dad said there was going to be a scary ghost story here,' Ash remarked. '*A Christmas Carol* isn't scary. It's full of Muppets.'

'Funnily enough, there aren't any Muppets in the book,' I told him. 'And yes, *The Signal-Man* is scary but it's not happening here until it starts to get darker. Frankly, I'm glad I won't be here. Ghost stories are too much. *A Christmas Carol* is about as scary as I get.'

'Oh, the irony,' Shona said, laughing.

'I wonder how long Jack will be,' I mused. 'I was hoping we could all go back together.'

As I spoke, I saw Jack peering round the crowd at me. He held up his hand, indicating that he'd only be five minutes.

'We're going back in the car,' I said apologetically. 'I'm really sorry. We'd give you a lift, but there won't be enough room.'

'Oh, don't worry about that,' Shona said cheerfully. 'Max loves the old bus, don't you? We might as well go and catch it now, because Pippa will be with the official crowd so there's no point waiting for her.' She linked arms with Max. 'See you back at the market. So exciting!'

'You must come to the teashop and try some of my Christmas cookies,' Max told us.

'His gingerbread mousse is to die for,' Shona added. 'Pop in if you get the chance.'

'Will do,' I assured her, my mouth already watering at the thought of gingerbread mousse. 'See you later.'

'*I* want some gingerbread mousse,' Freddie announced.

'Do you know what gingerbread mousse is?' Declan asked him.

Freddie shrugged. 'No, but I want it.'

I winced as the Braxton Hicks started again. So annoying! Like I didn't have enough to deal with already, since the backache hadn't eased.

'Hey, you made it!' I forced a smile as Jack ran up to us and hugged the boys in turn before putting his arm over my shoulder. If I let onto him that I was having these pains he'd bundle me home to rest, and there was no way I was missing out over something so trivial.

'What a palaver that was,' Jack said. '*Your Cotswolds* is here, as well as the *Courier*. Of course, they were more interested in Cain Carmichael than the Dickensian weekend, although they did admire the costumes that Callie and Brodie and little Immi were wearing.'

'Did you get your photo taken?' Declan asked, wide-eyed. 'Will you be in the papers?'

'And on the telly?' asked Ash.

'I don't know,' he admitted. 'They took loads of pictures, and the cameras were rolling, but who knows if anything of me will end up being used. Not that I'm bothered. All I want to do now is take my little family back to Rowan Vale and treat us all to hot chocolate at the market. Are we ready?'

'We're ready,' the boys chorused, clearly raring to go.

'I've got some news for you,' Jack murmured to me as we walked towards the car park. 'It turns out, Aubrey and Agnes have made up, and he's asked her to marry him.'

'Marry him?' I gave a puzzled laugh, not sure what to make of that. 'But how? I mean—'

'That old ghostly vicar Callie's told us about has offered to perform the ceremony. Callie says it's going to be on Christmas Day at All Souls after Amelia's finished the Christmas service and everyone's gone home. But don't let on, because Aubrey wants to tell you himself, and he's going to invite you. Us. He's going to invite all of us.'

'So why did Callie tell you?' I asked.

'Because...' He gave me a sheepish look. 'She wanted to tip me off, in case I decided to be funny about the whole Wyndham situation again.'

'And are you?' I asked, knowing the answer anyway.

'No, love. And really, I can't think of anything nicer than a Christmas Day wedding, can you?'

'Maybe one where we can see all the participants?' I suggested with a grin.

'Or one of them. That would be useful. As it is, there's only you who's going to see even Aubrey.'

'Ohhh.'

He gave me a suspicious look. 'What does "ohhh" mean?'

I linked arms with him and gave him a sweet smile. 'Nothing much. But there is something I forgot to mention. About Freddie...'

33

AUBREY

It was most gratifying, Aubrey thought, to be greeted with such warmth and kindness by their fellow ghosts, despite having hidden away from the village all those years.

Arriving arm in arm at the Magic Lantern Cinema for the final rehearsal of *A Christmas Carol*, a thrilled Florence by their side, they were hailed by Mr Swain, the station porter, who couldn't have sounded more delighted to see them.

Then those two bizarrely dressed young people, Danny and Brooke pushed past them at the entrance, issuing a cheery hello.

Peter the baker rushed over to greet them, seeming thrilled that they were out and about at long last. They had seen him a few months ago, when he'd turned up at the Hall to see young John and Robert, but it had only been a brief visit, and events had rather meant they'd had no chance for a real conversation.

'We must have a catch-up,' Peter told them. 'Perhaps you could come to my house one day? Or we could meet up in The Quicken Tree? I'm sure Isaac would be delighted to see you there again.'

As Agnes's eyes widened in horror, he added hastily, 'Or perhaps somewhere more suitable? I'm sure Polly Herron would welcome us at the teashop.'

'Perhaps,' Agnes agreed. 'After Christmas. It's very nice to see you again, Peter. Good luck with the play. I understand you're playing the role of Jacob Marley.'

'I am that,' he said proudly, 'and thank you kindly for your good wishes.'

Aubrey squeezed her hand approvingly as Peter headed over to the stage, and Florence said, 'Ooh, it's smashing in the teashop, Mother. You'll like it there. All them cakes and pastries wot smell so luvverly.'

'I sometimes wonder,' Agnes said with a sigh, 'if it's really worth continuing our daughter's elocution lessons.'

'Perhaps we shouldn't try to change her,' Aubrey suggested. 'After all, we love her just as she is, don't we?'

Agnes hesitated, then smiled, almost mischievously. 'We do,' she agreed. 'And perhaps we can find better things to do with our time once we are married.'

He gazed at her in wonder, thinking how much she'd changed since he'd proposed to her. Why, she'd become almost daring! He couldn't deny he loved this new side to her and hoped it would continue after their wedding, especially as she'd made it as clear as she could without actually saying the words that she would like them to share a room in future.

A thrill of anticipation had run through him when she'd cautiously suggested that perhaps, if he was agreeable, they should inform Mia that they would only need one photograph of Florence, after all.

He'd smiled, understanding. 'Quite so,' he'd said warmly.

She'd lowered her face and gazed up at him through her eyelashes, quite coquettishly, looking far younger and even more beautiful than usual. He had to confess, Christmas Day couldn't come soon enough for him, especially as Callie had discreetly suggested to him that Florence might like to spend their wedding night in Immi's room, having something called a sleepover.

He tugged at his shirt collar, feeling suddenly inexplicably hot. Luckily, his attention was drawn away from the forthcoming nuptials and the promise of their wedding night by Florence tugging on his hand.

'Gotta go, Poppa. The re'earsals are starting. Just sit right at the front so I can see you both, won't you?'

Agnes and Aubrey promised her they would indeed, and duly settled themselves in the best seats in the cinema as the final rehearsal before the Christmas Eve performance began.

It made him quite emotional when he saw his little girl acting the role of Bob Cratchit's daughter, although the part evidently required little from her other than to look poor but grateful until Tim – played by a terrified-looking Robert – passed away, whereupon she had to look poor but sad.

He doubted the cheerful wave she gave her parents was part of the script, but nevertheless he returned it, surprised and gratified to see that Agnes did, too.

Percy Swain was the epitome of festive jollity in his role of Fezziwig, while Peter clearly relished the role of Jacob Marley, issuing bone-chilling ghostly howls to make up for the absence of rattling chains.

Quintus Severus had failed to turn up, as he considered being on duty at the market far more important, and had decreed that, since his part consisted of nothing more than pointing and glowering, he needed no rehearsals.

No one was going to argue with that, so a delighted Ronnie Smith had agreed to be his understudy, although that sparked the inevitable argument with a jealous Bill Fairfax, and there seemed to be quite the kerfuffle backstage when the Ghost of Christmas Yet to Come finally made his exit.

Agnes complained that Walter Tasker was overacting his part dreadfully, and Aubrey privately agreed, but he had grown rather fond of Walter so gently reminded his fiancée that the man was a teacher by profession, not an actor, and his enthusiasm should surely be applauded. Agnes, quite the new woman, had graciously agreed and clapped even louder than Aubrey when the play finally ended.

'Well done, everyone,' Walter called, having clearly taken it upon himself to not only be the star of the show but the director, too. 'The next time we perform shall be on Christmas Eve in the ballroom at Harling Hall, with an audience of Mistress Chase, Sir Lawrence, and Miss Imogen. I expect you all to be word perfect. You are now dismissed.'

Like most of the ghosts, Aubrey, Agnes and Florence immediately left The Magic Lantern and headed for the Christmas market.

Florence, already hyped up from her star turn as Belinda Cratchit, grew increasingly excited as they neared the green. She gave a loud squeal.

'Poppa, look at the Christmas lights. Ain't they smashing?'

She sounded so thrilled to show them to him that Aubrey decided not to remind her that he'd already seen them strung all over the village.

'They do indeed,' he agreed.

'Quite beautiful,' Agnes said with a sigh. 'I'd forgotten how lovely the village is,' she admitted. 'It's so nice to be out of the grounds again. I have been such a foolish old woman.'

'We've agreed to put all that business behind us,' Aubrey said. 'A new start, remember? Do look at the shops! How beautiful the buildings look in the snow.'

'Like a Christmas card,' she agreed fondly. 'And just listen to the carols. How wonderful it all is.'

Christmas carols were indeed playing through the speakers and the hum of the excited crowds drifted through the air, causing Agnes to shiver slightly, being unused to so much activity.

'Are you well, my dear?' Aubrey asked anxiously, knowing what a momentous occasion this was for his betrothed and hoping she wouldn't change her mind.

'Perfectly well, thank you, Mr Wyndham,' she assured him. She'd reverted to addressing him formally, telling him that the emotion of his beautiful proposal had quite overwhelmed her, and she could only apologise for calling him by his Christian name, but that she would do so with pleasure once they were married.

They gazed in wonder at the scene before them. In the snow the little wooden huts with their strings of fairy lights looked even more enchanting than when Aubrey had caught sight of them upon leaving Honeywell House.

Although it had stopped snowing, Aubrey imagined it must be very chilly indeed, but that didn't seem to have deterred the crowds, who were milling around, chatting excitedly, queuing at the little stalls and strolling along the pavement outside the row of shops that edged the green – many of them dressed in costumes.

There were replica Fagins, Dodgers, Bill Sykes, Tiny Tims, Bob Cratchits and Mr Bumbles. One woman had made a real effort and looked incredible as an eerie-looking Miss Havisham.

Jasper Edgecumbe's photography studio was so busy there was a queue stretching along the pavement, and various tourists were cheerfully posing for photographs outside the Curiosity Shop, which had stuck a cheeky poster over its signage, adding the words 'The Old' to the start of its name.

'It's such a shame Lawrie didn't feel able to join us,' Agnes said with a sigh. 'He would have loved this.'

'I'm afraid his mobility is getting worse,' Aubrey agreed. 'And unfortunately, he's too proud and stubborn to use one of those strange little vehicles that Callie told us about.'

'Scooters, they are,' Florence said knowledgably. 'I've seen 'em. Old people scootin' up and down on 'em, looking like they're 'aving a great time. I reckon Lawrie's soft in the 'ead to say no.'

'Florence!' Agnes chided, 'Lawrie is certainly *not* soft in the head, as you so charmingly put it. He is a proud man. One cannot blame him for that.'

'I do think,' Aubrey said thoughtfully, 'that he is finding the stairs too much at the Hall these days. I really don't know what's going to happen. Oh, I say! Look who's here!'

Agnes followed his gaze, and he felt the shudder run through her. 'Good heavens!' she whispered, in awe. 'The Roman!'

Quintus Severus was truly a sight to behold, with his impressive centurion's uniform, complete with shield, spear and sword. A Roman African, who had reached an impressive age for the times he lived in, being somewhere in his late fifties, he had spent years guarding the Wyrd Stones as ordered by Sir Edward Davenport, before his mission had finally been ended by Callie.

Now he lived in the village, sharing a cottage with the elusive ghost of Hollywood actress Harmony Hill, and an oblivious elderly villager called Mrs Smithson. Callie had given him the new responsibility of policing the ghosts and making sure there was no disorder in the village.

As she'd explained to Lawrie one evening, within Aubrey's earshot, there was no real need for his services, but Quintus wasn't the sort of man who could be left without a role, and she wanted him to feel needed and useful.

Callie, Aubrey thought, was a most perceptive and compassionate young woman.

Now the centurion was marching up and down the green, not even bothering to dodge the living people who shuffled around the stalls, but walking straight through them without so much as a backward glance.

'Extraordinary man,' Aubrey murmured. 'How marvellous to see him here in the village at last. He must have been terribly lonely, spending all that time alone.'

'He does scare me a little,' Agnes admitted. 'Do you think he's safe? He looks rather stern, and one hears such stories about the Roman soldiers.'

"E's all right, Mother,' Florence assured her. 'Me and Immi have talked to 'im. 'E was telling us a bit about 'is life. Immi asked 'im if 'e'd come to the

'All and give us a lesson about the Roman Empire, and 'e said 'e'd think about it.'

'He did?' Agnes asked, amazed. 'I'm not so sure about that.'

'We 'ad to ask,' Florence said, smirking, 'just to see the look of terror on Master Tasker's face.'

Aubrey shook his head, trying to look disapproving, but his lips twitched with amusement at the thought.

''E used to live up in the norf,' Florrie explained. 'Guarding 'Adrian's Wall or sumfink, but then 'e was getting near retirement and 'is wife was from round 'ere so—' She broke off with an excited whoop. 'There's Immi! Look at 'er costume! Ain't it smashing?'

Before they could stop her, she'd run over to see her friend.

'I suppose,' Agnes said sadly, 'she's used to being without us when she's in the village.'

'Well,' Aubrey promised, 'that will change, soon enough. We'll make it up to her, my dear. You'll see.'

Within minutes they were surrounded by various female ghosts, who'd not had the opportunity to speak to them at the cinema and had evidently decided that they wanted to do so now.

There were lots of congratulations over their forthcoming marriage, which shocked them at first, as they'd thought to keep it a secret until after the ceremony.

'You can't keep secrets in Rowan Vale,' Polly Herron said with a laugh. 'Your Florence has been telling anyone who'll listen that she's going to be a bridesmaid.'

'Can I be a bridesmaid, too?' Millie, a teenager who'd sadly passed away in 1964, after falling from her bathroom window when she'd tried to sneak out to a Beatles concert against her parents' wishes, asked hopefully. 'I never got to be a bridesmaid when I was alive, and I'd love to do it just once.'

'Well,' Agnes said, rather flustered at all the attention, 'I don't know. I haven't thought that far ahead.'

'Well, you need to hurry up,' Polly warned her. 'You haven't got long to the big day, and by the way, are you going to ask John and Robert to be your pageboys? It would mean the world to them to be included.'

'John and Robert!' Agnes sounded appalled at the idea and Aubrey thought a hasty intervention was called for.

'Tomorrow,' he said firmly, 'Agnes and I shall sit down and make a plan, and when we've done that, we will let everyone know what we've decided. How does that sound?'

'Fair enough,' Polly agreed.

'But I really would like to be a bridesmaid,' Millie added. 'Just so you know.'

Finally alone again, Aubrey and Agnes strolled around the stalls, eyeing up the goods for sale and delighting in the delicious smells of roast chestnuts, sizzling onions, roast pork sandwiches, doughnuts, churros and chocolate.

'It's very odd, don't you think, that one can crave food one has never even tasted, just because of the smell,' Agnes said, gazing longingly at the doughnut stall. 'Oh! What on earth is going on over by the well?'

Aubrey glanced over to the old wishing well in the centre of the green. A platform had been set up in front of it, and a microphone placed upon it. A man with a cine camera on some sort of tripod was standing nearby, along with a young woman with a microphone in her hand, another young woman with what he recognised from Brodie's office as a machine for recording the voice, and an elderly man with a camera.

People seemed to be making their way towards the area, and out of the corner of his eye Aubrey saw Callie and Brodie leading a man bearing a remarkable resemblance to Mr Dickens' crotchety old character, Ebenezer Scrooge, towards the platform.

He turned away, more pressing concerns on his mind.

'Agnes, I was wondering,' he said, 'if you intended to ask Lawrie to give you away?'

Agnes's face lit up. 'Oh! I never even thought about that, but yes of course. Who else would I ask? Oh!' She looked suddenly subdued. 'Unless you wish him to be your best man, of course?'

'No, no.' Aubrey bit his lip, wondering how to put this. He decided, in the end, that he should be direct with her. 'Actually, my dear, I was considering asking Clara to be my best man.'

'Clara!' Agnes's hand flew to her ribbons, as he'd feared it might. 'But – but she's a woman!'

'Is that your only objection?' he asked cautiously. 'Because if it is, I have to say that I have heard that in these modern times, it is quite acceptable for a bridegroom to choose a woman as his best man, if that woman means something to him. And as Clara is my granddaughter – to all intents and purposes – I would really love to have her play a part in the ceremony. But of course,' he added, 'I will not do so if you feel uncomfortable about it, my dear. This is your special day, and I wouldn't do anything to spoil it for you.'

'I just...' Agnes swallowed. 'I cannot face her, Mr Wyndham. After everything I did. I am so ashamed. Perhaps she will not forgive me, nor accept me as part of your family? I could hardly blame her if that is the case.'

Aubrey sighed, knowing that no matter what he said she wouldn't believe him. Then his eyes fell upon the most welcome sight, and he straightened. 'Agnes, she's here. Clara. Look, they're all here. Jack and the three children, too.'

Agnes clutched his arm as she saw the Milsoms standing not too far away. The youngest child – Freddie, was it? – gave a grin and waved at Aubrey, and Agnes gasped.

'Does that child see you?' she whispered.

Before he could respond, Freddie had pointed to him, and the entire family turned to look. To his amazement, the two older boys stared directly at him, then tentatively waved. They could see him, too?

Aubrey waved back, and Clara said something to Jack. He shrugged, then nodded, and the Milsoms headed in their direction.

'Don't worry about a thing, Agnes,' Aubrey said reassuringly. 'Remember, they can't even see you.'

'You're here!' Clara smiled at him, and his heart lifted in delight. 'I was hoping you would be.'

'Who is he, Mum?' the eldest boy asked, staring at Aubrey in surprise.

'I can't believe this,' Jack said. 'You can see him, too, Ash?'

'So can I,' Declan said. 'He looks like an actor from one of those soppy films Mum always watches.'

'Oh wow,' Clara breathed. 'They can all see you! How amazing is that?'

'Fabulous,' Jack said with a sigh.

'Incredible,' Aubrey agreed. 'It's so good to meet you, boys. I'm your...' He paused, not sure what Clara wanted to tell them.

'Ashton, Declan, Freddie, this is your great-grandfather, Aubrey Wyndham,' Clara said firmly. 'My grandfather.'

Frantically, Aubrey blinked away tears. 'How do you do,' he said solemnly.

'You're a ghost?' Freddie asked, his eyes like saucers.

'Well, I, er—'

'Of course he's a ghost,' Ashton said. 'Immi's told me all about you,' he added politely. 'She's in my class at school. You're Florrie's dad, aren't you? Is her mum here with you?'

'Er, she is, yes,' Aubrey admitted.

'She is?' Clara asked. 'Oh, good. Because there's something I want to say to her.'

Agnes let out a little whimper, and Aubrey was about to leap to her defence when Clara winced suddenly and clutched Jack's arm.

'Are you all right, love?' Jack asked in alarm.

Clara puffed out her cheeks and nodded. 'Braxton Hicks,' she said, sounding a bit breathless.

'Braxton who?' Agnes said, frowning.

'Is it the baby?' Aubrey asked, feeling rather alarmed.

'No, no. Just practice contractions. Quite common at this stage,' Clara assured him.

'Are you sure?' Jack demanded. 'Because if you've any doubts, I'll take you straight home.'

Clara rolled her eyes. 'I'm fine. Stop fussing. I've got three weeks to go yet.'

'*Three weeks?*' Agnes whispered to Aubrey, as if they might hear her. 'She shouldn't be out in public! What on earth is she thinking?'

'Now.' Clara took a steadying breath, then continued. 'About Agnes. Is she still here?'

'Yes, she is,' Aubrey admitted, 'but I have to say—'

'No,' Agnes said bravely. 'Whatever she needs to say to me, I deserve it. Please, Mr Wyndham, I am prepared.'

Against his every instinct, Aubrey agreed and waited for the onslaught from Clara.

'I just want to tell you, Mrs – er, Agnes – that it's okay. I understand why you did what you did. I didn't behave any better than you, keeping secrets from Jack. You did what you thought was right, and so did I. I want you to know that there are no hard feelings, and even though I can't see you, I hope we'll be sort of – well, family, I guess.'

Aubrey felt a sudden and unexpected rush of affection for this young woman. He glanced at Agnes and realised she was quite overcome by Clara's words.

'I think,' she murmured, 'that your granddaughter has inherited her generosity of spirit from you, Mr Wyndham, along with a kind and forgiving nature. Will you please tell her that I am deeply sorry for my actions, that I am grateful for her understanding, and am truly honoured that she is willing to accept me into her lovely family.'

His voice thick with emotion, Aubrey relayed Agnes's message to Clara, who beamed.

'I have a present for her,' she told him, dipping into her handbag. 'I thought perhaps she would like it on her wall. Maybe Callie could frame it.'

She showed him a drawing which he and Agnes gazed upon in amazement.

'Why, Mr Wyndham, the artist has captured your likeness perfectly! How handsome you look!'

'You drew this?' Aubrey asked, astonished.

'Yes. After I saw you that day when I first came here. I didn't want to forget what you looked like, you see, after Lawrie said...' Her voice trailed off and she shrugged. 'Well, anyway, let's not go into all that again. Does Agnes approve?'

'Clara, my dear,' Aubrey said, 'she most certainly does. She is thrilled with your kind gift. Thank you so much, from both of us. And now we have a present for you, one I hope you will approve of. Agnes and I are to be married, and we would like you to attend the wedding. All of you, I mean.

'It's at All Souls' church on Christmas Day, and I was hoping... Clara, if it's not too much trouble, and if you feel up to the job of course, would you consider being my best man? I know it's not traditional, but then, there is nothing traditional about our circumstances, is there? Not that there will be much for you to do,' he admitted. 'It's not as if we can exchange rings, after all. But it would be nice to have someone stand beside me. Someone who is family.'

'Oh, that's wonderful news!' Clara told him. 'Congratulations!'

'Just don't ask us to be pageboys,' Ashton warned him.

'*I* want to be a pageboy,' Freddie said.

Aubrey wondered how many pageboys and bridesmaids they would end up with. At this rate the church would be full just with their attendants.

'I'd be honoured to be your best man,' Clara told him warmly. 'And I – oh!'

She gasped and bent over, clearly in pain.

'Braxton Hicks again?' Jack asked anxiously.

Clara nodded, clearly unable to even reply.

'Braxton Hicks, my eye,' Agnes said firmly. 'The woman's labours have begun. You must get her to her childbed immediately, young man.'

'Mummy, you've gone all purple,' Freddie observed.

'I'm fine,' Clara gasped.

'I don't think you are,' Jack said. 'We're going home.'

'I want to hear Cain Carmichael's speech,' Clara pleaded. She slowly straightened. 'Anyway, it's passed. I'm okay now. I can't miss the guest of honour.'

'That foolish old man?' Agnes asked incredulously. 'Why on earth would she want to hear *him* speak? Mr Wyndham,' she pleaded, 'you must make her go home. Anything could happen. She is hardly in the first flush of youth, after all.'

That was true enough, Aubrey realised, and he understood Agnes's concerns all too well. Even so, he hardly felt he was in a position to order Clara around. He'd only just found her. The last thing he wanted to do was antagonise her.

The microphone crackled and Callie spoke, her voice booming loudly across the green as she welcomed everyone to the Dickensian Weekend and thanked them all for coming.

Aubrey barely heard a word she said, so concerned was he about Clara. She was looking most peculiar, and he saw her taking long, deep breaths, as if trying to ward off the pain.

He hadn't been there when Elspeth had given birth to James. It had been made perfectly clear to him that his presence was neither required nor wanted, which, he had to admit, had been something of a relief. He had no idea what happened during childbirth, as he had spent the entire afternoon while Elspeth laboured in The Quicken Tree, nursing a tankard of ale bought for him by his understanding gamekeeper, and trying not to imagine what might be happening back at the Hall.

His ignorance meant that he was rather afraid that Clara's child would arrive at any moment, and he was torn between getting as far away from the scene as possible and watching her like a hawk for any signs that she was in danger. It was, after all, a risky business, and as Agnes had rightly pointed out, Clara was of an age when surely the risks were even greater.

A man's voice cut into his thoughts: the guest of honour, hired by Callie to open the Dickensian Weekend.

'It still blows me away me that, even though I've lived near 'ere all these years, this is the first time I've visited Rowan Vale. I was over the moon when Callie 'ere invited me to open the event, and I've 'ad a blast so far. Ridin' the steam train, lookin' round that station, it's bin a proper treat. To all those of you watchin' at 'ome, I say get yourselves 'ere if you ain't bin before, cos you don't want to miss out on this, trust me.'

'Good heavens, what can Callie have been thinking?' Agnes said, appalled. 'His diction is worse than Florence's.'

'Ohhh!'

All heads turned to Clara, who was gripping Jack's arm tightly.

'You need to go home,' he told her fiercely.

'Mr Wyndham!' Agnes sounded quite distraught. 'Please, trust me on this. The child is coming, and she must go to her bed.'

'Clara,' Aubrey said, terrified, 'I really think you should go home.'

Clara's hands gripped Jack's shoulders. 'Forget going home,' she gasped. 'Jack, get me to the hospital! My waters have just broken.'

34

Caitlyn Rose Milsom arrived at 1.37 on the morning of Sunday 21 December, weighing 6lbs 2ozs. She had rosebud lips, a button nose, dark blue eyes that stared sleepily at the world, her father's dark hair, and that delicious new baby smell that made me want to hold her tightly and never let her go.

'She's so beautiful.' Jack's voice was loaded with awe and wonder, as his little finger gently stroked our daughter's cheek. 'I'm so proud of you, Clara.' He kissed the top of my head and added, 'You did really well. I'm sorry it was so awful.'

'Totally worth it,' I told him, meaning it. At least it hadn't been as traumatic as when I'd had Freddie, and the hours of labour pains were already becoming a memory. 'Although if you miss that appointment for the snip in January, I'll hurt you far more than the op would, believe me.'

'I promise I'll be there,' he said, laughing. 'Four kids are more than enough. Oh, it's so good to have you both home.'

It was Monday afternoon, and Caitlyn and I had been discharged from the hospital just before lunchtime. Despite arriving three weeks early, she was a good weight, was feeding well, and the medical staff were very happy with her condition, which had been a huge relief.

The scene when I'd left the market was still a bit of a blur. I'd been so scared and in so much pain that I'd barely taken in anything that was happening, but Jack had evidently collared Brodie, who'd immediately run back to the Hall and brought his car as close as he could get it to the green, so I didn't have to walk far. He'd driven us straight to the hospital, while Callie, despite having a VIP guest and media people to look after, promised to keep an eye on the boys and said she'd take them back to Harling Hall where they could spend the night.

Jack told me later that he'd been so panicked he hadn't even thought about collecting my hospital bag, or anything for the boys, but he'd given Brodie our keys and Brodie had taken them back to Honeywell House to gather up their pyjamas, toothbrushes, and anything else they needed. He'd also grabbed my hospital bag and, after dropping our children back at the market, and taking Toby to the Hall, he'd driven all the way back to the maternity unit to hand it in, along with our keys, at the reception.

He'd even offered to stay so he could bring Jack home afterwards, but as we had no idea how long that would take, Jack had declined his offer and got a taxi home in the early hours of the morning. Even so, neither of us would forget how kind our friends had been when we'd needed them most.

We owed them a lot.

Callie had rung me that morning just after breakfast to assure me that the boys had enjoyed themselves tremendously, had bombarded Aubrey with questions about his life and his afterlife, which he'd apparently taken great pleasure in answering, and had had a wonderful few hours exploring the Hall, attacking each other and Immi with snowballs, and being fed all manner of delicious treats by Mia. She also warned me that Freddie had informed her he wanted a kitten.

Toby had apparently decided that having met Aubrey and suffered no ill effects, he could take Agnes and Florence in his stride. He'd been far more wary of Brian, funnily enough, and despite only being a few months old, the kitten had quickly realised he could wrap our gentle boy around his paw. Right now, Callie said, Toby was lying contentedly in front of the fire in Lawrie's sitting room, with Brian fast asleep on his back, the two of them having worn themselves out chasing each other round and round the snowy back garden.

The snow had fallen steadily all last night, and Rowan Vale was a picture of wintry beauty. I gazed out of the living room window to where our car was parked, thinking how odd it looked to see it there, but glad that the estate rules weren't so draconian that exceptions couldn't be made in cases of medical need. Jack bringing me and our baby girl home definitely counted.

I was longing to see my sons and introduce them to their sister, and I didn't have long to wait. The gate was pushed open, and I smiled in delight as I saw the boys, along with Callie, Brodie, Immi and Aubrey walking towards the house, Brodie carrying a big pink balloon with 'It's a Girl' written on it.

'Are you sure you're up to all those visitors, love?' Jack asked worriedly.

'Positive,' I said. 'I think, at this point, I'm running on adrenaline. The crash will come later.'

The boys raced in like mini tornadoes before Jack hushed them and led them sedately over to the armchair, where I was cradling Caitlyn.

Ash and Declan nodded approvingly.

'She's cute,' Ash said. 'And I got to choose her middle name, which is cool.'

'But I chose Caitlyn,' Declan pointed out smugly. 'It suits her. Are you okay, Mum?'

I was quite touched by his concern. 'I'm fine, sweetheart. Just a bit tired, but nothing a good night's sleep won't put right.'

'Not much chance of that for a while,' Callie said, smiling. 'Are we okay to have a closer look at her?'

'Of course,' I said. 'Come and see.'

Our four visitors edged closer.

'Oh,' Callie said longingly, 'isn't she just gorgeous?' She reached over and kissed my cheek. 'Well done! And congratulations.'

'She's like a little doll,' Brodie said, sounding awestruck. 'Look at those eyelashes! And those tiny little fingernails.'

'I'd love a baby sister,' Immi said wistfully. 'You are lucky, Ash.'

I glanced up at Aubrey, who had said nothing. He was staring down at my baby with the sweetest expression on his face.

'Well, Grandpa?' I asked him softly. 'What do you think to your new great-granddaughter?'

'Oh, Clara,' he said, sounding quite choked, 'she's as beautiful as her mother. Quite, quite beautiful.'

'Agnes and Florence are here, too,' Callie informed me. 'They wanted to see the baby, and they hope you don't mind.'

'Of course I don't mind,' I assured them. 'We're all family now, aren't we?'

Callie winked at me.

'Please, take a seat,' Jack told them all. 'I'll get that kettle on.'

'Freddie,' I said worriedly, 'you haven't said anything. Do you like your new baby sister?'

Freddie had been hanging back, clearly uncertain about our new arrival. Now he came forward, peering at her with curiosity. I watched him anxiously, hoping he wasn't going to feel pushed out, now that he was no longer the baby of the family.

'What do you think?' I asked.

He leaned forward and gave Caitlyn the gentlest of kisses on her forehead. 'She's nice,' he said with a shrug. 'I still want to call her Bluey, though. Mummy, can I have a kitten?'

35

AGNES

Christmas morning brought more snow, and scenes of chaos such as Harling Hall hadn't seen for many a long year.

If Agnes had managed to get any sleep, Imogen's excited cries at six o'clock that morning would surely have dragged her from her slumbers. As it was, she hadn't slept at all, as she was in such a state of nervous anticipation that she spent most of the night perched on the edge of her bed, gazing out of the window over the drive, her thoughts whirling faster than the snowflakes that had persisted, showing no signs of slowing.

Mr Wyndham had been a real gentleman, and with Clara's kind permission had spent the night on the sofa at Honeywell House, as Agnes had been afraid that if he saw the bride on the morning of their wedding, they would have bad luck.

He had left the Hall straight after *A Christmas Carol*, which had been staged in the ballroom. Callie, Lawrie and Immi had declared it to be thoroughly delightful and worthy of a West End run, which Agnes – having had the meaning of a West End run explained to her by Polly Herron – had thought was rather over-the-top praise for a play that had been mediocre, at best. Florence's performance excepted, of course.

As her thoughts turned to Florence, she realised that her daughter was in a state of excitement, too, not only over her parents' forthcoming nuptials but the fact that it was Christmas morning. Callie had bought her a DVD player and a whole bundle of DVDs of programmes she and Immi thought Florence would enjoy.

Not only that, but after the wedding, they were to be joined for Christmas luncheon by the Milsoms. Since Clara could hardly be expected to cook for her family this Christmas, and since Jack was apparently a terrible cook, Callie had invited them all over to the Hall, and Florence – who had taken a real shine to the boys – had been thrilled.

Agnes was happy about it, too. She rather liked the Milsoms. And, of course, Clara had been so kind and forgiving towards her that Agnes was perfectly content to welcome them to her home. They were, after all, Mr Wyndham's family, and she was pleased and relieved that Clara had evidently inherited her grandpa's kindly nature and seemed to carry no traces of the despicable Janie, Thomas, Elspeth or James.

She smiled softly, remembering how overcome Mr Wyndham had been when Clara called him Grandpa. It had moved him almost as much as when Florence announced that, in future, she would call him Poppa. Almost, but not quite.

That Mr Wyndham had a deep affection for his newfound family, Agnes had no doubt. But equally, she knew for certain now that they would never replace her or Florence in his heart. He was, first and foremost, a husband and a father.

She shivered in delight. Husband! Soon, very soon, she would be able to say that he truly was her husband. She had never believed the day would come, but here it was, and she couldn't wait.

She turned, her eyes roving over the bed she'd slept in night after night, alone for so many years. Tonight, she would share it with the man she loved. Tonight, he would hold her with a tenderness she had never experienced before. She knew it would be nothing like it had been with Cyril Ashcroft and felt no fear.

She would spend the rest of eternity making Aubrey Wyndham happy, and he would do the same for her.

She had never felt so blessed.

'Merry Christmas, Agnes,' she whispered to herself. A merry Christmas indeed.

36

AUBREY

Aubrey spent a restless night on the Milsoms' sofa, before being awakened at the unearthly hour of 4.35 a.m. by young Freddie, who'd decided that this counted as Christmas morning and it was time to get up and open the presents.

Since his cries of excitement roused the baby, Clara and Jack concluded they might as well give in to his pleas. Aubrey was politely turfed off the sofa with huge apologies from Clara, and within minutes the piles of wrapped presents under the tree were being torn apart in a frenzy of excitement by the three boys, while their poor, exhausted mother breastfed the infant.

A mortified Aubrey fled to the kitchen, where Jack, oblivious to his presence, stuck bread in the toaster and filled the kettle, yawning loudly and muttering about what he wouldn't give for a decent night's sleep.

Once all the presents had been opened, inspected and duly admired, and everyone had eaten and drunk while needlessly apologising to him that they couldn't offer him anything, thoughts had turned to the wedding.

Jack took Freddie to Harling Hall to join the wedding party, returning as fast as he could to change into a smart suit and help Clara with the baby while she got changed into the only dress she possessed that still fitted her and did her hair and make-up.

It was, he thought, quite ironic that, despite being the bridegroom, he was the only one who wasn't frantically rushing around making himself presentable for the event.

Really, while Clara and Jack dressed themselves and their children, all he could do was sit in the armchair by the window, gaze out at the wintry drive, and try to still his nerves. He wasn't even sure why he was so anxious. He was about to get everything he'd ever longed for.

Maybe, he thought, that was the problem. He was so close to having all his dreams come true that he couldn't quite believe something wouldn't go wrong at the last minute to prevent it from happening.

Surely he didn't deserve all this good fortune? To have found this wonderful living, breathing family, most of whom could see and converse with him, and seemed to find him interesting and not at all pathetic; to have a granddaughter who called him Grandpa; to live in a beautiful home at Harling Hall, with Callie and Brodie, Immi and Lawrie, and Mia.

To have a daughter who loved him.

To have a woman who adored him and was about to become his wife.

He shook his head, marvelling at the way things had turned out. Those long, lonely years he'd endured throughout his life were truly over.

He remembered the film the household had watched on Christmas Eve. *It's A Wonderful Life* had made Callie cry and Agnes dab her eyes. He'd felt rather choked up with emotion himself.

'It's a Wonderful Afterlife,' he murmured to himself and chuckled. He'd considered himself a failure, but the angel, Clarence, had said that no man is a failure who has friends, and he'd found so many now he could no longer deem himself worthless.

Joy and excitement replaced his anxieties, and he strolled happily to All Souls with his new family, Jack pushing the smart pram – which he'd hurriedly collected from the shop the Monday after Caitlyn's birth – with some difficulty through the ever-thickening snow.

It was only when they arrived at the church, and Aubrey discovered that all the ghosts in the village seemed to have turned out, that his nerves returned.

To his astonishment, Quintus Severus was standing guard by the church door.

'I wish you luck,' he told Aubrey solemnly. 'I never officially married my wife. We weren't allowed to marry while we served, you see,' he explained. 'I was about to leave the army and retire to her home town. We were to marry at last. I did not get the chance. I wish you all the happiness we never had.'

Aubrey hadn't known what to say to such a tale of woe, particularly as it was the first time he'd heard the Roman's deep voice, so he dazedly shook the man's hand and thanked him profusely.

Polly Herron was there, nodding and smiling at him, along with her newly rediscovered brother, Ray. Old Mr Swain greeted him warmly, apologising for the fact that Ronnie and Bill had also invited themselves.

'Don't you worry, though, sir,' he'd said determinedly, 'I've taken precautions and them two will behave themselves. Any trouble and they'll be out. Why do you think I invited Quintus Severus along?'

'We're so happy for you,' Brooke told Aubrey as he headed down the aisle. 'This is enough to give us all hope.'

She gave Danny a pointed look, but he didn't even seem to have heard her. He was sniffing into his sleeve and looked utterly miserable.

'Is he all right?' Aubrey asked, alarmed.

Brooke sighed. 'Yeah. Weddings. They get to him.'

He had no time to wonder why because Peter and Isaac hurried over to him, shaking his hand and wishing him the very best.

Amelia Davies, the current vicar, was also there, with Tully, her partner.

'Never had a wedding for ghosts before,' she told Clara cheerfully. 'Not that I'll see or hear any of this, of course, but I feel I should be here for it to wish the happy couple well. No doubt Silas is furious about it, but there you go.'

Silas, on the contrary, looked quite smug. 'She can't stop me now, can she, Wyndham?' he said, a wicked twinkle in his eyes. 'She can sit there, not able to contribute in any way, while I stand in *my* church and perform the ceremony. See how *she* likes it!'

'My dear Mr Wyndham,' Walter Tasker said, bowing low. 'Such an auspicious occasion. I wonder, have you any need of help with your vows? I was going to visit you last night to offer my services, but Mistress Chase advised me to stay away from Honeywell House, due to there being a new arrival. I have the perfect quote should you need it.' He struck a pose and said in his usual dramatic tones, '"Let me not to the marriage of true minds admit impediments—"'

'Thank you, Walter,' Aubrey said hastily. 'I have my vows quite clear in my mind, thank you.'

'Are you nervous, Grandpa?' Clara whispered.

Aubrey gave her a weak smile. 'Does it show?'

'Just a bit. You've got nothing to be nervous about. It's all going to go beautifully.'

They slipped into the front pew and waited for the arrival of the bridal party. Behind them on the second row sat Jack, nursing a sleeping Caitlyn, Declan and Ashton beside him.

Aubrey nibbled his thumbnail, his stomach feeling strangely queasy. Mia came hurrying up the aisle and he got to his feet, terrified.

'Is something wrong?' he asked anxiously.

Clara repeated the question to Mia who laughed. 'Nothing's wrong, Aubrey. I'm just bringing the music.' She held up the machine that had once stood on the kitchen worktop, blasting out popular tunes of the day, but which had in recent years been replaced with the pocket telephone that Mia insisted could do the job just as well. 'The bridal party has arrived, and we need music, don't we?'

Agnes had hoped to have the organ played at the wedding, but Amelia had warned Callie that Mrs Timmins, who played the church organ, might not be impressed that there was to be a ghost wedding at All Souls, and suggested it might be better if they found an alternative. After due consultation and much dithering, Agnes had finally selected the music she would like to walk up the aisle to, and Mia had duly promised that she would take care of it.

'The bridal party has arrived? Oh, my word!'

'It's okay,' Clara said kindly. 'Don't panic. Everything's going to be wonderful.'

If Aubrey hadn't known better, he'd have been sure he was sweating. He wiped his hands on his trousers just in case and straightened his cravat, which really didn't need straightening.

Across the aisle he saw Callie and Brodie slip into the front pew. Callie smiled and nodded reassuringly at him and Brodie gave a thumbs-up even though he couldn't be entirely certain where Aubrey was.

Then Mia pressed the button on the machine and the air was filled with the beautiful strains of 'Canon in D' by Johann Pachelbel.

A sense of calm flooded through Aubrey. What, after all, was there to be worried about? This was the happiest day of his afterlife.

He rose and stood before the altar, Clara at his side. He turned, his heart lifting as he saw Florence and Imogen walking down the aisle towards him. Immi carried a basket of rose petals, which she scattered as she walked. Behind them came the young pageboys: Freddie, beaming and waving at his proud parents and smirking brothers, with John and Robert just behind him, looking so proud they might burst. Bless dear Agnes for allowing them to be part of this special occasion.

Behind the pageboys walked Millie, looking blissfully happy in her indecently short dress and white boots.

And then, wonder of wonders, his beloved Agnes. Oh, how beautiful she looked as she glided down the aisle beside Lawrie, her dear face alight with joy and love.

She had fretted, he knew, that she was to be married in her night attire, and had said wistfully how wonderful it would have been to marry in a proper wedding dress. It was, alas, the one thing no one could do anything about, but he'd assured her repeatedly that she would be the most stunning woman in the church, and he hadn't lied.

She was.

As the music faded and Agnes reached his side, they smiled at each other and, ignoring the disapproving tut from Silas, took each other's hand.

The Reverend Alexander had done as he promised and created his own vows.

'Dearly beloved, we are gathered in this church today to celebrate the everlasting union of this man and this woman,' he began.

Aubrey tried to concentrate but his focus was all on Agnes, and the feel of her soft hand in his. He gently stroked her thumb with his own, giving her courage as he saw her trembling.

He realised suddenly that he was being asked to say his vows.

'I, Aubrey Thomas Wyndham, take you, Agnes Alexandra Ashcroft, to be my wife, to have and to hold from this day forward; on good days and bad days, free of earthly trappings and mortal concerns, I promise to love and to cherish you throughout eternity. In the House of our Father, before our friends and family, I make this vow.'

With bright eyes and a voice that was little more than a whisper, Agnes repeated her vows to him, her grip on his hand tightening as if reinforcing her every word.

'Good, that's that bit done then,' Silas said. 'Now, I believe you each have a quotation from a poem that you'd like to say to each other, which is a bit unorthodox, but given the circumstances I hardly suppose it matters. Go ahead.'

Aubrey turned back to Agnes and slowly, lovingly, recited a small part of a poem by the American poet, Elizabeth Akers Allen.

> *I fear not all that Time or Fate*
> *May bring to burden heart or brow,*
> *Strong in the love that came so late,*
> *Our souls shall keep it always now.*

Agnes closed her eyes for a moment as if dwelling on his words, then steadily, her head high, her gaze never faltering, she quoted the piece of poetry she'd chosen by Elizabeth Barrett Browning.

> *I love thee with a love I seemed to lose*
> *With my lost saints. I love thee with the breath,*
> *Smiles, tears, of all my life; and, if God choose,*
> *I shall love thee better after death.*

Silas cleared his throat. 'Well then, all very lovely, I'm sure. Now that Agnes and Aubrey have exchanged their vows, the ceremony is complete, and I declare that they are husband and wife for all eternity. Don't just stand there, Wyndham. You know the drill!'

And to loud cheers from the congregation, Aubrey kissed his bride.

EPILOGUE

I lay quietly on the sofa in the living room at Honeywell House, gazing sleepily at the fire. It was ten o'clock at night, and the boys were sound asleep in their beds. It had been a long and exciting day for them, and they were worn out.

Beside the sofa in her carrycot, Caitlyn gave a soft sigh and sucked contentedly on her knuckles. She'd just had a feed and had finally fallen asleep, giving me the much-needed chance to relax and unwind at last.

Over in the armchair by the window, Jack slept, his head propped in his hand, as he'd been too exhausted to climb the stairs to our bedroom.

Toby snored gently from his usual place on the rug. It had been a day of excitement for him, too, as he'd been brought to Harling Hall after the wedding ceremony and had spent the afternoon being fussed over and spoilt by the entire household. Like all animals, he could see the ghosts and seemed completely unfazed by them now.

What a day! As if Christmas wasn't hectic enough, the wedding had added even more excitement. I wouldn't have missed it for the world and was glad that Caitlyn hadn't chosen to arrive today instead of Sunday.

Callie had told me that Aubrey and Agnes had looked really sweet together and were clearly so much in love that even Silas had been in a good mood. I'd definitely seen the joy in my grandpa's eyes, and I couldn't be happier for him.

After the ceremony, we'd crunched through the snow to Harling Hall. Callie and Brodie had rigged up some music in the ballroom for the ghosts to dance to, so they could celebrate the wedding in their own style, while the living among us headed to the dining room for a traditional Christmas lunch, cooked to perfection by the super-competent Mia.

After I'd fed and changed Caitlyn, we'd joined the ghosts in the ballroom, and even though I could only see Aubrey, and poor Jack and Brodie couldn't see any of the ghosts at all, we'd had a lovely time. The ghosts, the boys, Immi, Callie and Brodie danced to a mixture of classical and festive music, while I sat, gently rocking Caitlyn, in the company of my lovely husband and a smiling Lawrie. Lawrie had, after the ceremony, apologised to me for his past behaviour, and we'd agreed to put the whole sorry business behind us and get on with enjoying this wonderful day. After all, everyone else was.

Apparently, the only ghostly wedding guest not present at the Hall was Quintus Severus, who'd returned to Appleseed Cottage to keep the reclusive Harmony Hill company. The vicar had also apparently gone home. Callie thought being so nice and cheerful had probably worn him out.

Agnes and Aubrey had kissed Florence goodnight and promised they'd see her in the morning before quietly slipping away to their suite to spend their wedding night together, even though it was only seven o'clock.

'Bless them,' Callie said, smiling, 'they can't wait. No one deserves this happiness more than they do.'

The boys had thoroughly enjoyed being at the Hall. Ashton, who'd at first found hanging out with Immi embarrassing, had to admit that she was pretty cool as she could see all the ghosts, and Immi was happy to act as a go-between as the two eldest excitedly asked questions of them.

Evidently, Declan was particularly interested in hearing about Peter's time in the village pillory, while Ash wanted to know why Walter Tasker hadn't steered William Shakespeare well away from writing, because it would have saved him an awful lot of boring homework if Will had become a glovemaker like his father instead.

At half past eight, Jack and I decided it was time we headed home, and he went off to round up our sons.

'Not to push you,' Callie had said hesitantly, 'but have you thought any more about what you're going to do about getting a job? Are you still intent on selling tickets for the model village?'

I'd glanced over at the pram where my sleeping baby lay.

'Hardly seems important right now,' I'd admitted. 'And to be honest, I'm sure I can find something better when I'm ready to start work again.'

She nodded. 'We're moving the model village over here before the end of January,' she said. 'That will give us plenty of time to set things up, make sure it's in the right location, get the path sorted, that sort of thing. Thing is, we're thinking of putting the ticket office in the old stables, and setting up a gift shop there, too. It's time we began seriously marketing Rowan Vale and the Wyrd Stones. We really want the estate to make enough money to keep everything maintained well and to invest in new projects, so we have to up our game.'

'Sounds like a good idea,' I said, yawning.

'Yes, we think so. So, I was wondering if you'd reconsider doing some artwork for us.'

My yawn died immediately. 'Artwork?'

She nodded eagerly. 'Yes! Honestly, Clara, you're so good, and I think we could be a great partnership. Think about it. Your paintings and drawings on jigsaws, cards, notebooks, fridge magnets – all sorts of merchandise. I really think this could be a profitable endeavour for both of us.'

'Are you serious?' I asked.

'Of course! And you could do them in your own time. I totally understand that right now you have other priorities, and if you do decide to go into business with us it would be ages before you have anything to offer us, but I just want you to give it some thought. I have every faith in you, and I know Jack does, too. He can't rave about your artwork enough.'

I saw Jack heading back towards us, chivvying the boys along. 'I'll think about it,' I'd said, getting up from my chair. 'I promise I'll let you know.'

'That's all I ask,' she'd said. 'No pressure.'

Now, as I lay on the sofa in the stillness of this December night, my family sleeping while my thoughts tumbled over themselves, I remembered her offer and wondered...

I knew Jack had faith in me. I knew Callie and Brodie thought I was talented. I remembered how my old work colleague, Jenni, had raved about my paintings.

Was I really good enough to go into partnership with the Harling Estate? Maybe it was time I had faith in my own abilities.

I eased myself off the sofa and padded over to the sideboard, where I quietly slid open the junk drawer and pulled out the sketch pad and a pencil.

Sitting down again, I turned the pages, gazing with a critical eye at the drawings of Jack, the boys, Toby, the platform at Harling's Halt which had been the first sketch I ever made when I arrived here, and the glorious old mill, with its huge waterwheel and tall, brick chimney.

I'd never attempted to draw Harling Hall, or the church, or the shops, or the riverside, or the inn, or the farm. I'd never even picked up a paintbrush since I moved here.

But I remembered sitting on the Leyland bus on Saturday morning, gazing out at the winter landscape, and the longing that had stirred within me to capture the scene on canvas.

For a long moment I hesitated, then I turned over the page, picked up the pencil and began to write.

Sketchbooks
Round brushes
Watercolour paints
Watercolour panels...

* * *

MORE FROM SHARON BOOTH

Another book from Sharon Booth, and the first in another enchanting series, is available to order now here:
https://mybook.to/SkelseaCrossBackAd

ACKNOWLEDGEMENTS

Thank you so much for reading *Christmas Spirits at Honeywell House*.

I can't believe that I'm already at the end of the third book in my Ghosts of Rowan Vale series. Time seems to have gone by so quickly – possibly because I love spending my days in this little Cotswolds village so much. Being in the company of my ghostly characters is so much fun, and I really hope you enjoy reading about them as much as I enjoy writing about them.

I'd like to say a huge thank you to everyone at Boldwood Books for enabling me to bring this series to my readers. It's such an incredible team and I feel so lucky to be part of it. You're simply the best!

Extra special thanks go to my wonderful editor, Francesca Best, whose input is invaluable and so insightful. It's a pleasure to work with her and I feel so lucky that she 'gets' my work and knows exactly how to improve it.

Thanks also to Debra Newhouse for the copyedits (which are never a chore!) and to Jacqueline Beard MBE for the great job she's done with the proofreading.

Thank you to Rachel Lawston for another beautiful cover. I feel so lucky to have Rachel working on my books as her illustrations and design skills are superb. And thank you to Karen Cass for the brilliant job she's done narrating the audio book. She was my first choice as narrator and I'm truly grateful that it's her voice telling my stories for me.

Thanks to the wider team at Boldwood – to Niamh, Wendy, and (very patient) Claire, Ben, Issy, Kate, Megan, Marcela and everyone else whose names I'm still learning! There are so many people working behind the scenes to produce our books and they all deserve thanks, especially Amanda Ridout our CEO who made it all happen. Amazing!

When it comes to family and friends, I know I always thank the same people, but the truth is they never fail to support me and help me, and I don't know what I'd do without them.

Thank you to Jessica Redland, my best friend and sounding board. Without those long, long conversations (where we go over our writing plans, story tangles, half-baked ideas, character quirks, and ridiculous plot twists that could never really work... could they?) writing would be a lot more difficult and a lot less fun. She's earned many grateful hugs from me for always accepting my mad ideas, encouraging me, supporting me, laughing with me (and sometimes at me, in the nicest possible way!) and being there when I need her.

And I'm lucky to have other writing friends to discuss this crazy job with, too. Eliza J Scott is so lovely and very supportive, and since our meetings usually happen over cheese scones it's even more of a pleasure when we catch up every couple of months!

The Write Romantics – my writing family – are always there when I need them. Thanks to Jo Bartlett, Alexandra Weston, Helen Phifer, Helen Rolfe, Deirdre Palmer, Jackie Ladbury, Rachel Thomas, Lynne Pardoe, and of course, Jessica, for their invaluable friendship over the last twelve or thirteen years.

Jessica and I are also members of a local writing group, The Beverley Novelists. Our monthly meetings are fantastic, and we love catching up with Val Wood, Cass Grafton, Jenni Fletcher, Alex Weston, Linda Acaster, Jeevani Charika, Kate Kenzie, Sylvia Broady, Lynnda Worsnopp, Karen Drury, and anyone else who happens to turn up.

Outside the writing world, my husband is the patient star of the show, and I'll be forever grateful to him for his support and encouragement, for not letting me give up this writing lark when I almost did, for all the coffees he brings me, and for always pretending to be interested when I go over "work stuff" with him. He's much better at faking fascination than I am when he tells me about *his* "work stuff", or starts talking about football or fishing! If he has one fault it's that he can't resist interrupting me to show me some ridiculous video he's seen on TikTok. Still, I suppose no one's perfect. But he's pretty darn close.

Finally, thank you so much to everyone who buys my books, reads them on Kindle Unlimited, listens to the audio versions, or borrows them from the library. Thanks to those of you who subscribe to my newsletter/s, read my blog, visit my website, chat to me on social media, comment on my posts, share my news, or help in any way to spread the word about my books. I couldn't do this without you, and I'll be forever grateful. Thank you so much!

Lots of Love
Sharon xx

ABOUT THE AUTHOR

Sharon Booth is the author of feel-good stories set in charming, quirky locations, and now writes cosy romances with a magical twist for Boldwood. She lives with her husband in East Yorkshire, England.

Sign up to Sharon Booth's mailing list for news, competitions and updates on future books.

Visit Sharon's website: www.sharonboothwriter.com

Follow Sharon on social media:

- facebook.com/sharonboothwriter
- instagram.com/sharonboothwriter
- youtube.com/@sharonboothwriter
- bookbub.com/authors/sharon-booth
- pinterest.com/sharonboothwriter

ALSO BY SHARON BOOTH

Ghosts of Rowan Vale
Kindred Spirits at Harling Hall
Loving Spirits at the Vintage Teashop
Christmas Spirits at Honeywell House

BECOME A MEMBER OF
THE SHELF CARE CLUB

The home of Boldwood's book club reads.

Find uplifting reads, sunny escapes, cosy romances, family dramas and more!

Sign up to the newsletter
https://bit.ly/theshelfcareclub

Boldwood

Boldwood Books is an award-winning fiction publishing company seeking out the best stories from around the world.

Find out more at www.boldwoodbooks.com

Join our reader community for brilliant books, competitions and offers!

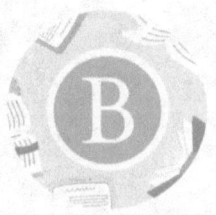

Follow us
@BoldwoodBooks
@TheBoldBookClub

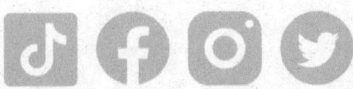

Sign up to our weekly deals newsletter

https://bit.ly/BoldwoodBNewsletter